Compelled by Memory

The Lewis Land Monuments 1994–2018

Will Maclean with **Marian Leven** and **Arthur Watson**

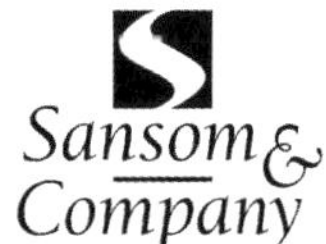

Sansom & Company

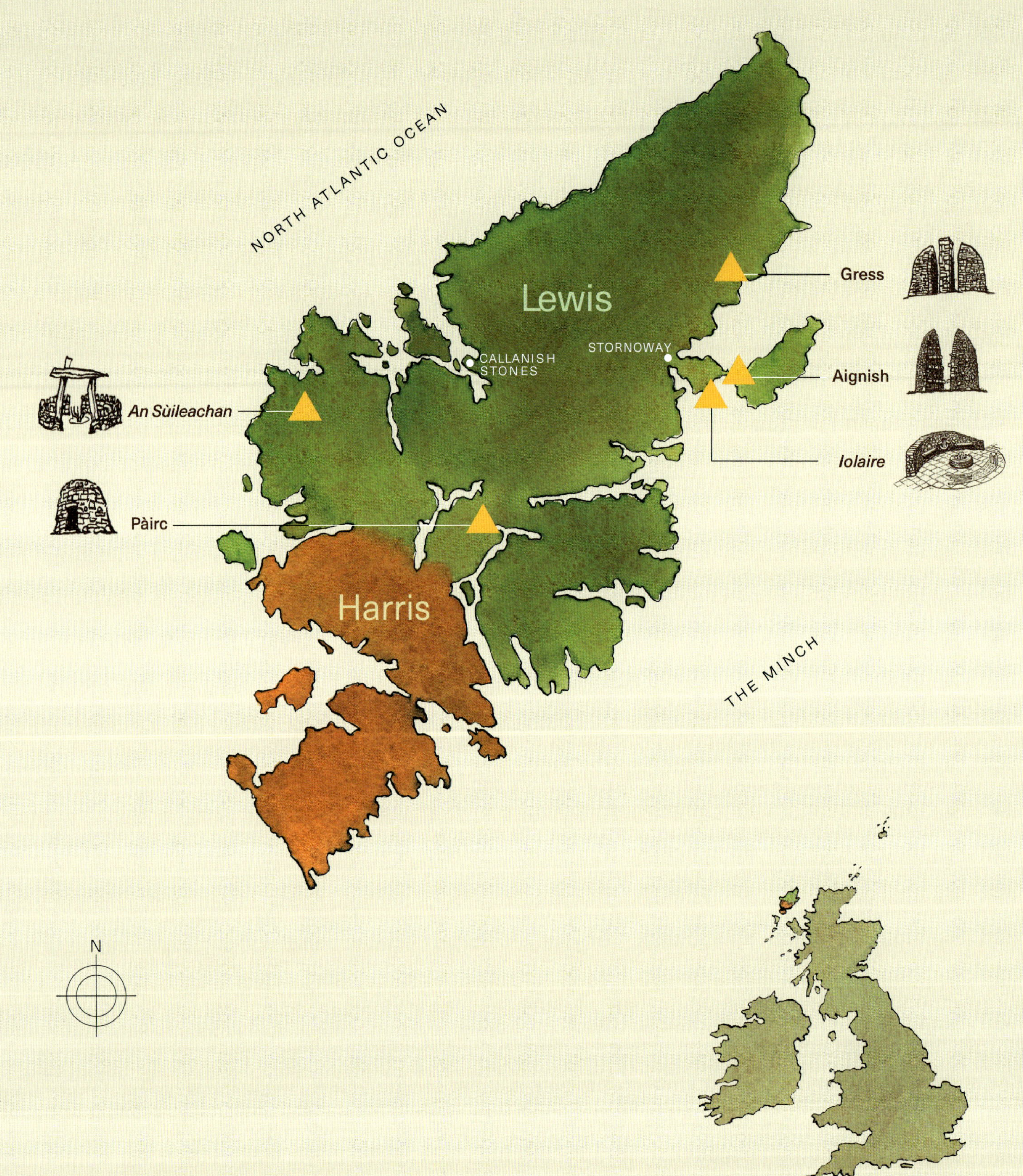

-6°
NORTH ATLANTIC OCEAN
Lewis
Gress
STORNOWAY
CALLANISH STONES
Aignish
58°
An Sùileachan
Iolaire
Pàirc
Harris
THE MINCH
N
MAP AND DRAWINGS BY CLARE HEWITT

Contents

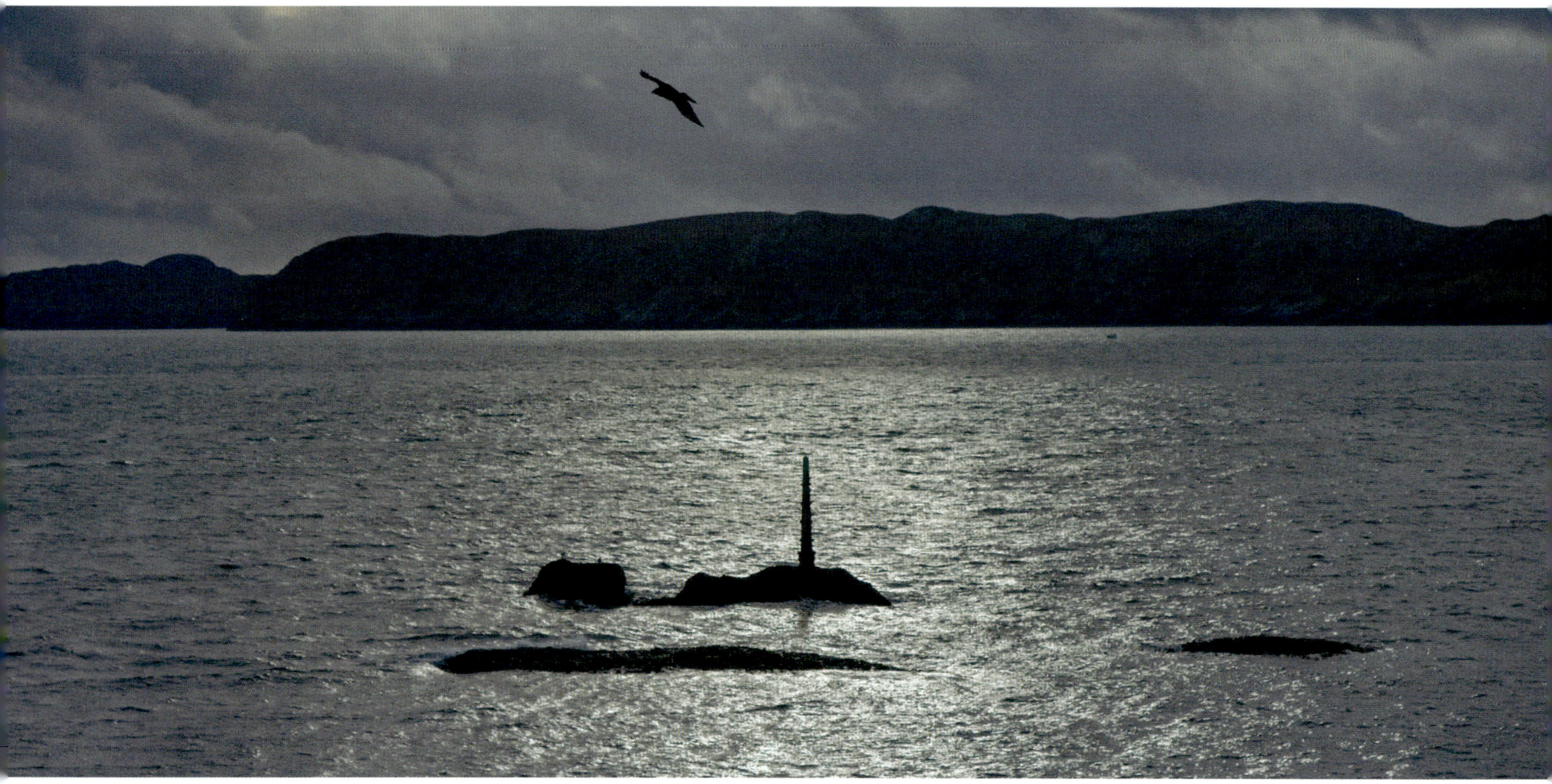

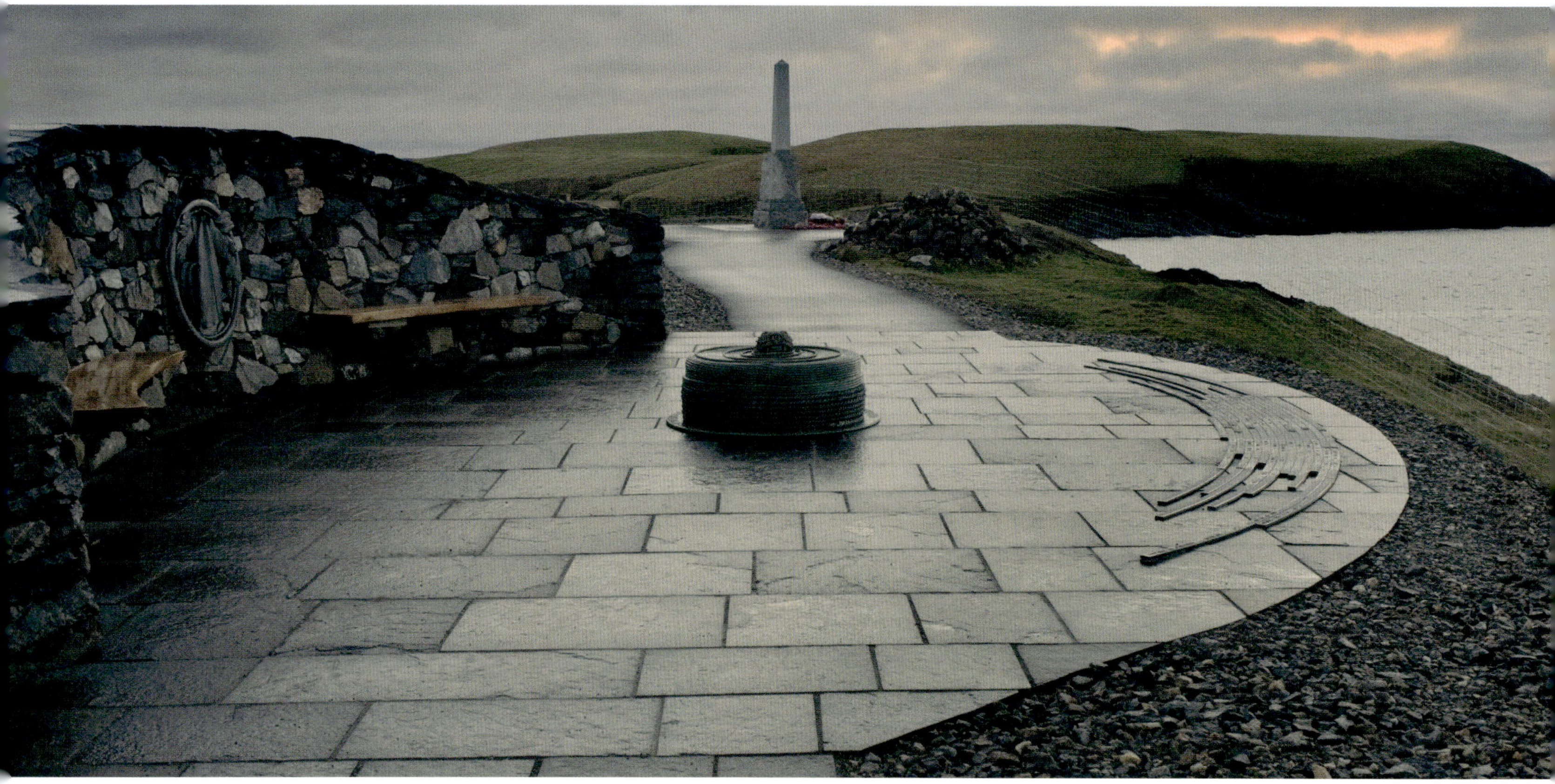

TOP View of the marker where HMY *Iolaire* sank on New Year's Day 1919
BOTTOM The *Iolaire* memorial, looking south east

Introduction

Monuments, even memorials, are mostly about power. They have become controversial in recent years because other events have made people acutely aware of this: how, in them, the power structures of the past are perpetuated in the streets and squares of the present. Indeed, remembering the Duke of Sutherland on his pillar at Dunrobin, they are even on the hilltops. In Scotland, however, there is also one grand exception to this rule: a monument, not for the powerful, but for those whom Lindsay Blair, in her essay for this book, calls 'the voices from below'. The Scottish National War Memorial in Edinburgh was built after the First World War in an extraordinary collective effort by a team of artists and craftspeople led by Sir Robert Lorimer and funded by wide popular support. It overthrew the age-old delusion of the glory of war and seized back for the community – from the powers that had precipitated the most terrible waste of human life in recorded history – the commemoration of Scotland's dead. With no delusions of glory, the monument articulated the nation's terrible sense of loss and its hope that peace would now prevail. Such a monument that subverts the power of the few to reclaim it for the many is indeed rare.*

The monuments on Lewis celebrated in this book do, however, share that distinction. The first three were built to commemorate the actions of the 'heroes of the land raids'. Theirs were emphatically voices from below, but they confronted power nevertheless. Will Maclean was the designer for these monuments under the leadership of the organisation Cuimhneachain nan Gaisgeach (Commemoration of Our Land Heroes) but, as with the National Memorial, they too were in a real sense collective endeavours. The project grew from wide consultation initiated and led by the late Angus Macleod of Stornoway. Maclean then brought it to fruition, first in the Pàirc Deer Raid cairn and then with the Aignish cairn and the memorial sculpture at Gress River. He took no fee and always worked in cooperation with others.

These first monuments commemorated specific events at specific sites. The two that followed, however, An Sùileachan, and the Call na h-*Iolaire* (The Loss of the *Iolaire*) monument, were slightly different. Will Maclean says of the first of them, An Sùileachan, undertaken with his wife, Marian Leven: 'while commemorating the land raiders, [it] was designed to look forward to the future of the community of Reef now under trust ownership'. The Call na h-*Iolaire* monument, on the other hand, again undertaken with Marian Leven and also with Arthur Watson, marks the centenary of the tragedy of the wreck of HMY *Iolaire*. In a terrible storm on New Year's Day 1919, 201 men returning from the war perished when their ship was driven onto the rocks outside Stornoway harbour. As Tom Normand puts it in his contribution to this publication, these two monuments 'pay homage to the crofters' riots and to the Iolaire disaster – this is written into their respective narratives – but each of these monuments is also a communal and a meditational site. They are created in order to memorialise and to heal. They offer places where the commonweal is remembered and

*See Duncan Macmillan, *Scotland's Shrine: The Scottish National War Memorial*, Lund Humphries, London, 2014

refreshed. They are works of art that simultaneously recollect the past and signal a belief in the future. This is their power, and their rare dignity.' Normand's words could just as exactly summarise the achievement of the National War Memorial. There is also a direct link to it in the Iolaire monument, for the names of those who were lost in that tragedy are recorded both on the monument and in the rolls of the dead in the National War Memorial. The Gress River cairn, too, is linked directly to the First World War. It commemorates a confrontation immediately after the war's end when, instead of the promised 'land fit for heroes', men returning from the war found only dispossession and landlessness.

Although they were two very different projects, what Sir Robert Lorimer achieved in the War Memorial and Will Maclean and associates in the Lewis monuments was to articulate a powerful sentiment widely shared in the community, but which had until then found no collective voice to memorialise it and so pass it on to posterity. The essays in this book tell how, on Lewis, the people found their voice and how in the five monuments described here it has been given a memorial form that will resonate down the generations. Both Maclean and Lorimer drew on the sense of community and the sense of place that underpinned a collective need for remembrance. Indeed as these three essays argue, all these monuments are rooted in place, and in the history acted out in that place. These things have shaped their siting, their form and their fabric. Thus, as they are set in the landscape, they also reflect the preceding millennia of unknown history that have already left their mark on it – all the great continuities, in fact, of the ancient place that is Lewis. One of the most telling details in any of the monuments is the arch in An Sùileachan, built from stones found nearby that seem to have been prepared thousands of years ago for use in some Neolithic monument, planned but left unbuilt. Thus these monuments join the great rhythm of the centuries without missing a single beat.

The people of Lewis were pushed too far by those with the power to summon armed soldiers to assert their will, yet in spite of the odds so stacked against them, they fought back. What they were defending was their collective identity built up over many generations in their intimate relationship with the land. Patrick Geddes, pioneer town planner and ecologist, who articulated so many of these things, had a favourite three-word slogan to summarise what it is that gives a community its identity: Work, Place, Folk. These were also precisely the things that the men and women of Lewis fought for: the right to work on the land that was their place and so maintain their community, their folk. None of these things had any meaning singly. The place with no work was unviable. Work without place was equally so to the crofters. With neither work nor place there could be no community. The crofters saw all this very clearly and Joni Buchanan's essay contribution quotes a magnificent riposte from them to Lord Leverhulme in the confrontation at Gress: 'You have bought this island. But you have not bought us, and we refuse to be the bond slaves of any man. We want to live our own lives in our own way, poor in material things it may be, but at least it will be clear of the factory bell; it will be free and independent.'

Will Maclean was an inspired choice to design the first of these projects, the Pàirc Deer Raid memorial cairn, and then naturally the others that followed. Indeed he was really the only choice. In an interview with *Studio International* in 2012, he described his own motivation as an artist and how he was already engaged with the culture of his people when he was at art school: 'I had been reading around my family history in Skye and Wester Ross-Shire and my first attempts to describe my reactions visually came in the form of figure compositions relating to the Highland clearances.' Then a little later in the same interview, he described how he wanted to give visual expression to the voice of the Highland people, how that voice 'has come historically through music, song and poetry', but he would like 'to contribute to a growing realisation that the visual arts can have a place in contemporary Gaeldom just as they did in the Celtic culture of old'.

If this was his ambition, he has succeeded superbly in a body of work that can stand alongside that of the Gaelic poets, who have kept their own tradition so vigorously alive. As Lindsay Blair makes clear, however, far from turning inwards to stay within the safe but narrow horizons of peevish self-regard, Maclean has exercised his 'spatial imagination'. He has done what the poet Sorley MacLean did with such authority and has ranged across the world, not only to follow the Gaels in their diaspora in resonant works about emigration, but also to see their community with the people living on the northern edges and indeed the explorers who went beyond them. There is power in maps just as there is in monuments. Maclean turned the map around and it made the world look different. His dedication to the idea of finding a visual form of expression for Gaelic culture and history has been heroic, but he was not entirely alone. Lindsay Blair traces the fight back against the marginalisation of the north, citing Ian Finlay writing in the 1940s and others in the Scottish tradition, but she also widens the argument as it must be widened to place it where it belongs in the European tradition of radical thought.

The three essays in this book complement each other beautifully. Lindsay Blair places Maclean and those he worked with in the context of a wider cultural rebellion against the hegemony of imposed values that do not match the history and real cultural geography of the north. This is in different form the same hegemony against which the land raiders fought so valiantly. In a vivid set of narratives (provided also in Gaelic at the end of the essay section), Joni Buchanan tells the story of the events that are commemorated in these monuments and of the courage with which the people, both actually and metaphorically, bared their breasts to the bayonets of the powers ranged against them and, too, why this struggle was rooted in a sense of place. Tom Normand tells us about the monuments themselves, their iconography and the subtle ways that it records and indeed recalls the events that the landscape witnessed. With this record and interpretation to set them in their context of landscape, history and people we can be confident that, through these monuments, those voices from below will now be clearly heard on Lewis for many generations to come.

Duncan Macmillan, September 2021

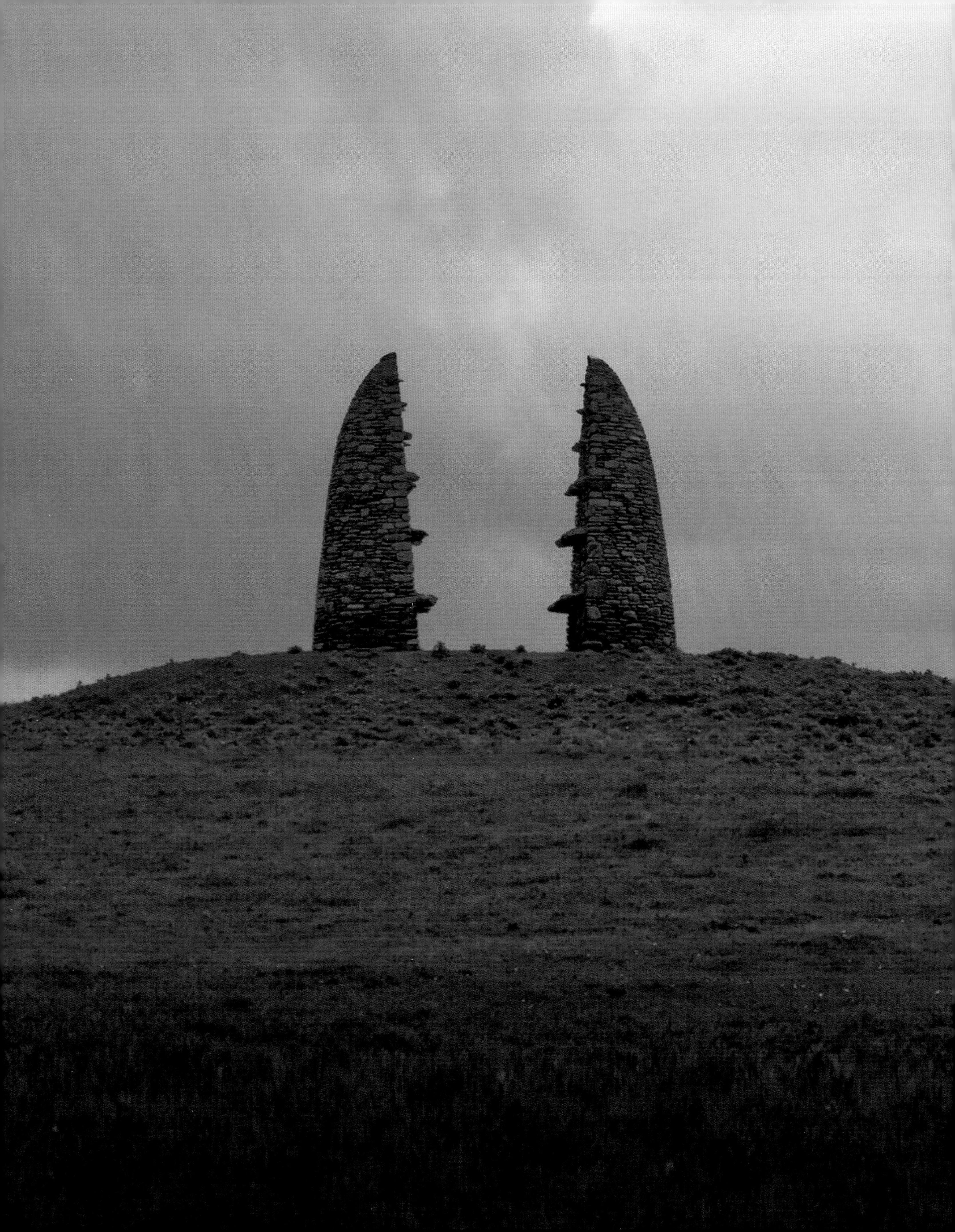

A History of Struggle behind the Lewis Land Raid Memorials

This set of essays is provided in Gaelic, on page 71

Joni Buchanan

Will MacLean's commemorative monuments sit in the wild and rugged Lewis landscape.[1] Each one symbolises a distinctive narrative connected to its location, commemorating the men and women who stood up to historic injustice. Their actions ensured that communities continue to survive today on this remote edge of Europe.

To differing degrees, in the 17th and 18th centuries, western European countries experienced a disintegration of their socio-economic order and the development of new capitalist conditions. In the Scottish Highlands and Islands there was a particularly harsh, 'inexorable and convulsive shift from a traditionalist to a commercialised society'.[2] To engage in the capitalist endeavours of the age, Highland Clan Chiefs supplanted 'kin' obligations with strictly commercial relations. Clan members became rent-paying tenants and Chiefs turned themselves into private landlords committed to maximising rental income and controlling production.

On Lewis, the first phase of capitalist land organisation, initiated by the island's owner Lord Seaforth, involved the reorganisation of village arable land into individual lots or crofts and removing vast areas of traditional grazing land from crofting use in order to augment the land given over to sheep farms and sporting estates. In addition, many crofters became semi-industrial labourers employed to gather and process kelp to extract alkaline from seaware. It was a short-lived industry but extremely lucrative for Seaforth and other landlords. Rents and taxes (raised on the whim of estates) could be met while kelping flourished but when it failed they became an additional burden on a peasantry which was, by then, perennially in debt. The intensive labour requirements of kelping, which engaged whole families, as well as raising cattle for rent and the subdivision of crofts, led to a sharp decline in agricultural practice and the emergence of the potato as the main subsistence crop.[3]

Within the first half of the 19th century kelping failed, potatoes rotted in the ground and much of the population was thrown to the four winds. Those with the wherewithal sought hope in other lands before that same involuntary fate befell them. There was no capacity to cope with crisis and the landlords' preferred solutions proved catastrophic for generations to come.[4]

Systematic clearance, beginning around 1819 on the peninsula of Pàirc, left an estimated thirty villages deserted. By the 1880s, when the Pàirc Deer Raid (the subject of the first Maclean monument) took place, up to 70,000 acres had been removed from crofting.

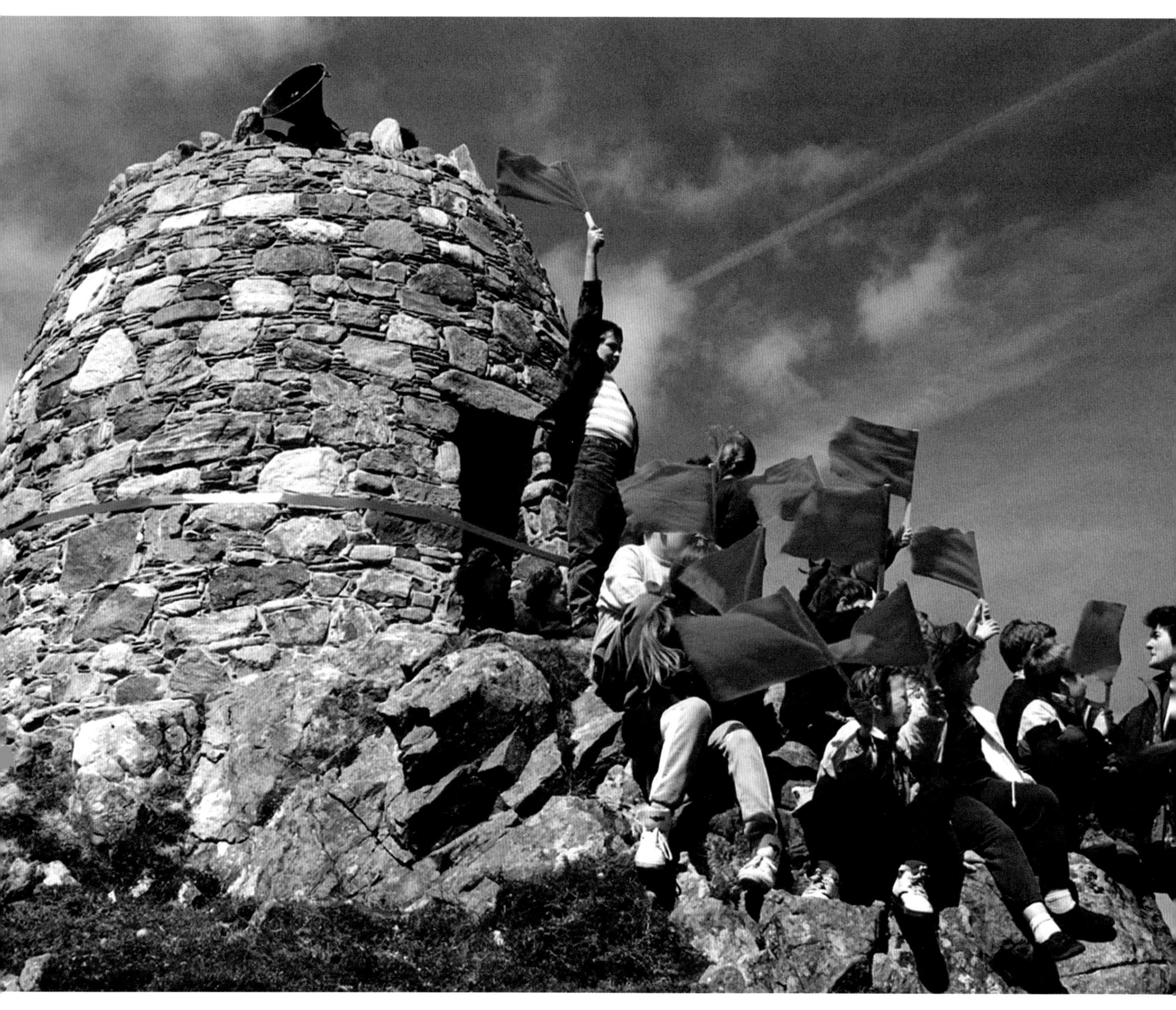

ABOVE Local children at the opening ceremony of the Pàirc memorial cairn at Balallan (Photo: Sam Maynard)

Clearances were continued by Sir James Matheson, who bought the island in 1844. A native
of Sutherland, he was a partner in the insurance and shipping company Jardine Matheson,
which traded tea, fine silks and most lucratively opium in lands then known as the Orient.

By the mid-19th century, two-fifths (over 1,000 individuals) of the population of Uig in the
south-west of Lewis (where the monument, *An Sùileachan*, is located) had been cleared.
Forty thousand acres of Uig were in the hands of seven tenants by the 1870s, three of whom
allocated their land to sporting estates. Reduction in the land available meant that crofting
villages became overpopulated, with as many as three families (one tenant and two landless
cottars) living on the one croft. Critically, crofters also remained tenants-at-will, with no
security of tenure and no redress in law. If they dared protest, fines or eviction followed.

The Bernera Riot in 1874, which erupted in response to eviction notices being served on
56 families, was indicative of the start of a more militant resistance. A few years later, in 1882,
crofters at Braes in Skye adopted the tactic of the Irish Land League, refusing to pay rent and
resisting notices of removal. In the face of growing unrest and political action, the government intervened in crofting affairs for the first time since contributing to the relief of destitu-
tion in the 1840s by establishing the Royal Commission on the Highlands and Islands.
Its report, published in 1884, shows a consistent picture of landlord injustice and growing
impoverishment.

In January 1886, four 'Crofters' Party' Members of Parliament were elected. The new Liberal
administration passed the first Crofters' Act, which conferred security of tenure, allowed
compensation for improvements and set up a form of land court, the Crofters' Commission.
This represented a great step forward for the crofters' cause. However, the Act did nothing
to alleviate the predicament of the landless cottars. Neither did the legislation return land
to the crofting population, which ensured that agitation continued. The Maclean monument
at Aignish, in the Point district of Lewis, creates a powerful image of the 1888 confrontation
between crofters seeking the return of land given over to a single sheep farm and Royal
Marines, drafted in to quell unrest. Partial victories were won before the process ground
to a halt with the outbreak of the First World War.

For returning ex-servicemen, there was much unfinished business. When it became clear
that the Lewis estate, now owned by Lord Leverhulme, was implacably hostile to breaking
up farms, land raiding resumed. The third Maclean monument recalls the stand-off between
crofters and Lord Leverhulme at Gress Bridge in 1919. Collectively, these works reflect
a noble history of struggle which shaped Lewis down to the present day.

---

1. The fourth sculpture, *An Sùileachan*, in Reef, was co-designed by Will MacLean and Marian Leven, and the fifth,
    the *Iolaire* memorial at Holm, co-designed by Maclean, Leven and Arthur Watson
2. A. I. Macinnes, *Clanship, Commerce and the House of Stewart, 1603–1788*, Tuckwell Press, East Linton, 1996
3. Sir John MacNeill Report, 1851
4. *The Napier Commission* report, 1884, by the commission of inquiry into the condition of crofters and cottars
    in the Highlands and Islands (which was appointed in 1883 with Lord Napier as Chairman).
    See also my *The Lewis Land Struggle: Na Gaisgich*, Acair, Stornoway, 1996

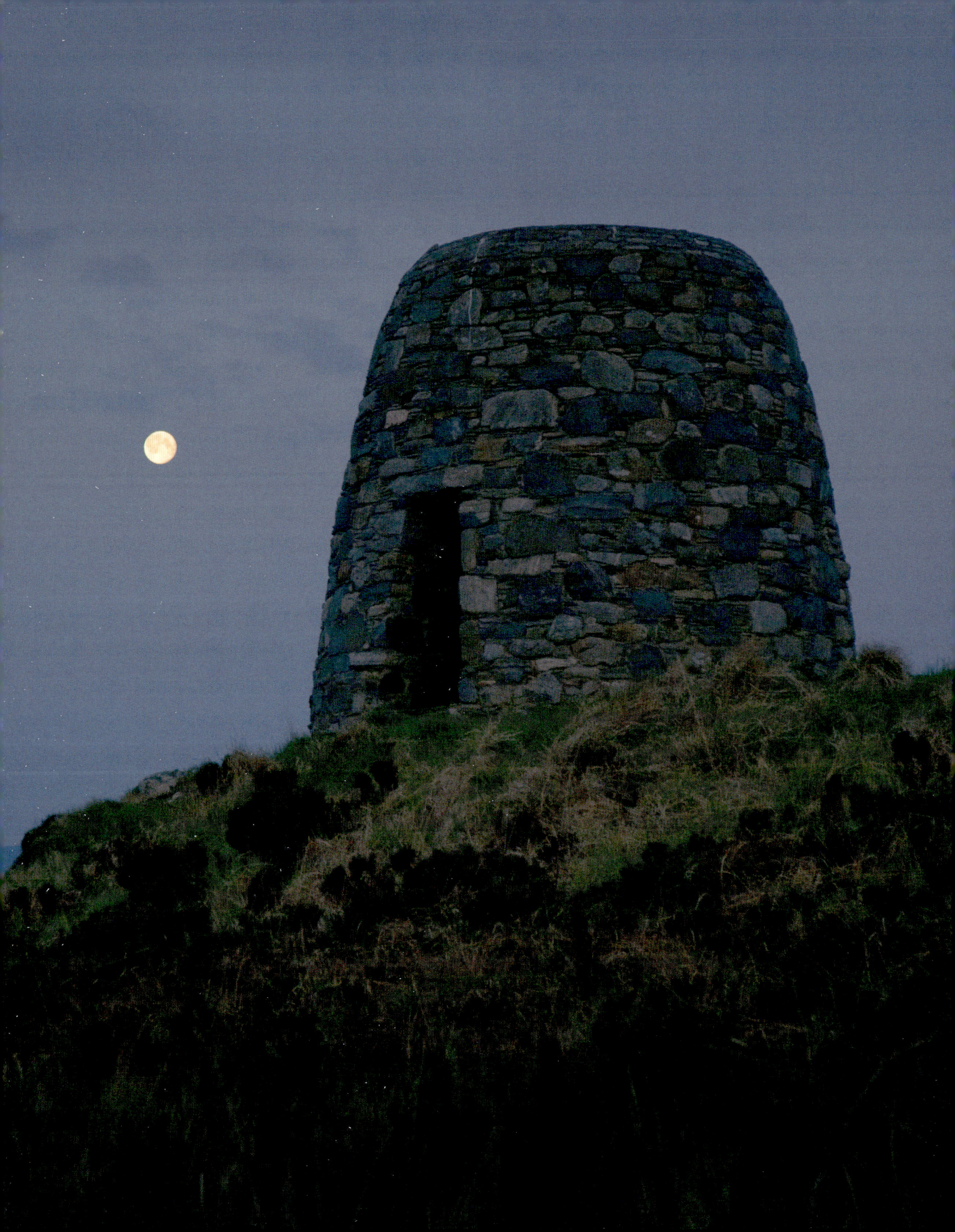

The Pàirc Memorial

Scene of the 1887 Pàirc Deer Raid in Balallan in the District of Lochs

Designed by Will Maclean / Construction completed in 1994

Joni Buchanan

'Park [Pàirc], which nature seemed to mean for man, with all its arable lands, hill pasture, and bays of the sea, offering grand opportunities for comfort, as a reward for human industry, was quite unprecedentedly relieved of the inhabitant population of twenty-eight townships. To the perpetrators of such deeds the discontentment and bitter feelings of the fugitive inhabitants appeared as nothing at all compared to the peculiar pleasure they enjoyed from the fact that now the sheep and the fleet-footed deer could graze on the meadows and on heaths impiously depopulated.'

The Napier Commission (report of commission of inquiry into the condition of crofters and cottars in the Highlands and Islands of Scotland), Vols I – V, here Vol. II, p.1,139, Edinburgh, 1884

John Smith of Balallan, in the district of Lochs, was eight years old when his family was caught up in the enforced exodus from the peninsula of Pàirc. Beginning around 1820, dejected people, young and old, wandered in small groups away from their villages. They became part of an itinerant population. These scenes remained with John Smith all of his life, and as an old man giving evidence to the Napier Commission he recalled that they were 'Dealt with as a herd of sheep driven by dogs into a fank'. Some 'were evicted to America', others 'scattered here and there' on small, poor patches of land.

The Pàirc evictions continued, intermittently, over a forty-year period. Those who remained were crowded into evermore impoverished living conditions. By the 1880s almost 2,000 people were squeezed into nine villages in the whole area of Lochs, on 181 crofts of about an acre each. As many as a fifth were squatter families with no land.

In 1881, when the lease for the Pàirc sheep farm was up for renewal, the people of Lochs petitioned the widowed proprietrix, Lady Matheson, for a portion of the land, pleading: 'Unless some means are devised to extend our holdings we must either have to emigrate or become a burden on the estate.'

Twice their pleas elicited no response. When they warned that they might 'be led to resort reluctantly to such steps as many of our unfortunate countrymen are forced to adopt',

 The Pàirc memorial cairn by full moon

Lady Matheson's rejoinder was unequivocal. She dismissed the petitioners as authors of their own misfortune and proceeded to let the sheep farm (26,000 acres) of Pàirc as one unit with no small tenants, while 42,000 acres were let as deer forest to Joseph Platt, an English machine-maker married to a member of the aristocratic Thorneycroft family.

These circumstances set the scene for an event immortalised in Will MacLean's monument overlooking all of Pàirc, which contains amongst its many stones a selection from the homes of the men and women who exposed their plight and alerted the conscience of a nation. By coincidence, or what many regarded 'as a kindly act of providence', the new headmaster at Balallan school was Donald MacRae from Alness, a veteran Land Leaguer who understood that, to be effective, political action must be well organised and widely publicised.

Throughout the autumn of 1887, MacRae and village representatives agreed a strategy to be executed on 22 November. They resolved that 'groups of crofters and cottars, principally the latter, should leave the various townships and . . . proceed into the forest of Pàirc in one body and shoot all the deer they come across or drive them into the sea'.

On the appointed day two hundred men, led by pipers and carrying rifles and provisions, marched into the forest of Pàirc. Women, old men and children lined the route, cheering them on their way. A telegram hurriedly dispatched from the Stornoway Sheriff to Dover House in London declared 'They threaten to remain until all deer are exterminated, they will listen to no remonstrance.' Within hours, a detachment of Royal Marines, based at Maryhill Barracks in Glasgow, were requisitioned to set sail for Stornoway. Adding to the general ferment, Mrs Jessie Platt, wife of the Pàirc forest lessee, portentously insisted in a telegram to the Scottish Office: 'Delay may be fatal.'

Publicity was central to MacRae's strategy. Newspapers were notified in advance and eye-witness accounts appeared in the national press. *The Scotsman*'s correspondent arrived by boat some one hundred yards from the camp. He wrote: 'The scene was the most impressive and not a sound broke the stillness save the swish of the oars. Suddenly sweeping around a point the gleaming of firelight was seen. A tent, made of cabers and covered with canvas boat sails, had been erected at Airidh Dhòmhnaill Chaim. Small fires burned, pipers played and food was being prepared. Visiting reporters were asked to listen to the cause which induced them to resort to such methods of hunting for food, and to invite them to partake of a share'.

The following day Sheriff Fraser arrived on the scene and implored the Raiders, in his native Gaidhlig, to go home. When they refused he read the Riot Act and, fearing immediate arrest,

Interior of Pàirc memorial cairn with stone no. VIII, from Donald Macmillan's house (see Notes to Illustrations)

they agreed to leave the forest. Before nightfall all the raiders had withdrawn, having peace-fully and effectively put their case to the nation.

Meanwhile, military preparations continued. 'It would be unwise to make any changes until sufficient arrests are made to vindicate the law', thundered the Lord Advocate. Sixteen men gave themselves up and were charged with 'mobbing and rioting', though only six were sent to trial. On 14th January, proceedings commenced at the High Court in Edinburgh, with Lord Justice Clerk Moncrieff and Lords MacLaren and Lee on the Bench. At the end of the hearing the jury took just half an hour to return verdicts of not guilty on all charges. The verdicts were received with 'loud and prolonged applause in the court'. Donald MacRae was lifted shoulder-high and carried along the High Street, stopping at the steps of St Giles to thank the crowd. He said the trial and defence had cost them nothing, 'We were defended by advocates and by agents who would have done credit in any area of Scottish history, and the result was proof of their ability and devoted-ness.' A victory was won but the battle continued.

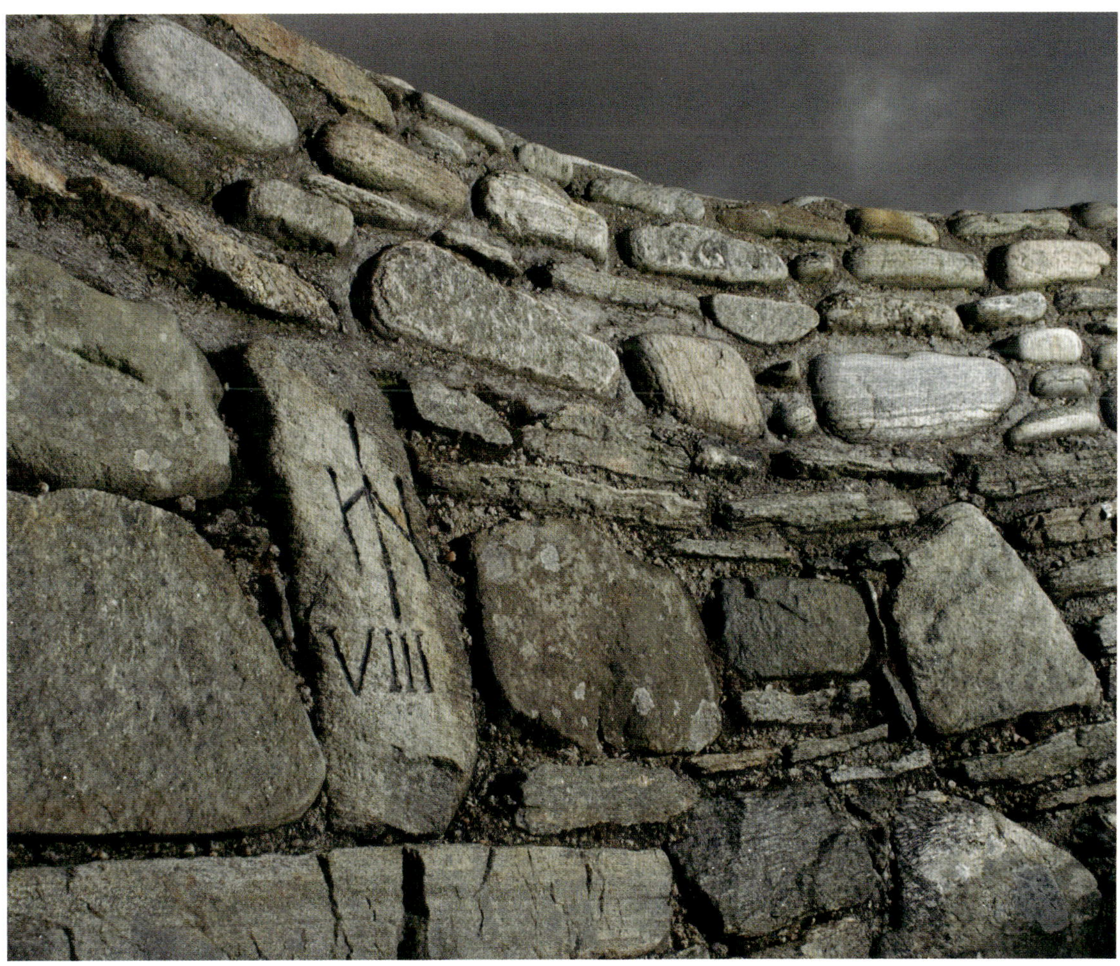

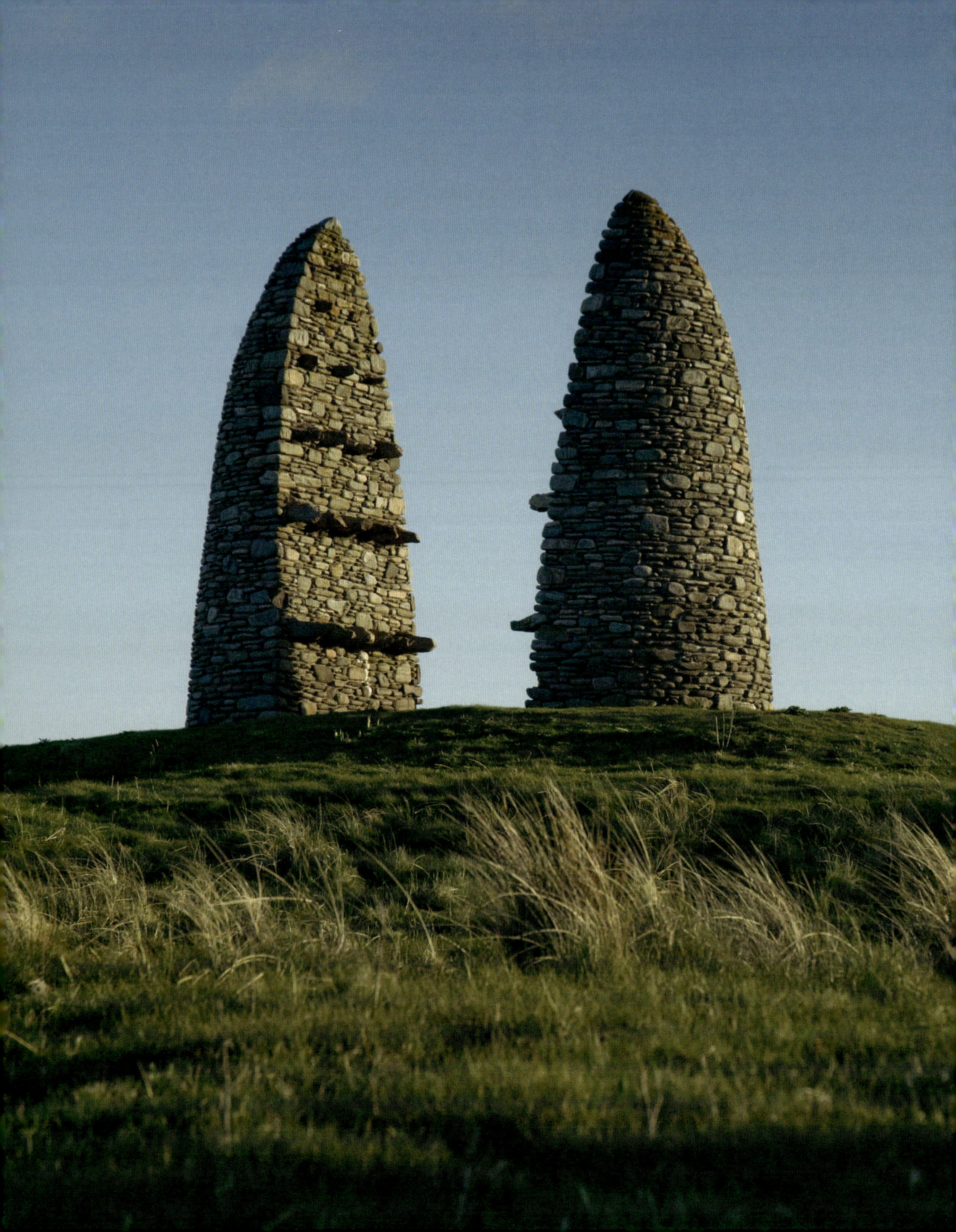

The Aignish Memorial

Site of the 1888 Aignish Riot at Point

Designed by Will Maclean / Construction completed in 1996

Joni Buchanan

'They say Cape Horn is a wild place. Now this place where I live is exposed to the winds that blow down upon one side from Cape Wrath and upon the other from the Butt of Lewis – two places that are quite as wild as Cape Horn. Our shore is so exposed from these two quarters, that while we could work well enough at sea, we are not able to save our lives or our boats when we reach land. If we had a place of refuge there, since we can work well, we would be able to take our living out of the sea as other people in Scotland are able to do.'

The Napier Commission (report of commission of inquiry into the condition of crofters and cottars in the Highlands and Islands of Scotland), Vols I – V, here Vol. II, p.1139, Edinburgh, 1884

Between 1860 and 1886 there were six drowning tragedies in the district of Point. In each case all the crew were lost, usually six men. 'My own son, along with four of a crew, was drowned by the capsizing of the boat at our own door', John Stewart of Bayble told the Napier Commission. Landing places were open and dangerous. Many of the crews were landless squatters, wholly dependent on their fishing income. 'I take my living for my family out of the sea. What I take out of the croft would not support my family for one week', said John Stewart. Danger at sea and denial of access to land – here was an unsustainable predicament that created sheer desperation.

The Matheson estate's heavy hand was backed up with the constant threat to any who complained: 'You will be deprived of your land'; Kenneth Macleod from Garrabost told the Napier Commission: 'We are so depressed that the fear of the estate management . . . has taken the courage out of us.' Like crofters elsewhere on the island they had no security of tenure and their rents were incommensurate with the poor pieces of land they cultivated.

The same issues were being played out across the Highlands. Increasingly, people were taking a stand against injustice and the oppression of landlords. A particularly infamous Lewis factor for the Matheson estate, Donald Munro, was regarded as being the very embodiment of oppression; as the late Iain MacArthur wrote in *Na Gaisgich*, 'It is not surprising that the curse of the population followed Munro to the end, so much so that they could not give him the honour normally afforded the dead. Pile it [the dirt] upon him, put it upon him', they said, as they closed the grave, 'As he put upon us'.

It is not fear alone that is symbolised in Will MacLean's monument at Aignish. The struggle
of brave people tired of scraping a living is embodied in its story and so too is conflict.
The two columns stand opposite one another on the east side of the cemetery of Aoidh,
on a narrow stretch of land between high walls at the head of the bay. They are fashioned
from handsome stonework in the local tradition and curve in towards each other in a show
of deep antagonism. Here and there sharper stones protrude from the structures, like
bayonets aimed at the opposing force, just as happened on the appointed day of the riot.

The difficulties experienced on land and at sea finally came to a head towards the end
of 1887. In many respects the moment was apposite. Just a couple of months previously
the Pàirc raiders had heightened awareness of the injustices which existed on Lewis.
During the closing weeks of the year, two meetings were held in Garrabost Free Church
at which plans were laid for militant action against the landlord and his tenant farmers.

Talk of preparations in Point to follow the Pàirc raiders' lead spread and soon reached
Sheriff Fraser and estate authorities in Stornoway. Two constables, accompanied by
a reporter from *The Scotsman* newspaper, were the first to be sent to the farm and
to await any sign of disturbance. Around midnight on New Year's night a group of men
appeared and set about dismantling the farm dykes; the constables took them by surprise
and managed one arrest. The others fled into the dark night.

Tensions were raised but this was a prelude to the appointed day of the full-scale riot,
the 7th of January 1888, which witnessed the clash of forces depicted so dramatically
in the Maclean monument. Over five hundred men and women gathered at daybreak
on a hill above the farm. They quickly set about driving the stock away from the farmland.

By then, plans by the authorities to subvert the riot came into force. Eighty Royal Marines and
Royal Navy personnel, as well as about twenty constables, were at Sheriff Fraser's disposal.
The Royal Marines had been dispatched to nearby Melbost the previous night and the navy
ratings came ashore in the morning and hid in the farm outbuildings. It is doubtful, however,
that they anticipated the numerical strength of forces which assembled against them.

The Riot Act was repeatedly read in Gaelic but each time, *The Scotsman* reported, the crowd
responded: 'Our families are starving. We need the land.' Within an hour, a thousand people
were scattered over the farmlands. The incredulous *Scotsman* reporter noted: 'They simply
did not pay any attention to the Marines . . . They did not desist until every hoof had been
driven out at the other end of the farm.'

Arrests were made and this created the focal point for confrontation with the crowd, brand-
ishing their sticks at the armed soldiers and police. Sensing the danger of serious bloodshed,

the Marines backed off and awaited reinforcements of Royal Scots from Stornoway. Eventually, they escorted away the arrested men, while the crowd hurled earth, stones and sticks at the retreating column.

The leniency shown towards the Pàirc raiders had caused political outrage and a hard-line judge, Lord Craighill, was appointed to the case. He handed down prison sentences of between 6 and 15 months to 16 men. *The Scotsman* reported 'great dismay and anger amongst the people'; when this news was posted in Stornoway shop windows, the Land League called on crofters 'to manfully maintain the agitation'. Aignish became another indelible landmark in the long march towards justice and land reform.

As Iain MacArthur concluded in his account of the riot in *Na Gaisgich*, 'It's possible that people didn't understand the effect of the riot at the time. But, it raised awareness again of the poverty of islanders, the rioters shaped their destiny, they sought their freedom and their legal rights. What precious achievements! They churned the milk but it was the next generations that tasted the butter.'

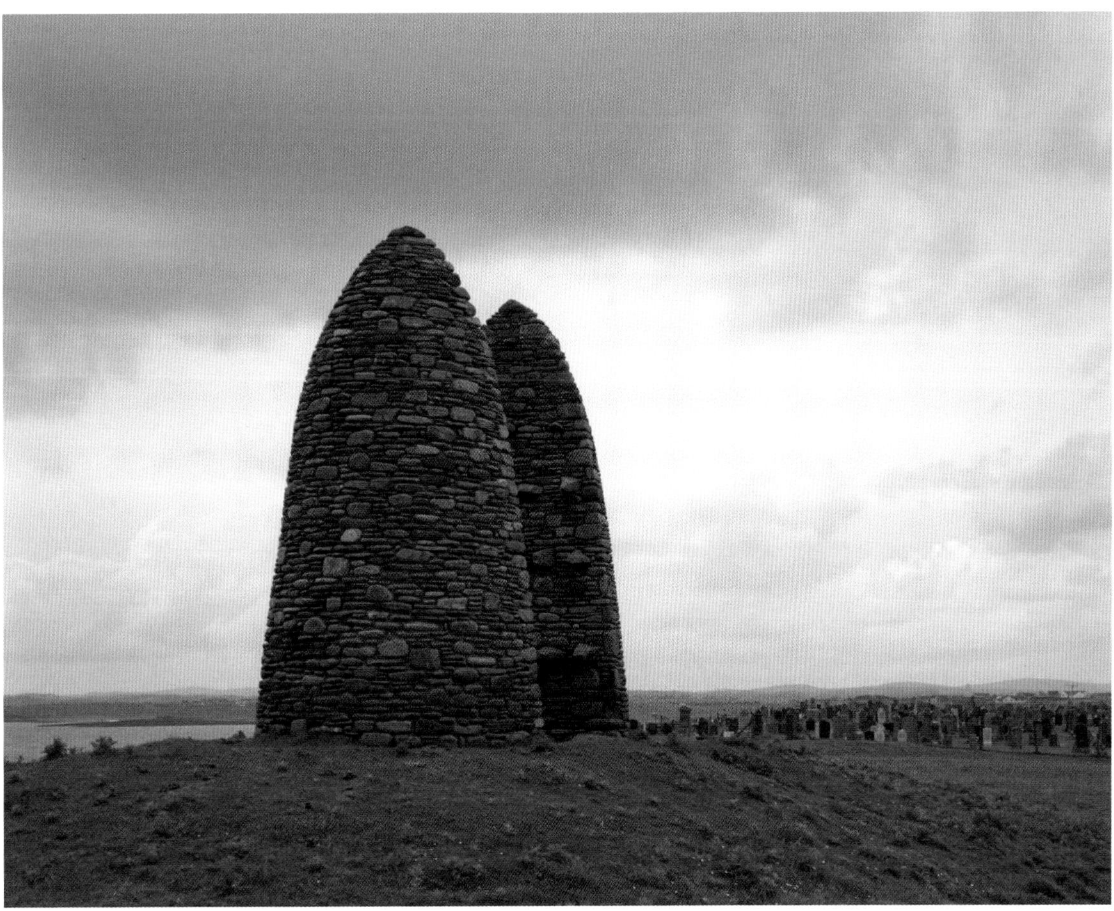

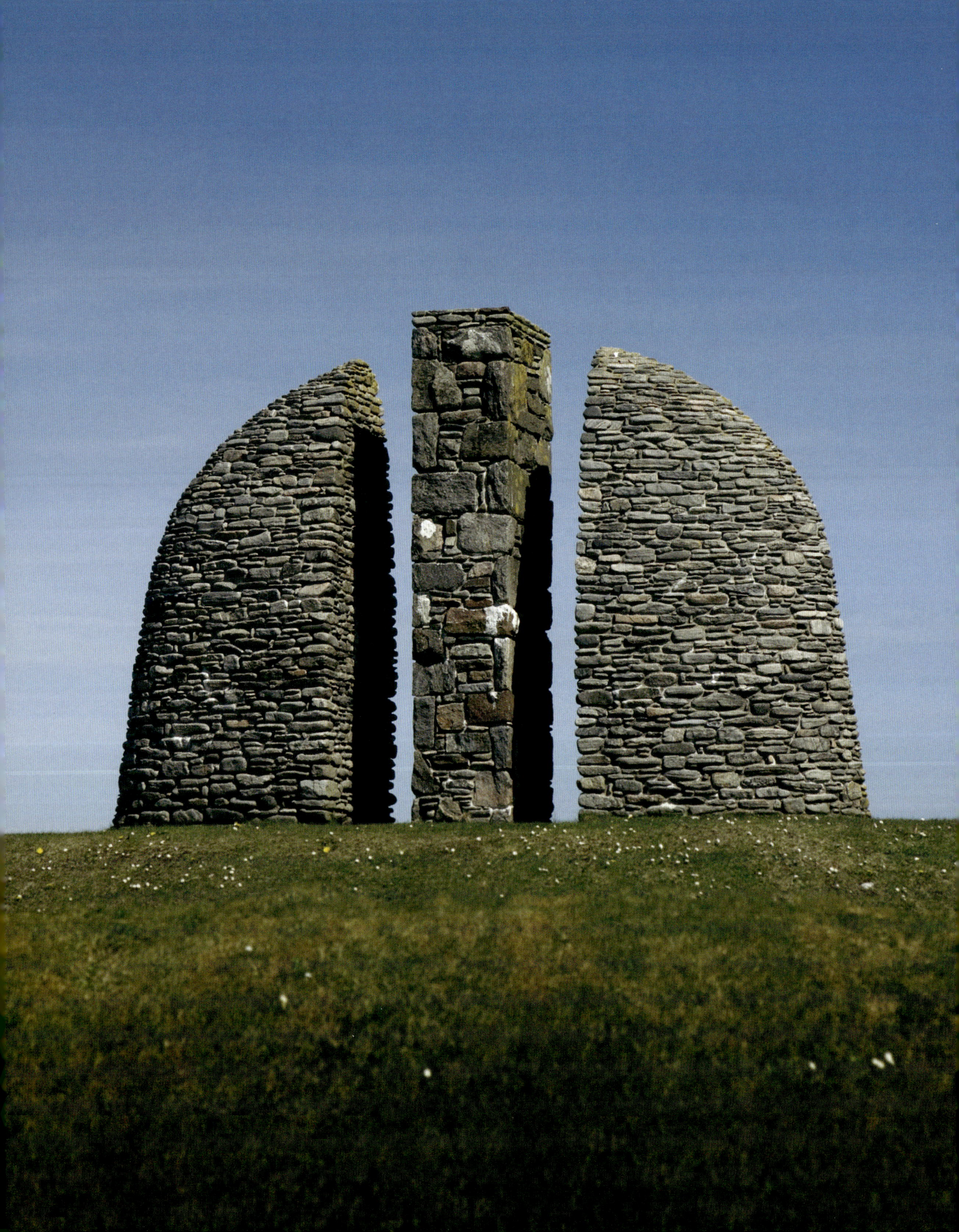

The Gress Memorial

Scene of the 1919 meeting between Lord Leverhulme and the Coll and Gress crofters in the District of Back

Designed by Will Maclean / Construction completed in 1996

Joni Buchanan

Emotional threads run deep through the columns of ancient rock and the rise of earth that encircles Will MacLean's monument at Gress Bridge. The earth is symbolic of the trenches from which the ex-servicemen who led the struggle for the resettlement of Coll and Gress farms had just returned. Lord Leverhulme, founder of a huge industrial empire, Lever Brothers, which in 1918 acquired the Isle of Lewis, is represented by the central pillar, powerful and unyielding. At the outer edges, two curved forms evoke the listening crowd, weary but resilient, huddled against the wind. The gaps between central and outer shapes symbolise the philosophical distance between the protagonists.

An application for the break-up of Gress farm had been lodged by the Board of Agriculture with the Land Court in July 1914. Forty new holdings were to be created. Fraught negotiations between the Board and Matheson estate delayed the process. With the country at war, the Board was reluctant to pursue costly litigation and opted instead for 'an indefinite postponement of the resettlement schemes'. Even before hostilities concluded, preparations to relaunch the Lewis schemes were back on the Board's agenda. In September 1917 they issued Compulsory Orders in respect of the Lewis farms. By then, however, a whole new dimension had emerged. The last of the Matheson proprietors was in the process of selling to Lord Leverhulme, who on acquiring the island in May 1918 wrote: 'My object with the Isle of Lewis is not business, but to find a delightful home in a beautiful island among a people I greatly admire and respect.'

Leverhulme, however, was the quintessential self-made man and business was never far from his thoughts. By the autumn of 1918 he had developed plans to turn the town of Stornoway into the 'finest city in the West of Scotland', with new industries, railroads and homes for workers – all welcome in a depressed post-war economy.

The land question was still very much alive, and in the General Election of December 1918 all three candidates believed it was the political and economic priority of the age. They acknowledged the great potential of Leverhulme's schemes and assumed both agrarian production and industry to be perfectly compatible, as they felt they had always been. Just before the election, and as a reminder of the urgency of their claim, landless families in Coll and Gress wrote to the Board urging them to 'cut out Gress farm as soon as possible, before Spring so that we can build our houses during the good weather'; further delay, they threatened, would only lead them to 'take the law into our own hands'.

On New Year's Day 1919, Lewis awoke to the unspeakable tragedy of the *Iolaire* disaster. In the weeks that followed, work began on Leverhulme's employment schemes and they provided a rare shaft of optimism in an atmosphere of stunned and incomprehensible grief. It soon emerged, however, that crofting did not feature in Leverhulme's plans for the island; he regarded crofting as 'the worst possible form of tenure . . . the constitution of additional small-holdings would only extend and aggravate a system thoroughly bad'. He demanded from the Board of Agriculture a moratorium on resettlement schemes for 'several years'.

For the first time in history the law was on the crofters' side. They had the support of the Scottish Secretary, Robert Munro, and the Land Settlement (Scotland) Act 1919 greatly increased funds available to enable the Board to compulsorily purchase land. The Government also understood the pressure to make good the slogan 'Land fit for Heroes'. One of the crofters' leaders, Angus Graham, wrote a letter to Munro on 3rd March 1920: 'We are demanding nothing but the promise that was made to us when we was ploughing the green ocean, and when we was in the earth holes in Flanders up to our knees in mud.'

Will MacLean's monument at Gress Bridge depicts the first stand-off between Leverhulme and the raiders, which took place on 12th March 1919. The landlord stood on an upturned barrel at the centre of a crowd numbering over a thousand and announced: 'So great is my regard for Lewis and its people that I am prepared to adventure a big sum for the development of its resources and its fisheries.' He would, he said, spend £5 million on a great fishing fleet, a fish-canning factory, railways, a garden city . . .

It took a brave man to interrupt his flow, but Leverhulme was dealing with intelligent people. Alan Martin intervened to address the crowd in Gaelic, which Leverhulme's interpreter translated as: 'Come, come, folk! This will not do! This honey-mouthed man would have us believe that black is white and white is black. We are not concerned with his fancy dreams, that may or may not come true! What we want is the land, and the question I put to him now is, Will you give us the land?'

Leverhulme's answer was emphatic: 'No I will not give you the land; not because I'm vindictively opposed to your views . . . I believe if my views are listened to, if my schemes are given a chance, the result will be enhanced prosperity and greater happiness for Lewis and its people.'

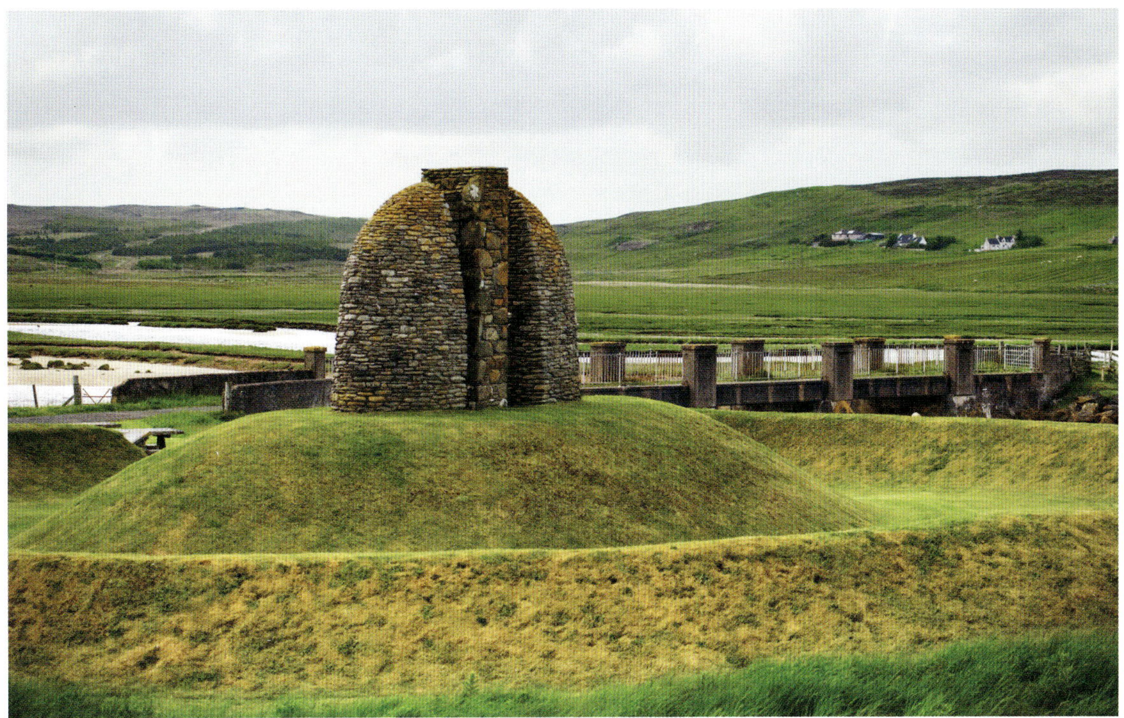

Again, he was interrupted, this time in English, by another raider, John MacLeod: 'I would impress on you that we do not oppose your schemes of work; we only oppose you when you say you cannot give us the land and on that point we will oppose you with all our strength. You have bought this island. But you have not bought us, and we refuse to be the bond slaves of any man. We want to live our own lives in our own way, poor in material things it may be, but at least it will be clear of the factory bell; it will be free and independent.'[1]

The scene was set for a classic and protracted conflict. The farms were raided on three separate occasions. Leverhulme proved an unreasonable opponent, using every tactic to divide opinion. He barred raiders from employment then halted all work until raiders withdrew. When they did withdraw he failed to restart the schemes. By January 1921 the raiders had left the disputed farms and the government acceded to Leverhulme's demands for a 10-year moratorium on land settlement providing the work schemes were resumed.

Crucially, Lever Brothers were by then facing financial difficulties – arising from their West African operations and a deepening recession in the domestic economy – and Leverhulme pulled the plug on his Lewis schemes. Early in 1922, the Board of Agriculture took over the farms of Coll and Gress as well as North Tolsta and Orinsay, creating 180 new crofts and 81 enlargements of existing holdings, while Leverhulme's grand schemes were consigned to history as a mirage that had come and gone.

---

1 Colin MacDonald, *Highland Journey*, Moray Press, Edinburgh, 1943. Colin MacDonald was a Board of Agriculture officer sent to Lewis to negotiate with Leverhulme.

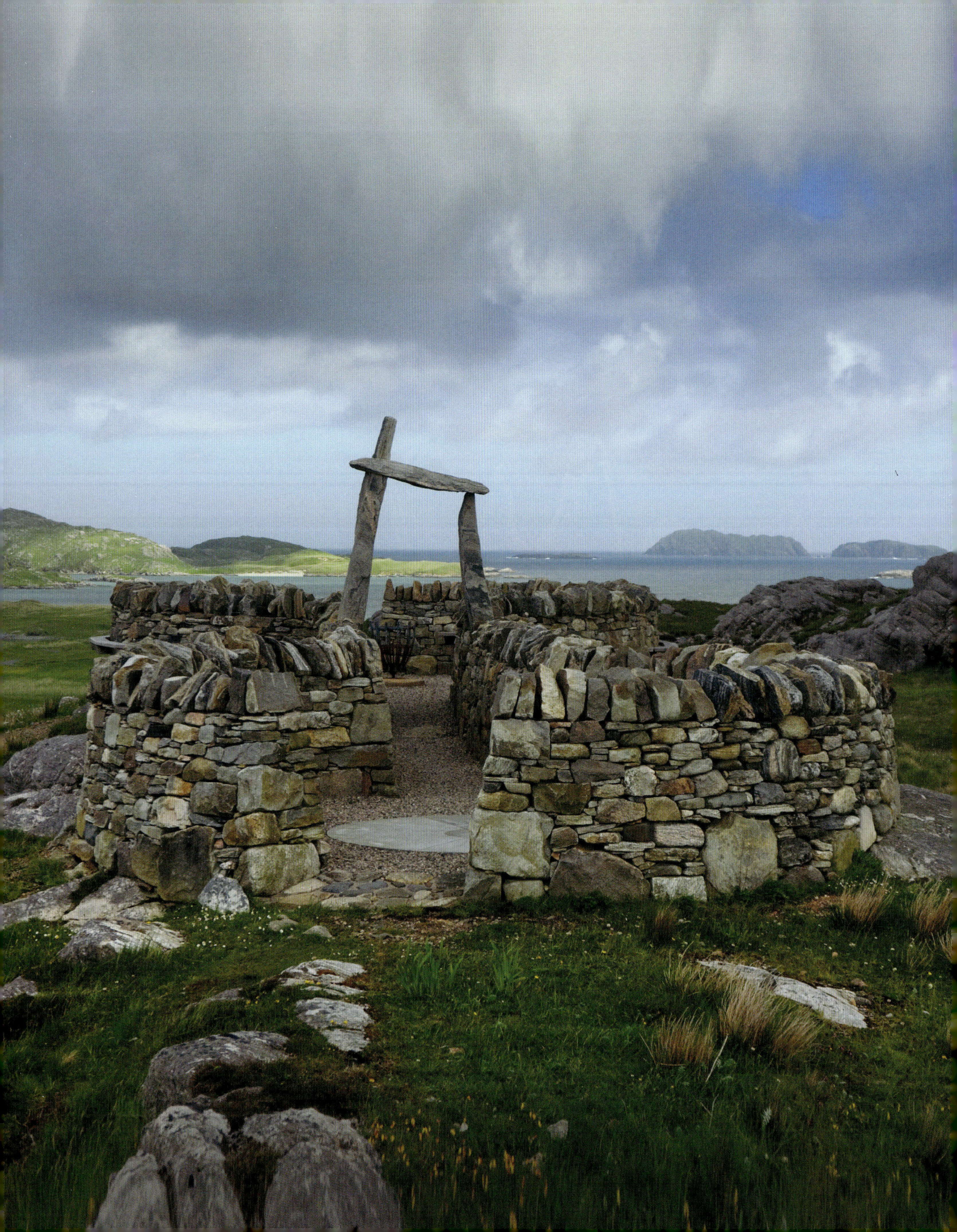

An Sùileachan

Scene of the Reef Land Raids 1913/14 and 1920/21

Designed by Will Maclean & Marian Leven / Construction completed in 2013

Joni Buchanan

Spread across the brow of Eicleat Bheag, a rocky hillock that straddles the western flank of the village of Reef, lies *An Sùileachan*, the fourth commemorative structure commissioned to honour those who resisted the absolute power of landlordism and restored land to the crofting population of the Bhaltos peninsula.

An Sùileachan, designed by Will Maclean and Marian Leven, symbolises a journey through time. It draws the visitor back in history to the 1850 evictions and salutes those who later regained the land. On the southern aspect of *An Sùileachan* a stone portal built from slabs of magnificent Lewisian gneiss moves the visitor metaphorically from the past through to the present and invites us to gaze at the land around, now held in trust by the villagers themselves, and to ponder what the future might hold for this tranquil place.

For three years, 28 Reef families peaceably resisted all attempts by the estate of Sir James Matheson to remove them, but in 1850 they were forcibly evicted from their homes: some scattered on the island, others removed to America. Neil Maclennan, of Breasclete, told the Napier Commission: 'Those of us who came here [the Breasclete moorland] brought the roofs of our houses with us. Others left these things there and they went useless.'[1] A year after the Reef evictions a further fourteen Bhaltos and Kneep families were removed.

By the late 19th century the remaining population of the peninsula, known traditionally as the 'fourteen penny lands', were crowded into two villages with no access to the surrounding land, which had been added to large farms. Amongst them were 31 landless families.

Over the period in excess of 40,000 acres of land in Uig had been taken out of crofting use and given over to seven sheep-farmers and three big sporting estates. The first act of popular resistance against the absolute and arbitrary power of the Lewis estate was in 1874, when the people of the Island of Bernera, also in Uig, resisted the removal of 56 families from their traditional grazing lands. The Bernera resistance was indicative of the beginning of a more forceful stand against injustice.

Reports of unrest in south Uig began to filter through in the early 1880s. In December 1884, HMS *Assistance*, with a force of up to one hundred Marines, arrived in Loch Roag to arrest eight men accused of placing stock on offshore islands for grazing and deforcing Sheriff's Officers. They were tried at the Court of Session and summarily imprisoned. The following year ten men and seven women were fined for similar activities. The women were charged with 'mobbing and rioting and breach of the peace'; their fines, five shillings each, were paid by the London branch of the Highland Land Law Reform Association.[2]

On two occasions, in 1891 and in 1896, the Deer Forest Commission recommended that Reef should be resettled as a crofting village, but the estate refused to comply. In 1909, the Matheson estate agreed to give up the farm of Reef in return for 'a perpetual guarantee of rent' from government. However, the Board of Agriculture for Scotland took refuge in the view that Reef was 'quite simply statute-barred' (because it fell below an overall figure of £80 in annual rents). Actually, as confirmed in official correspondence, they feared that if they bought the farm (as they were legally entitled to do under the Small Landholders (Scotland) Act 1911) this would 'let in the deluge'.[3]

Believing the Board to be obstructionist, the landless squatters notified their intention to raid, proclaiming 'This was our forebears' place . . . and in spring we will plant it.' In the late winter of 1913 and twice in the New Year they drove the farmer's stock from Reef farm. The raider Alasdair MacKay told the parish policeman: 'You can have plenty of prisoners now. We've waited too long . . . now we have made up our minds to take it, whatever may happen to us.'

In late January 1914, the crofters began to turn the ground in Reef in preparation for cultivating in the spring. They were interdicted to stop all work by the Matheson estate. When the interdicts were defied, 18 men were cited to appear at the Court of Session in Edinburgh. A subscription was raised in Stornoway before they could leave for the capital, where at the Court of Session each was sentenced to six weeks' imprisonment.

At this critical point, the issue at stake was driven into abeyance by the outbreak of war. Most of the men went off to fight and those who survived came back more determined than ever to claim their own 'land fit for heroes'. The contrast between their country's call to arms in this terrible war and its continuing failure to make good promises of land was incomprehensible and impossible to accept.

By February 1920, the crofters and cottars could wait no longer. Eleven of the original raiders wrote to the Secretary of State for Scotland: 'We are demobilised soldiers and sailors unemployed since September . . . we are compelled to begin spring work on Reef Farm. If you will send the Commissioners of Small Holdings to us for the purpose of dividing the farm into crofts and putting us in possession as we trust you will, we will delay our operation to the 1st of March. If they are not here by that time we will be under the necessity of beginning work as a means to our livelihood.'

By this time, the new landlord, Lord Leverhulme, was locked in dispute with the Scottish Office and offered up the Uig farms as pawns in his resistance to breaking up the ones closer to Stornoway. Finally, in 1921, the land of the Bhaltos peninsula was restored to the people. The fact there is a population here today and a future for this community is due to the struggles undertaken by those who secured a just outcome at that time. *An Sùileachan* is a magnificent memorial to these struggles.[4]

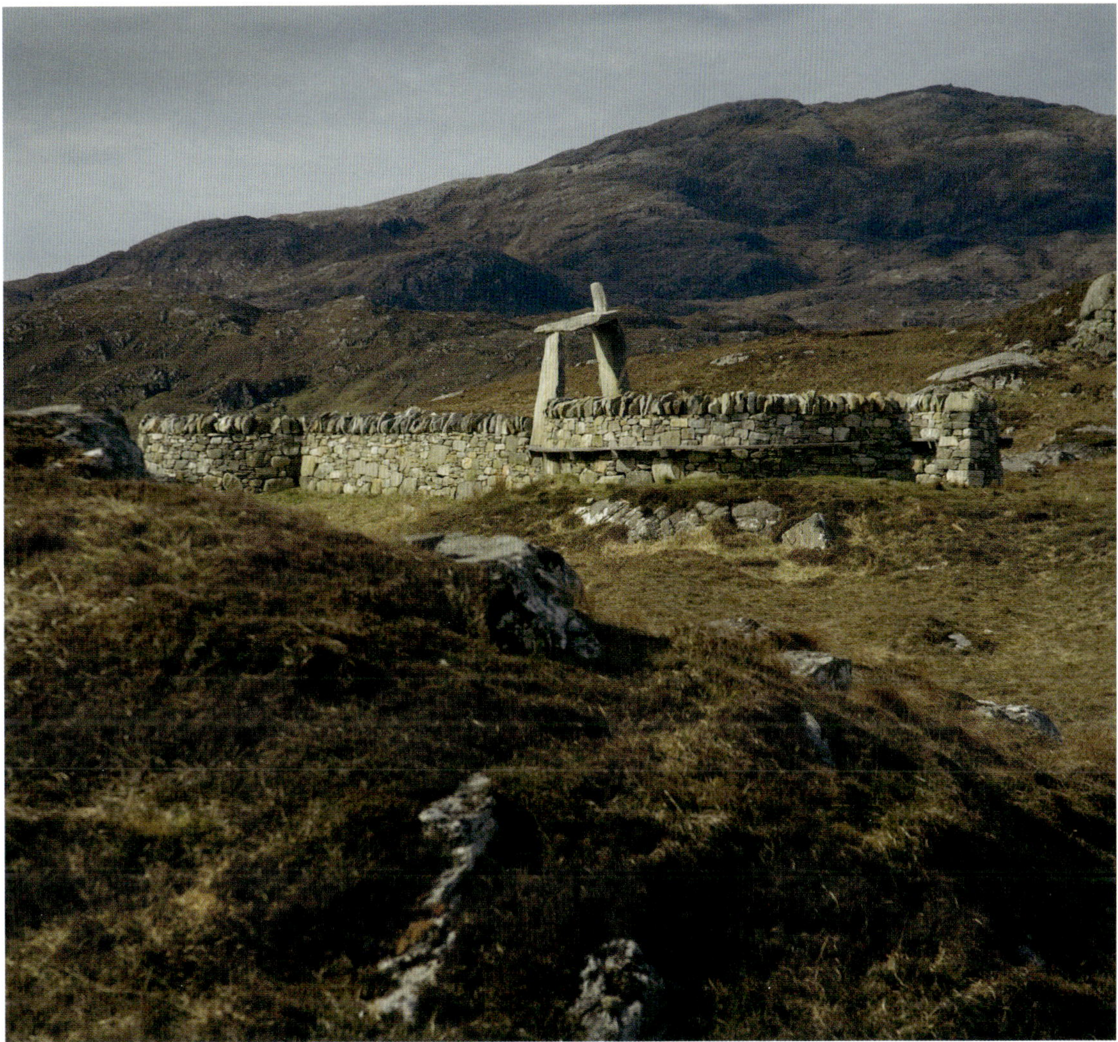

1. J M Mackenzie, *Diary 1851*, Acair, Stornoway, 1994
2. *The Napier Commission* report, 1884, by the commission of inquiry into the condition of crofters and cottars in the Highlands and Islands of Scotland (all five volumes of the report are now digitised and hosted by the West Highland College UHI and transferred to the Centre for History; see www.uhi.ac.uk)
.3 Deer Forest Royal Commission of Inquiry, 1892
4. Scottish Records Office, AF 59; AF 67/61; and AF 67/62

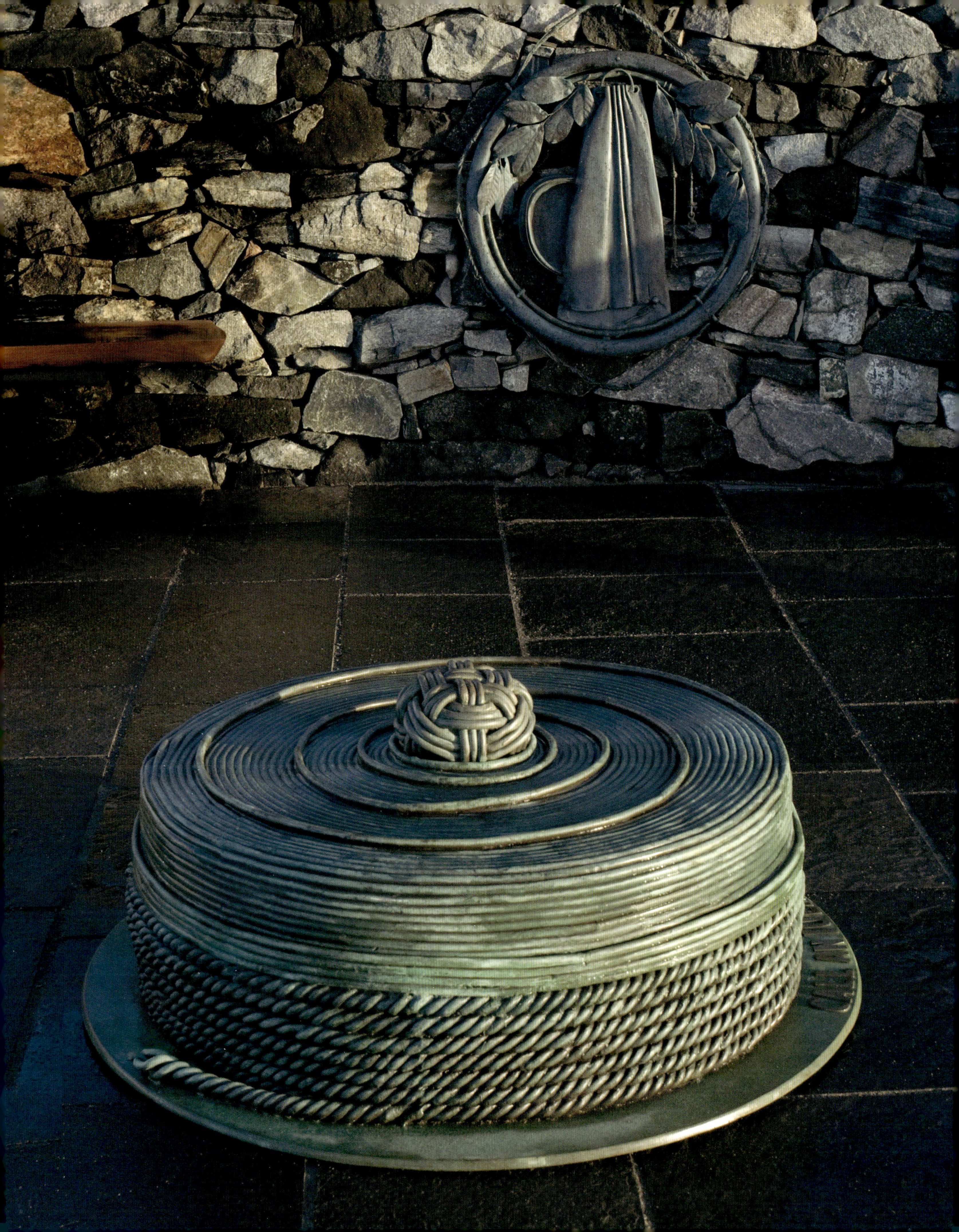

The *Iolaire* Memorial

Marking the tragic loss at Holm, 1st January 1919

Designed by Will Maclean, Marian Leven, Arthur Watson
Construction completed in 2018

Joni Buchanan

Over the course of the First World War, up to 6,000 young Lewis men volunteered, or were later called up, to fight at sea and on the front line. A fifth of that number never returned. The casualties of those four cruel years were more than the sum of lives lost, leaving the island depleted of its lifeblood, and still the Armistice did not bring an end to the squander. At the very dawn of peace and within sight of their home 201 men drowned, including 174 from Lewis and 7 from Harris, in the sinking of HMY *Iolaire*. Few villages escaped the loss of youth on that night; the pain was everywhere, desolate and incomprehensible.

The Stornoway Gazette's fine editorial described the dark cloud that descended on Lewis on New Year's Day, 1919. 'Islanders', the paper reported, 'have been mourning as they have never mourned before and they refuse to be comforted. Death has come to them in an appalling tragedy, cruel, crushing and bitterly poignant.' It remained the country's worst maritime disaster in coastal waters of the 20th century. Instead of a joyous homecoming for survivors of war, it left still more young women widowed, children without the presence of their fathers, grieving parents and lost loves. Its impacts continued to be felt through succeeding generations while knowledge of the *Iolaire* disaster remained largely confined to the island that had been so devastated by it.

Among a range of commemorative projects to mark the 100th anniversary, Will Maclean RSA, Marian Leven RSA and Arthur Watson RSA were commissioned by An Lanntair Art Gallery in Stornoway to create the centenary memorial in bronze and stone. It looks out over a short – and because of its proximity to shore deceptively benign-looking – stretch of sea, towards the sharp and craggy rocks known as the Beasts of Holm/Biastan Thuilm, where the unspeakable catastrophe took place.

Arthur Watson created a bronze coiled heaving line and hawser, placed centrally on a surface of slabbed granite, with bronze lettering in curved bands carefully listing the names of each lost naval rating. On the stone wall, Will Maclean's bronze wreath fuses motifs of life and death, with laurel leaves and rendered details of a rating's belongings, evocative of the haunted spirits of the dead, the memories, and the deep and enduring sorrow at their loss.

On the wall is Will Maclean's bronze wreath, with Arthur Watson's bronze sculpture of the hawser and heaving line placed on the granite floor

The nautical forms of the sculptures represent the island's ties with the seas: reliance, fear, knowledge and respect – that everlasting dialogue. They signify, especially, the chaos of that terrible night; of seeing brothers, cousins, neighbours and friends tossed into a dark and terrifying sea, being hurled against the rocks, emerging, and then sucked back into the abyss by the relentless might of an undertow, never again to resurface. Amidst all this, there was also a story of hope and the resilience of the human spirit; of one man, John Finlay MacLeod, jumping into the sea with a rope, a lifeline, and managing, through that remarkable act, to save the lives of 40 of his comrades.

When John Finlay told his story to the BBC in 1961, he said it was so difficult to talk about it publicly because he did not want to hurt anyone by reviving painful memories of things that had passed.[1] I expect he was slightly less reticent about talking to the BBC as the conversation was in his native Gàidhlig, though his account was as tactful, understated and modest as the man himself.

He explained that the night was so dark and stormy that you could not see a thing. As the ship became impaled on the rocks a flare launched from the stricken vessel momentarily lit the surrounding area and only then did he realise, when he saw the beacon (marking the dangerous rocks), that the Iolaire had hit the Beasts of Holm. He said:

> I made up my mind to take the heaving line in my hand, and I jumped out of the back with it, to try and get ashore. I didn't expect the rock to be as difficult as it was. But when I reached the bow the rock was above me and the current pulled me back, but if I had struck the rock there would have been nothing [left] of me, I was then pulled further back with the current than I had been before. And when three large waves went over me, the third one, I went ahead of that one, and I was thrown on my chest onto the steep rock, that's how I got ashore and I held onto the line the entire time.

John Finlay was from a family of boatbuilders and seamen, each generation passing to the next their deep knowledge of the intricacies of seas and of tides. His son John Murdo MacLeod, also a boatbuilder, wrote down his father's detailed account of his actions and explained the significance of the third wave:

> Maybe he was fortunate that he was somewhat familiar with that coastline. He used to come up there on a trading smack that my grandfather had. Having decided on his course of action, he gave the end of the heaving line to a fellow beside him and told him he must not let it go. He didn't put the rope round his middle, but two times round his left hand and locked the end of the rope with his thumb. Then he dropped into the water.

> At the first attempt the surge carried him away from the shore. With extraordinary presence of mind, he then took stock of the situation. Local knowledge again told him

that the *fath* of seven smaller waves was followed by the *claith*, three bigger ones. He reckoned that if he could let himself go on the third high wave, with luck he would be carried over the rocks and land on the slope. That is what happened. After four had come ashore on the heaving line, he realised it would not hold and the hawser line was sent across. In all 40 lives were saved and he was at the end of it until finally there was nobody else coming ashore.[2]

Lifeboats, the only other hope of survival, were lowered and loaded with young men, but as Donald MacDonald from Cromore recalled,

> We were used to mines, torpedoes and shell fire but this struck fear in our hearts. We knew we were trapped and no lifeboat could live in that maelstrom … Pieces of the lifeboats on the wind side were being hurled over our heads. Some sailors were trying to get two boats out the lee side. I descended to the bulwarks to jump into one of the boats. Thank goodness I missed it by seconds. It was loaded. I watched it churning and spinning and in an instant down it went. I could see little black spots in the foaming froth. Something determined me from jumping into the second boat. I gazed at it as I shoved off, then a mighty backwash wave seemed to fill the boat. It seemed to glide up to their shoulders, their heads – and no more. I could not see any survivors from any of the boats.[3]

Even when the men leapt into the sea and somehow managed to find the lifeline, the merciless current still swept them away from the rope. Donald MacDonald from North Tolsta, who came ashore on the rope, could see some of the men who had leapt before him being torn away from it by the ferocious strength of the outgoing waves:

> The tragedy was when the waves were going out, one after another and sweeping the men off the rope. I was watching for so long as I had vowed to myself not to leave the vessel. I began to think if I did catch the incoming waves I would be borne onto the shingle beach like a fish before the sea turned again. The returning waves were sweeping the rope bare. You can't comprehend the ferocity of that sea. Many had now lost heart to go onto the rope as they saw what was happening. I thought I would take my chance of life or death when the next sea would be going landwards. As the waves hit her side I got onto the rope and with a death grip I hung on. I felt the sea receding and the rope curving with its force but by then I was amongst the rocks. Clinging to the rope I made my way through the rock – that's how I got away – my time hadn't yet come.[4]

In the days following, islanders were thrown into a stunned and indescribable grief; they had been dealt an overwhelming hand, a trauma the likes of which had never before visited their shores. The morning cast light on the grimmest scenes – the torn, tattered remains of young men and then the desperate search on the shore, on the rocks, in the tangle of seaweed, for beloved sons.

The bodies were laid out in a makeshift mortuary at the Battery, the naval base where the man in charge of operations was Lt Frederick Townend from Hull. Townend later recalled,

Watching the relatives of missing men searching for their dead was the most harrowing experience of my life, especially when an identification was made. For months after it was over, I saw in my dreams, rows of naval-issue boots, with numbers chalked on their soles.[5]

In the villages, preparations for the special homecoming were quietly put away. Fathers and brothers, sometimes mothers and sisters, left with their horses and carts for the town to claim their dead. There are so many stories, too many for this brief account, but Donald MacPhail from Shawbost, who travelled to Stornoway with a neighbour Roddy Murray who was searching for his son, conveyed the scene of terrible pathos at the mortuary when he spoke to Fred MacAulay in 1961:

I left for Stornoway – I remember it was dawn – with a horse and cart, myself and two other boys and the father of one of the lads who had been lost. And we went down to the Battery where the bodies were laid out for identification. I remember they had tickets on them… Leurbost, Shawbost, Tolsta… and the man who went over with us, his son was there and I remember he was so handsome that I could have said he was not dead at all. I remember the colour of his face, I remember that fine yet.

His father went on his knees beside him and he began to take letters from his son's pocket, and there was money, silver and paper money. And the father was reading the letter that he found and the tears were falling from him and splashing on the body of his son. I think it is the most heart-rending sight I have ever seen, and that was only one of many to be seen on the Battery that day and for many days afterwards.[6]

They carried the bodies home, slowly. Chirsty Morrison from Lional, Ness, remembered: 'as though the great weight of their anguish slowed every step they took . . . a terrifying anguish. War had ended and everyone expected them home.'

---

1. John Finlay MacLeod interviewed by Fred MacAuley, BBC Radio nan Gàidheal, 1961
2. *West Highland Free Press*, December, 1993
3. T. C. Dòmhallach, *Call na h-Iolaire*, Acair, Stornaway, 1978
4. M. Macdonald and D. J. MacLeod, *Call na h-'Iolaire': The Darkest Dawn, The Story of the 'Iolaire' Tragedy*, Acair, Stornoway, 2018
5. *ibid.*
6. T. C. Dòmhallach, *Call na h-'Iolaire'*

See also:
BBC Radio nan Gàidheal, Fred MacAulay interviews: Kenneth Maciver, 1986, 1987; Jo MacDonald, 1989; Annella Macleod, 1999; and Nan S. Macleod, 2008. *Eilean an Fraoich Annual/Stornoway Gazette*, 1977; Ness Historical Society Archives; J. MacLeod, *When I Heard the Bell: The Loss of the 'Iolaire'*, Birlinn, Edinburgh, 2009

Arthur Watson's bronze sculpture of the hawser and heaving line with the lettering, and a view of the marker where HMY *Iolaire* sank.

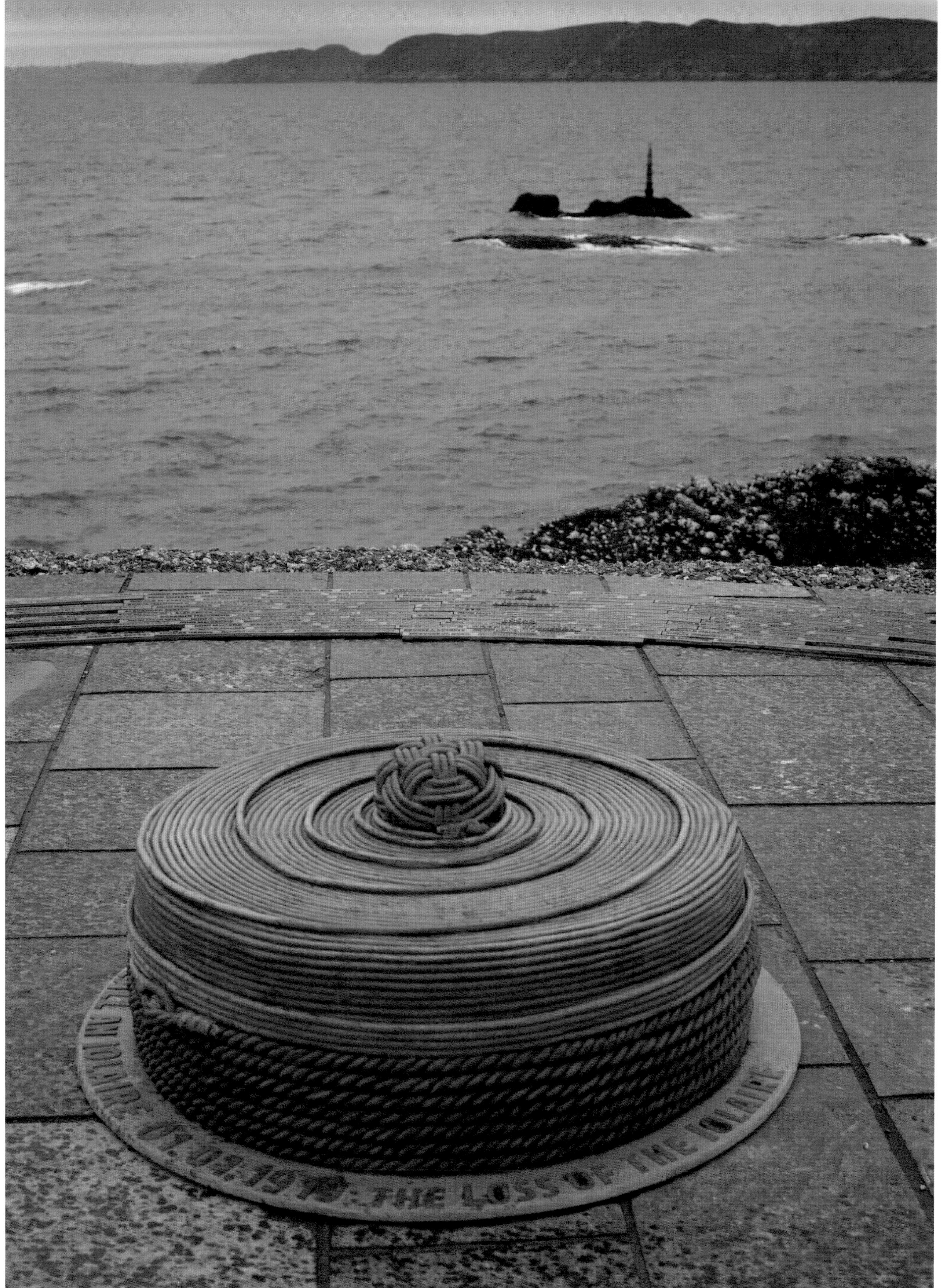
THE LOSS OF THE IOLAIRE

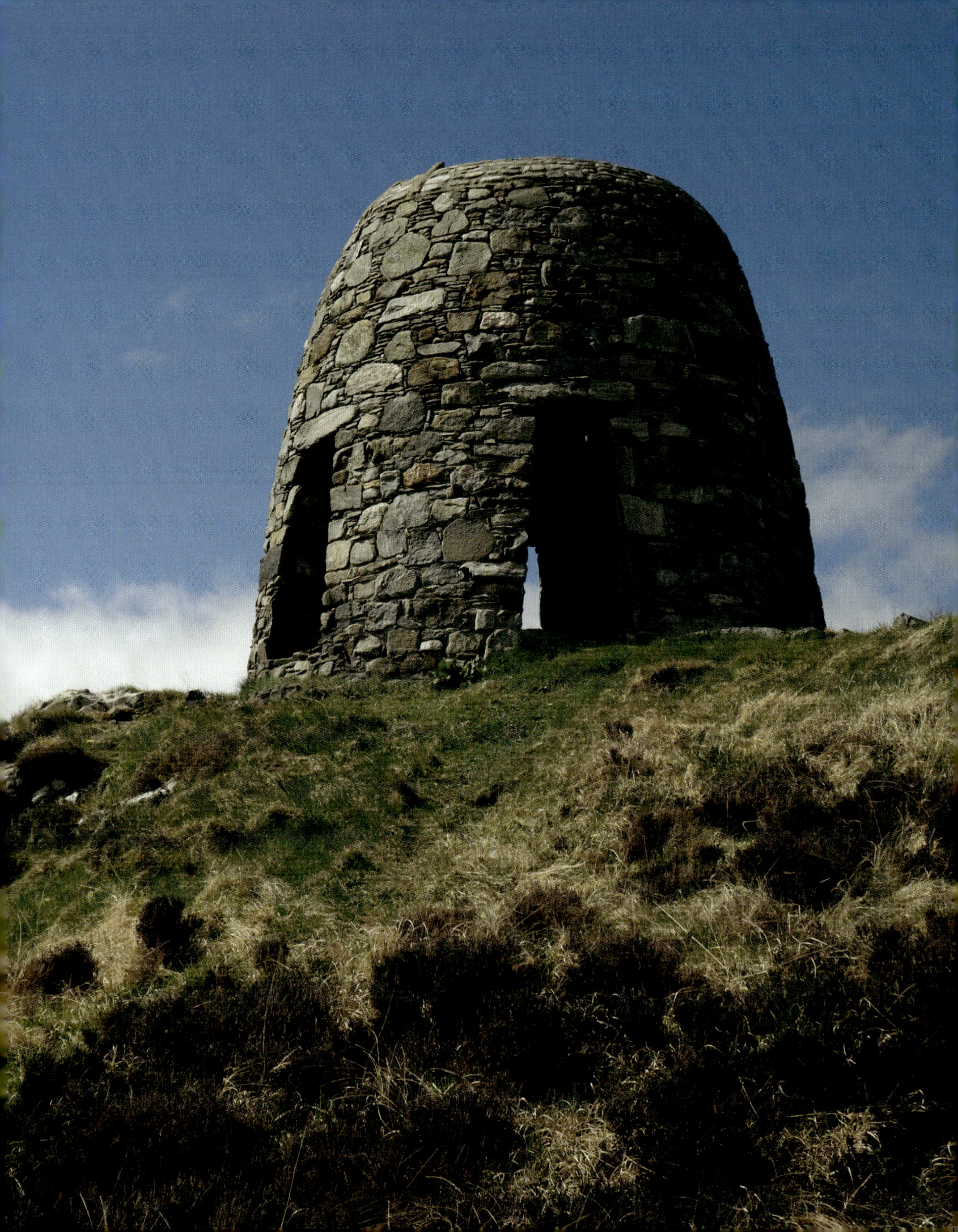

Memory, memory-places
and memorials

Tom Normand

To visit the Isle of Lewis in the Outer Hebrides is to experience a landscape that is awe-inspiring. Its jagged coastline is jewelled with small beaches, rolling sand dunes and wind-blown machair plains. Rocky outcrops and fjord-like sea lochs corrugate the island's shore-line. The central moorland is replete with great washes of peaty marshland and everywhere the fertile land supports rare plants, impressive birdlife and a startling array of mammals, insects and amphibians. Stornoway is the main port and by far the largest town, while the island is studded with smaller townships and villages in different parishes. The marks of a deep island history are laced through the landscape in prehistoric settlements, stone circles, ancient brochs and 'cleared' homesteads. Truly, this journey is breathtaking in its natural and historic associations. But also, to journey on Lewis is to encounter some of the finest examples of contemporary memorial land art in the British Isles.

These 'memorial cairns', as they are referred to, were made in direct response to the community's own vision. Through the expert initiative of the local polymath and activist, the late Angus 'Ease' Macleod, who established the organisation Cuimhneachain nan Gaisgeach (Commemoration of Our Land Heroes), the brief for a meaningful and creatively ambitious series of memorials took root.[1] This was developed at every level by the island's peoples and their ownership of the project spread through public meetings and careful negotiations, often with the assistance of the local arts centre, An Lanntair, in Stornoway. During the monuments' construction, the craftspeople and artisans of the island became fully engaged in the building process, most especially through the knowledge of the engineer John Norgrove and the skilled hands of the Lewis stonemason, James Crawford.

With the support and guidance of Malcolm MacLean, Director of the National Gaelic Arts Project, Will Maclean set about creating three such monuments between 1994 and 1996. Conceived and developed by an individual who is acknowledged as one of Scotland's most eminent contemporary artists, they pay homage to different aspects of Lewis's history and its people. Maclean's commission was to commemorate the struggles of islanders in the land agitations from 1887 to 1920: those defining moments when the indigenous crofters united to resist the changes being imposed on their land and culture.[2] The requisition of traditional

 Pàirc memorial cairn, Balallan

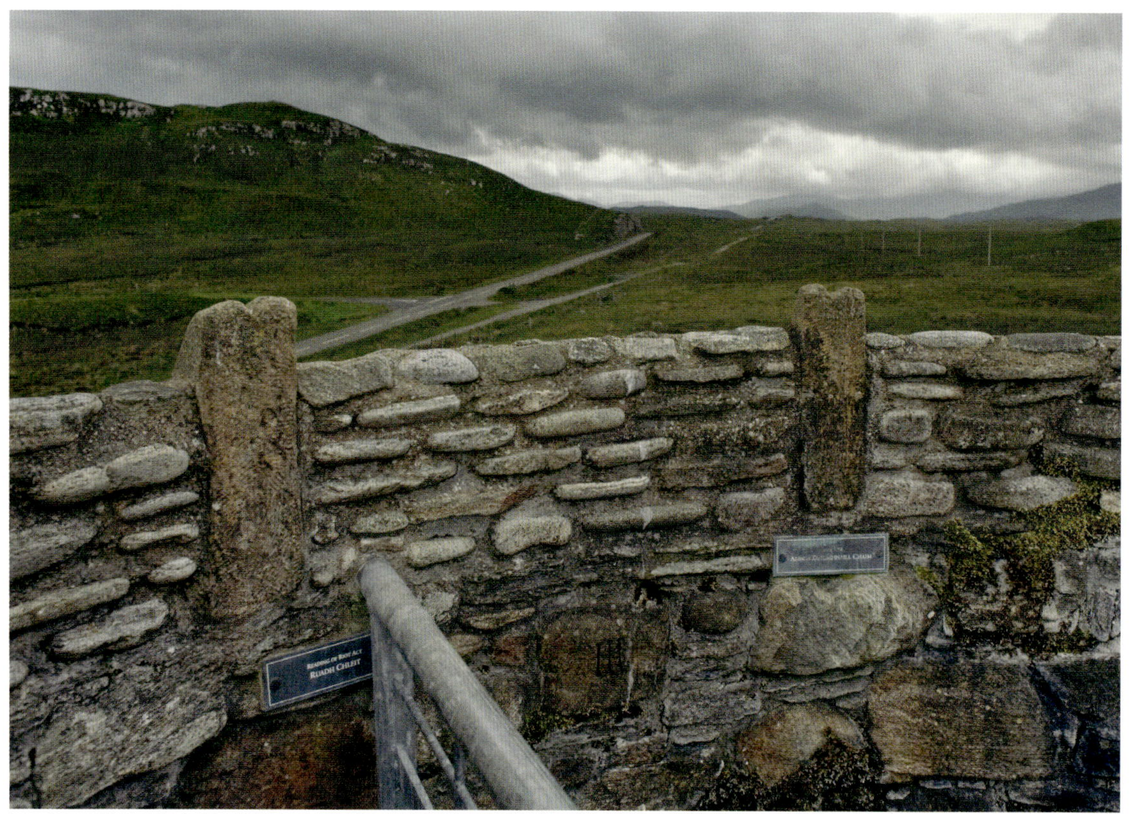

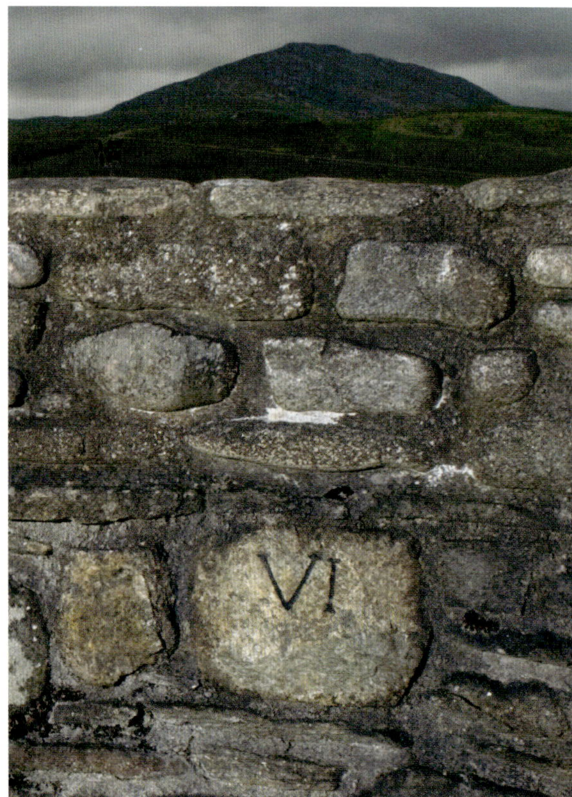

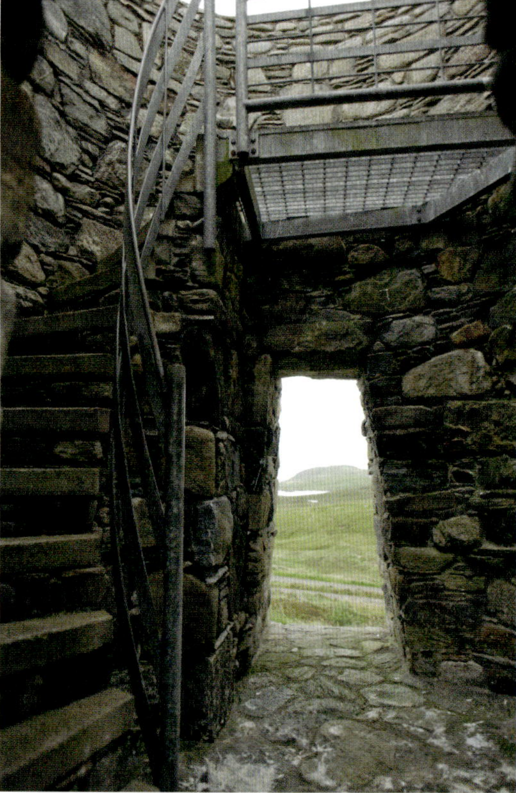

TOP Sighting stones directing the viewer to the three scenes of the riots
BOTTOM LEFT A stone marker, no. VI, taken from Murdo Macdonald's house
BOTTOM RIGHT The stone stairway to the Pàirc memorial's viewing platform

crofting grounds was ordered by landlords ostensibly with a view to modernising agricultural practices. Inevitably this modernisation led to the displacement of tenant farmers and the destruction of a centuries-old way of life and custom. Maclean's eloquent monuments mark sites of resistance and disruption in a manner that alludes to details of the historical events themselves. That is to say, the monuments are, collectively, a chronicle written in stone.

These three monuments, the Pàirc memorial, from 1994, the Aignish memorial and the Gress memorial, both completed in 1996, have become landmark 'memory-places' in Lewis. They are sites for contemplation and reflection, and identity-markers for the whole of the island's population. They are bound into the consciousness and the lived sentiments of the community in their richness and distinction, while they also stand for the islanders' painful memories. Though these are quite evidently exceptional examples of contemporary land art, the monuments are deeply rooted in the island's own landscape, anthropology and culture. Each is designed to connote the historic building types, including elements of traditional cairns, 'black-houses', wheelhouses, beehive structures, brochs and duns. The carefully laid and bonded stone has been gathered from local beaches and from ruined cottages, and the walls of the cairns are constructed and crafted in sympathy with local custom and terrain. As such, these memorials appear both ancient and profoundly modern. They are, in all these features, secular sites that invoke a profound spiritual memory, and they have generated a culture of collective affirmation.[3]

The first of these monuments is the Pàirc memorial, some 15 miles south-west of Stornoway. Standing on a rocky outcrop near Balallan village in the parish of Lochs, it is an imposing and recondite structure. Its shape echoes the form of the island's most famous 'broch', the now ruined Iron-Age fortification of Dùn Chàrlabhaigh, known in English as Dun Carloway.

The Pàirc memorial is circular. Its wide footprint tapers towards its uppermost platform, created for the visitor to view the landscape where raids occurred.[4] Three separate entrances give access to the monument, and an internal circular stairway leads to the viewing platform. Here, three sighting stones project upwards from the topmost tier of the stone wall and each is indented with a sighting line. These direct the viewer's attention to the sites of the principal events of the raid. In November 1887, the crofting community in the parish of Lochs reacted to cumulative pressures on their lives and culture and engaged in a 'raid' on their ancestral lands. The first of the significant sites highlighted by the memorial was the campsite at Airidh Dhòmhnaill Chaim where some 160 crofters, led by the local schoolmaster Donald MacRae, occupied the parkland, established an encampment and burned peat fires in order to create a feast of venison. It was these actions that led to the deployment of the Sheriff's Officers, and the Riot Act was read at the second site, Ruadh-Chleit. The third sighting stone indicates the landscape at Ceann-a-Carraigh, where confrontation between the two groups broke out. All this led to the arrest of crofters' leaders and their trial in an Edinburgh courtroom.

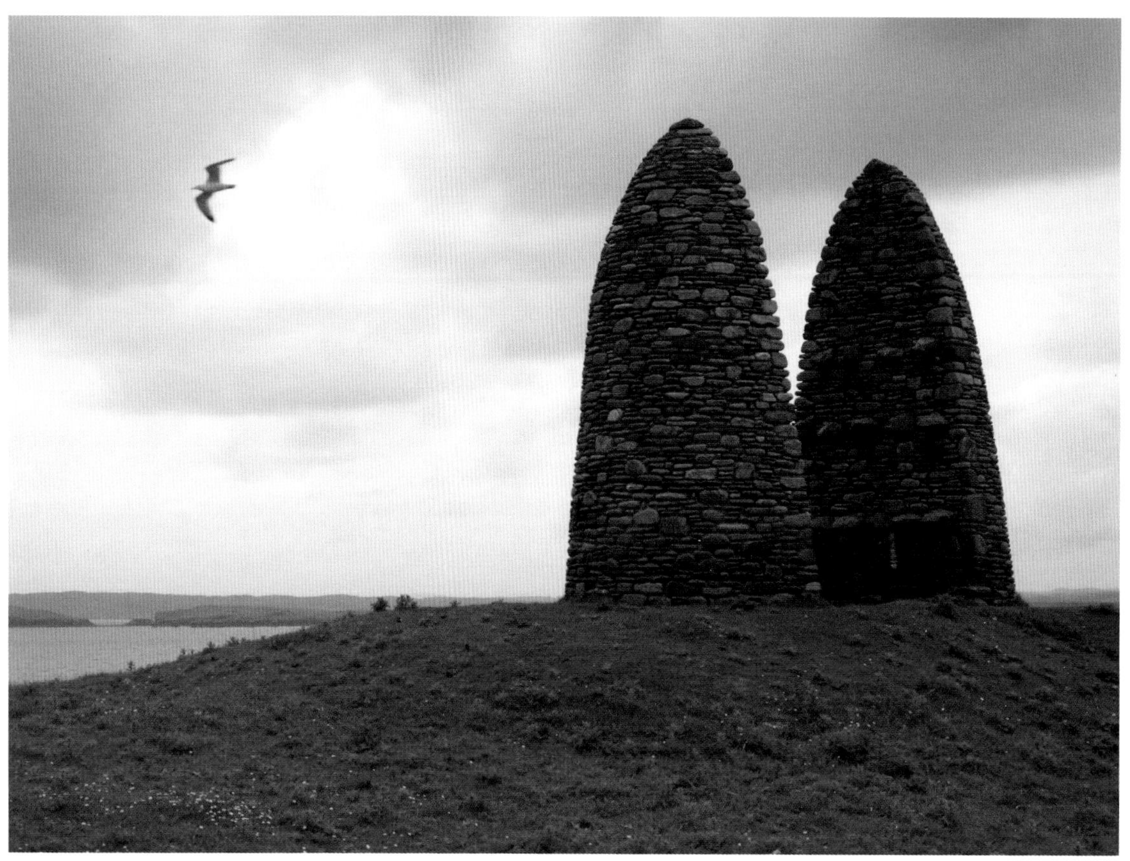

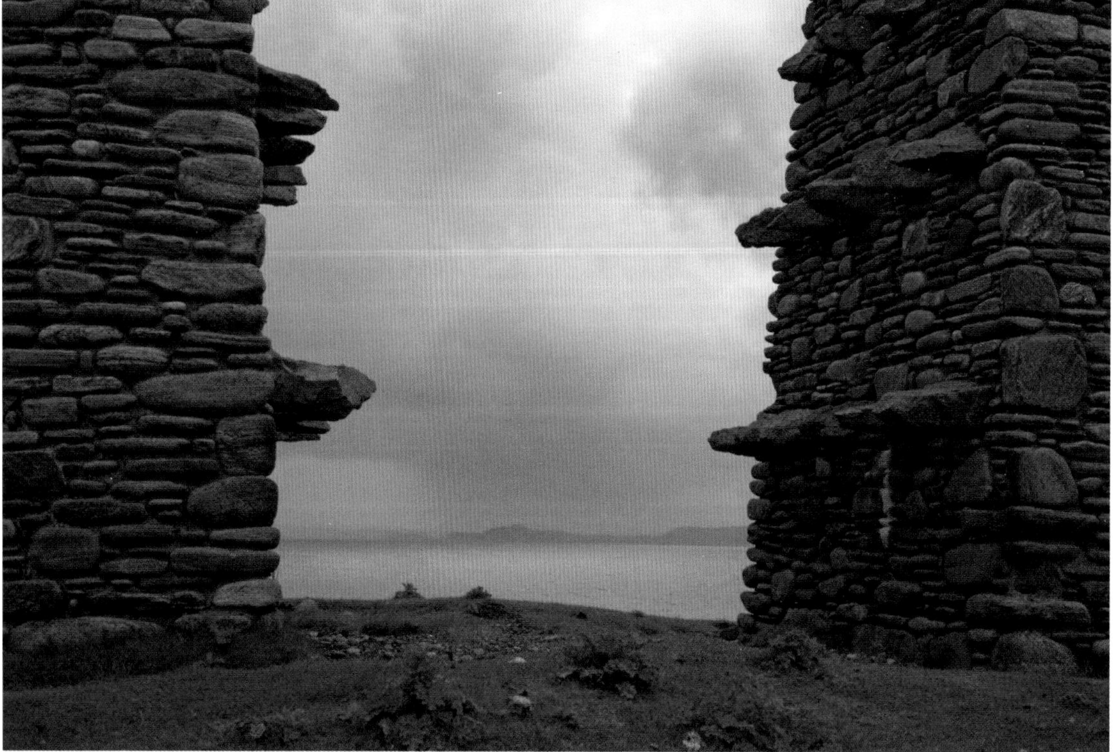

TOP Aignish memorial cairn
BOTTOM View through the opposing Aignish structures

Though the marker stones direct the visitor to these specific places, the monument itself contains discrete references to the events that are commemorated. The three entrances to the memorial are aligned to the three communities that invoked the raid: the peoples of Pàirc, Kinloch and North Lochs. Numbered stones within the monument are dedicated to the key protagonists and to those placed on trial. Significantly, some of the stone used to build the monument was gathered from the ruins of crofters' homes in the parkland. The imposing and impressive memorial presents a charged narrative that reflects historical events and presents them to the people as material culture.

The Pàirc Deer Raid memorial cairn was completed in 1994 after four years' work, and such was its success that it served to remodel the idea of a cairn from that of a simple marker to a compelling work of art. In consequence Maclean was commissioned to undertake two further memorial cairns: one at Aignish and the other at Gress River. These would develop the language of commemorative monuments as works of imaginative land art and create on Lewis a fundamental currency of memory and celebration.

A few miles north-east of the parish of Lochs, across a narrow isthmus, is the Eye Peninsula, also known as the district of Point. Here, in 1888, only two short months after the Pàirc Deer Raid, a crofters' rising occurred in the farmlands near the village of Aignish. Again, crofters were reacting to the takeover of traditional croft lands and their conversion into large tenanted farms. But here the conflict was especially acute. Landlords were now aware of the crofters' strategy and determined to resist their actions. Crofting families had set out to occupy the land, tear down fences and re-establish the ancient crofting grounds. At Aignish the Sheriff's Officer called upon a contingent of Marines. The gathered crofting families came to number nearly 1,000 men, women and children, and, as the confrontation intensified, the Marines drew bayonets and confronted the group; the crofters are said to have bared their breasts and stepped towards the unsheathed bayonets. Subsequently, a further cohort of Scots Guards was called upon and arrests were made. Thirteen men were jailed.

In response to the intensity of this confrontation, Maclean's Aignish memorial is forceful and potent. Sited on raised ground, it has the shape of a large cairn. Constructed from gathered stone its two halves stand in opposition to one another. From the flat inner surface of one part, sharp projecting stones, in the manner of bared 'teeth', are arranged in parallel lines, mimicking the drawn bayonets, while the opposite part is given more rounded projecting stones, symbolising the human vulnerability but also the determination of the crofters.[5] The whole structure is strange and unsettling; it has the psychological intensity of a 'surrealist object', writ large, evoking Man Ray's *The Gift* of 1921 – a flat iron with its smooth surface designed to iron out creases from cloth, transformed into a torturous object sporting an upright column of menacing thumb tacks. Maclean's monument articulates dispute and crisis, and it channels the raw anger unleashed in the defiant actions of the local people faced with the brutal reactions of officialdom.

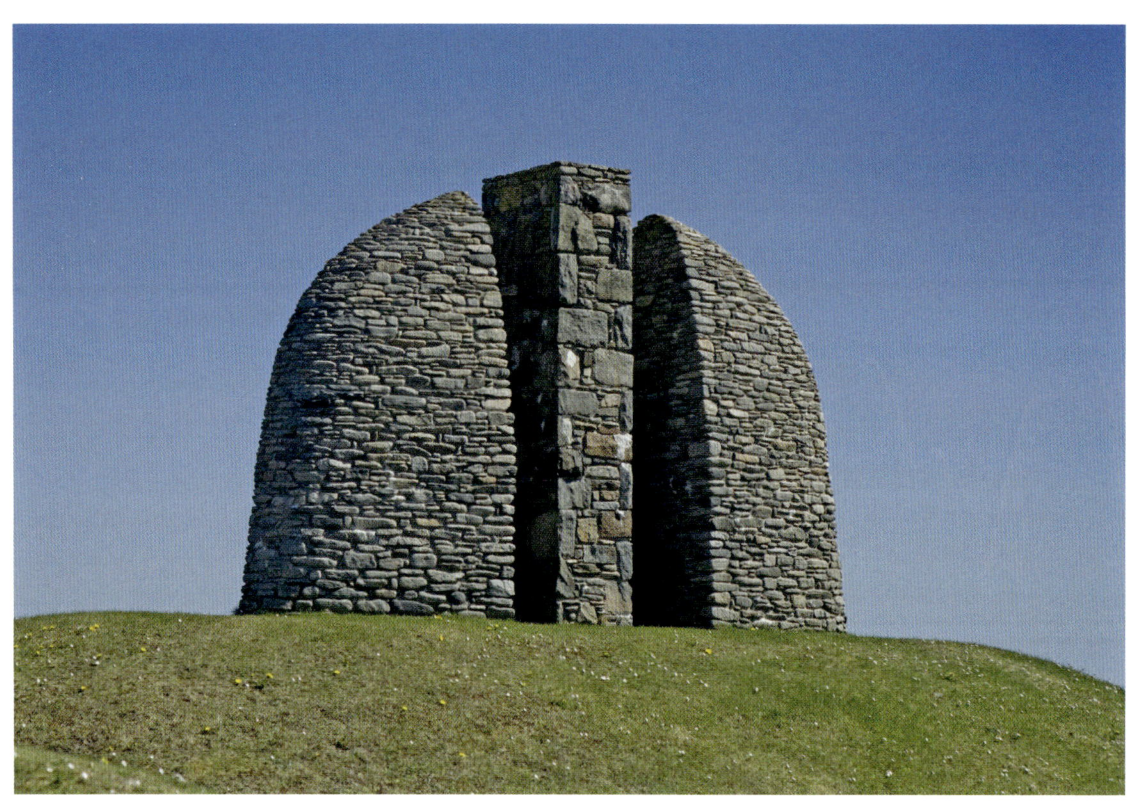

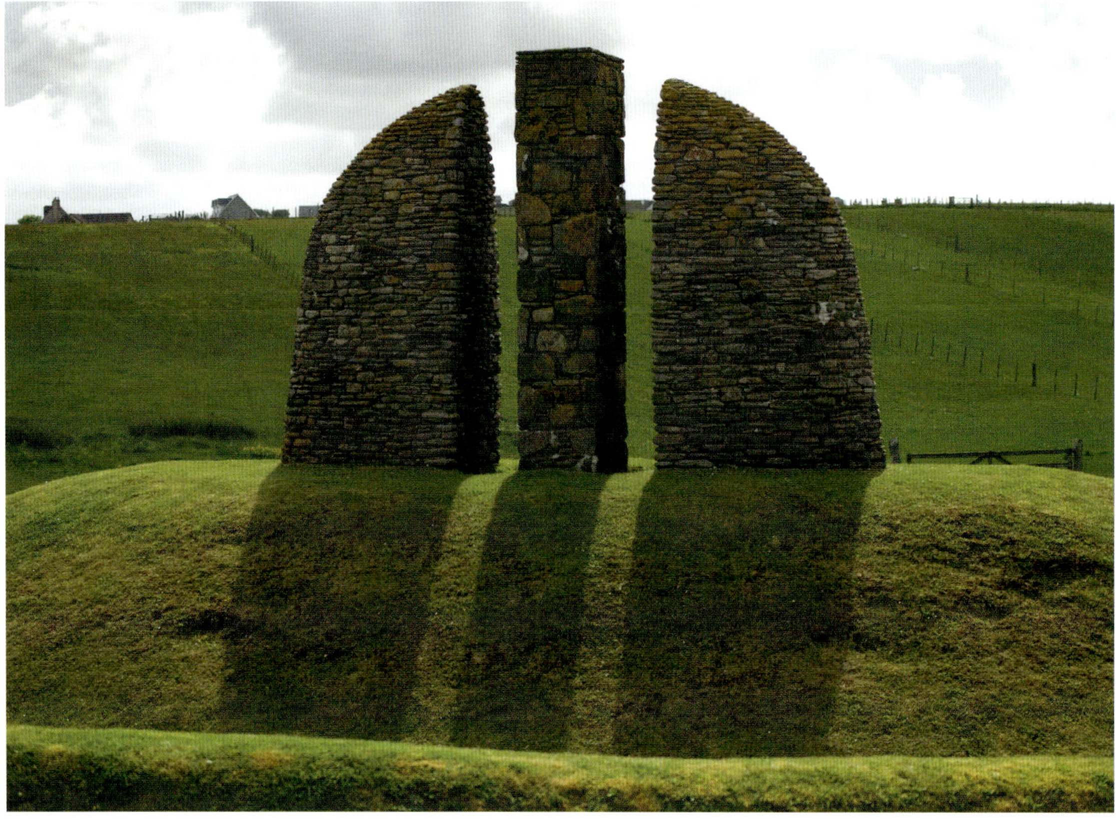

The tenor of Man Ray's extraordinary work is extended to the Gress River memorial, which is sited to the north of Aignish and some nine miles from Stornoway. Like the Aignish monument, this was completed in 1996 and, similarly, the Gress memorial is designed as a bifurcated cairn, reminiscent of an upturned boat. Two curved forms built from rough, gathered stone are separated by a 3.5-metre-tall rectangular pillar,[6] constructed by contrast from smooth dressed stone that alludes to Lord Leverhulme,[7] the resolute individual who had divided the community with his plans for development.

The earthworks that form the stage for this monument are notable: the raised earth platform, the ditch and the earthen rampart all reference those fortifications, those 'trenches', familiar to all who had experienced the First World War. The Gress memorial fuses the crofters' claim to their own culture with a more general tribute to those who had died in the cataclysmic conflict that had affected the whole of the western world.

The subtle narratives in the Balallan and the Aignish monuments come to a head in the memorial at Gress River. Whereas the previous monuments referred to crofters' rebellions in the 19th century, the Gress River structure memorialises the extension of these grievances into the period after the First World War. In the wake of the Crofters Holding (Scotland) Act of 1886, there had been tentative steps to return the large enclosed farmlands to traditional smaller crofts. Some modest momentum towards this redress had been made in the early years of the 20th century, but that stalled when the island was sold to Lord Leverhulme, the soap magnate, who sought to 'rationalise' the economy of Lewis and to create an infrastructure that might accommodate industrial expansion. These developments were suspended during the First World War when the people of Lewis responded to the call to enlist. In 1919, as Lewis survivors returned to the island, they recognised that Leverhulme was intent upon changes that would further erode their crofting rights and would challenge those ameliorations instigated by the Crofters Act. Once again, the outraged crofters rebelled, raiding the farms at Gress and in the surrounding area. They attempted to re-establish the pre-war settlement by dividing the lands into crofts. Compromises ensued, and there were attempts at arbitration up to 1920, at which point Leverhulme ran into financial difficulties and abandoned both the project and Lewis itself. In 1922 the Board of Agriculture took control of the land and at last had it divided into crofting plots.

With the realisation of the memorial at Gress River, Maclean's commissions from Cuimhneachain nan Gaisgeach were complete. The island community had appropriately recognised its 'land heroes' and had done so in a way that identified the Isle of Lewis as a locus for significant contemporary memorial land art. Inevitably, the success of these first monuments, at a local and an international level, created a desire for others to complete the narrative.

OPPOSITE TOP Gress memorial cairn
OPPOSITE BOTTOM The setting, with earthworks resembling the trenches from the First World War

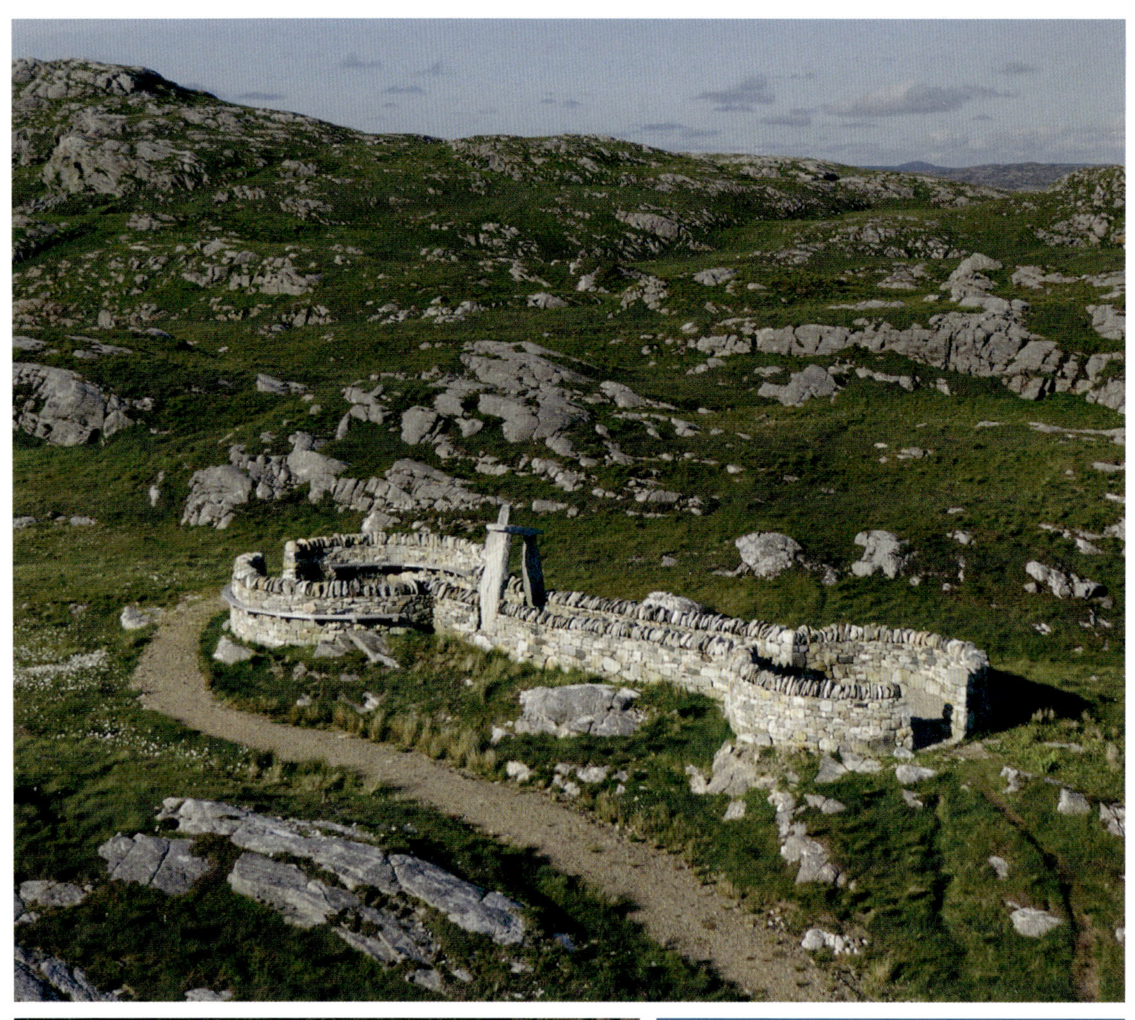

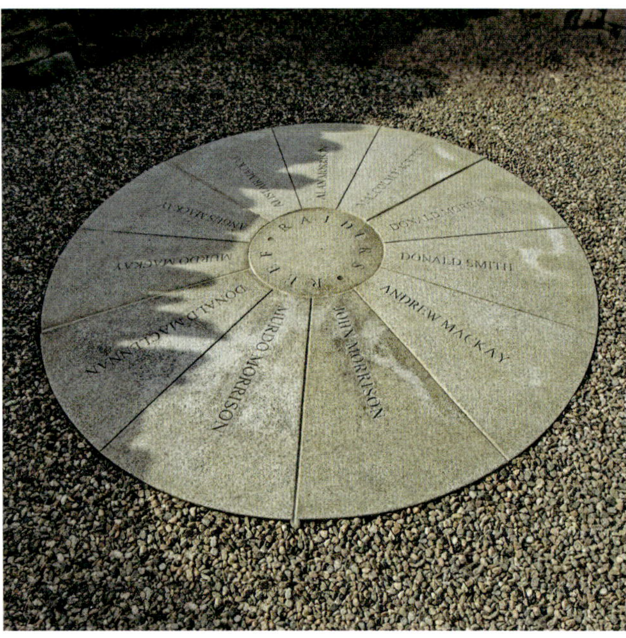
RAIDHA R
DONALD SMITH
ANDREW MACKAY
JOHN MORRISON
MURDO MORRISON
DONALD MACLEAN

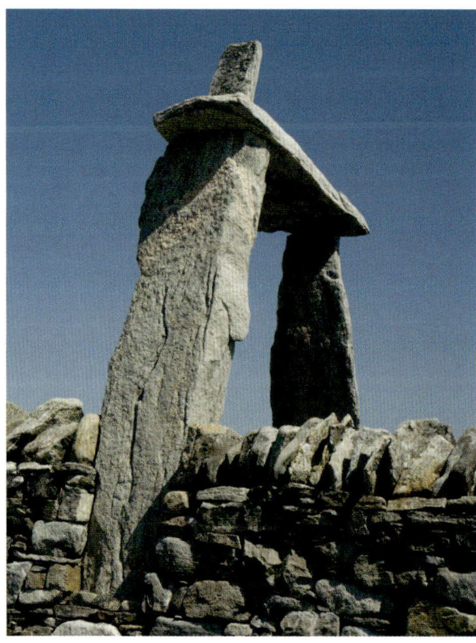

On the far west coast of Lewis, some 34 miles from Stornoway and above the village of Reef in the Parish of Uig, is an area of machair and beach known as Traich na Beirghe. A short distance north of this, the Bhaltos Community Trust (which was formed in 1998 to raise funds when the opportunity to purchase the Bhaltos estate from the landlord arose) identified a site for *An Sùileachan*. They offered the commission to Maclean and artist Marian Leven, who worked in close collaboration for this monument – and subsequently for the *Iolaire* memorial.

Dramatically situated on two flat rocky outcrops, with easterly views to the village of Reef and westwards to the island of Pabay Mor, *An Sùileachan* was completed in 2013. More than any other, this commission therefore combines a commemoration of crofters' struggles with a strong sense of resolution and peace. It is a participatory work, inviting the gatherings that are now a regular feature for the community, including anniversaries, weddings and baptisms, or simply offering a place of rest and contemplation.

Skilfully built from local, gathered, stone, it echoes the shape of the Pictish 'double-disc', or 'double-sun', pattern frequently found inscribed on the symbol stones of north-east Scotland. Openings at the east and western ends of the circular structures give access, and the opening to the west looks out to the Atlantic Ocean, where many islanders, cleared from their lands, embarked on a journey of emigration to the New World.

The walled passageway between the circular enclosures is a processional route where the visitor passes beneath an open archway in the form of an asymmetric trilithon. This arch is created from three significant monolithic stones rescued from nearby Loch Roag, close to the world-renowned Callanais stone circle. These long-abandoned stones, discovered serendipitously by the stonemason James Crawford, were possibly cut in Neolithic times.[8] The skill set required to construct *An Sùileachan* was readily to hand and deepened the community's engagement. Working with James Crawford on the local style of stone wall building was Ian Smith; John Macleod was in charge of the iron work, the woodwork was overseen by Angus MacLeod, and the engineer John Norgrove again offered his services.

An Sùileachan creates an intimate and ataractic space. The double-disc provides integrated seating on the outside and also within the larger, western, circular space, where on top of a well-worn millstone, an iron fire basket has been placed, reflecting the shape of a beacon. It is designed to hold peat for making fires to celebrate and commemorate, and serves to welcome community engagement as a beacon of hope. The past is marked in the eastern enclosure, which contains a flat granite circle with the inscribed names of 14 local 'land-raiders'. This restrained reference links the work to the narratives of the earlier memorials. Walking from one circular area to the other may be understood as both a physical and a metaphysical journey. Proceeding under the archway allows for multiple metaphoric

TOP Aerial view of *An Sùileachan*
BOTTOM LEFT A granite disc with the names of 14 land raiders
BOTTOM RIGHT The arch formed of Neolithic stones located nearby

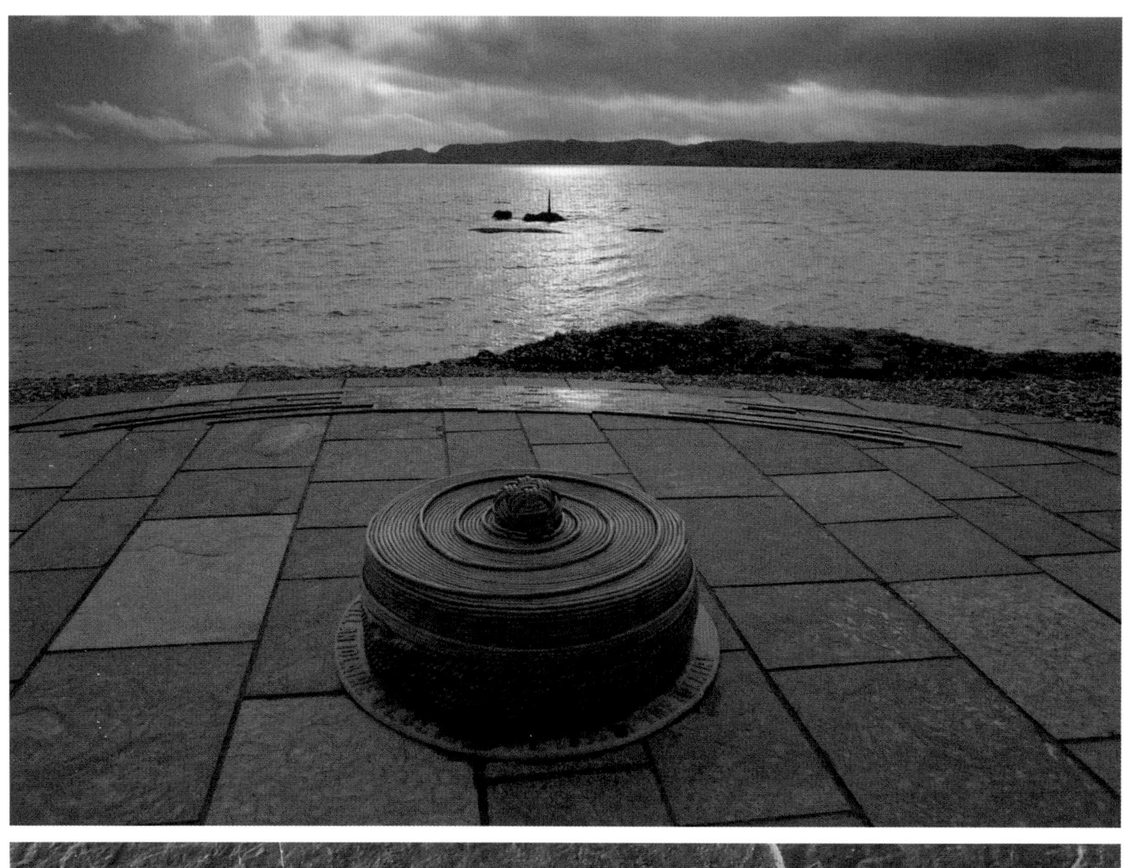

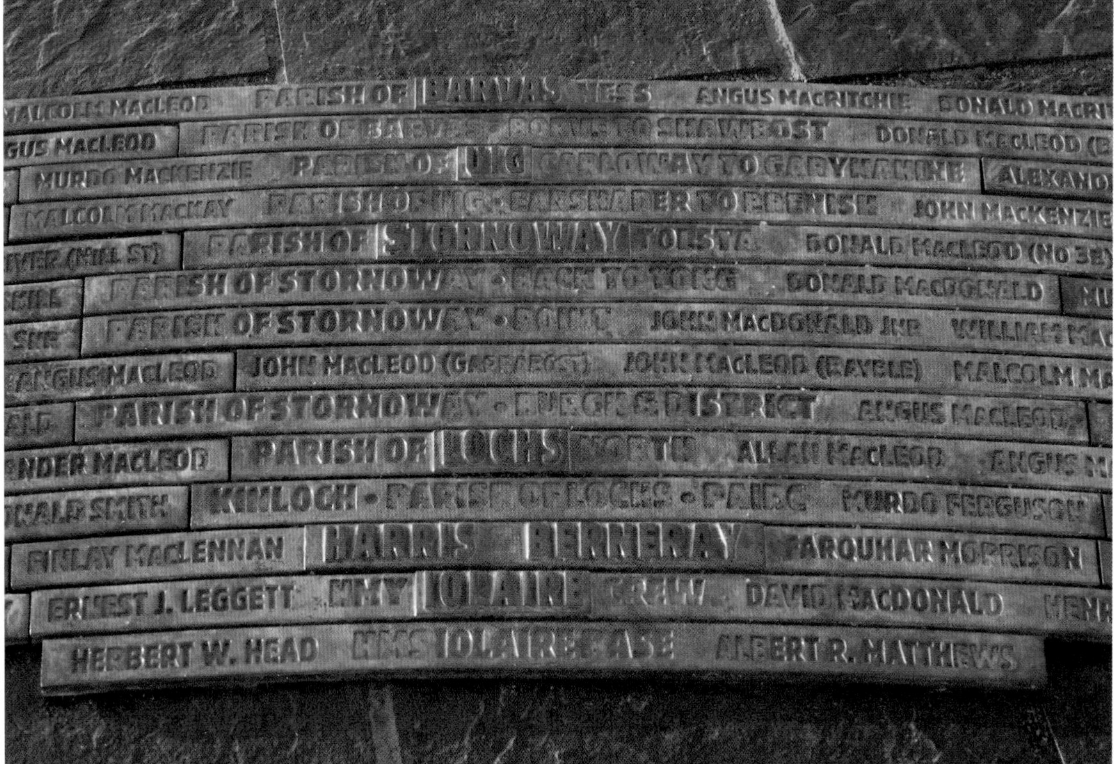

progressions from the past to the future, from history to prospect, and from the material world to the intangible sublime.[9]

The very title *An Sùileachan* relates to the Gaelic for 'eye', a point referenced for Maclean and Leven by the Gaelic scholars Finlay and Norma Macleod. As with most translations from the Gaelic, the simple definition masks a host of subtle allusions. The sense of 'eye', in this context, certainly bears witness; it recognises events and records their significations. But the connotation of 'eye' also proposes a 'seer' in the mystical sense, encompassing the notion that insight can be both magical and mysterious. Moreover, this deeper sense of 'envisioning' implies a level of understanding that can move from passionate indignation to benevolent tranquillity. In *An Sùileachan*, the intimation, the promise, of a future harmony has been written into the form and the materiality of the structure.

At the close of the year in 2018, Maclean, Marian Leven and the sculptor Arthur Watson completed a memorial to a different Lewis tragedy, one which was described in *The Stornoway Gazette* as 'the blackest day in the history of the island'. This was the sinking of His Majesty's Yacht *Iolaire*, on the morning of 1st January 1919.

The details of this terrible tragedy (which are extensively documented in the recently published book *Call na h-'Iolaire'. The Darkest Dawn: The Story of the 'Iolaire' Tragedy*[10]) are described previously by Joni Buchanan (pp.31 – 4). Briefly, the *Iolaire* was commissioned to carry sailors returning to the port of Stornoway after service in the First World War. In the early morning of that fateful New Year's Day, the ship's course took it within a few metres of the shoreline, and barely a mile from Stornoway Harbour, where she foundered on an outcrop of rocks known as the Beasts of Holm. The record shows that 201 men died, of which 179 were from the Isle of Lewis. Some 79 men were recorded as survivors, at least 40 of them rescued by John Finlay MacLeod, from the village of Ness. He managed to swim to the shore with the hawser, along which the survivors pulled themselves onto the wintry, rocky coastline. As day broke the people of Lewis searched among survivors and amongst the dead, seeking out fathers, husbands and brothers. Most families found themselves in mourning.

For a hundred years this tragedy has haunted the island and the islanders. A modest stone monument was erected after the First World War on a knoll to the south of the village of Sandwick, overlooking the site of the disaster. It takes the form of an obelisk, with an inscription recording the details of the disaster below the crown-and-anchor symbol of the merchant fleet. With the centenary of the First World War approaching, the island community resolved to commission a more resonant memorial, titled in Gaelic *Call na h-'Iolaire'* – The Loss of the *Iolaire*.

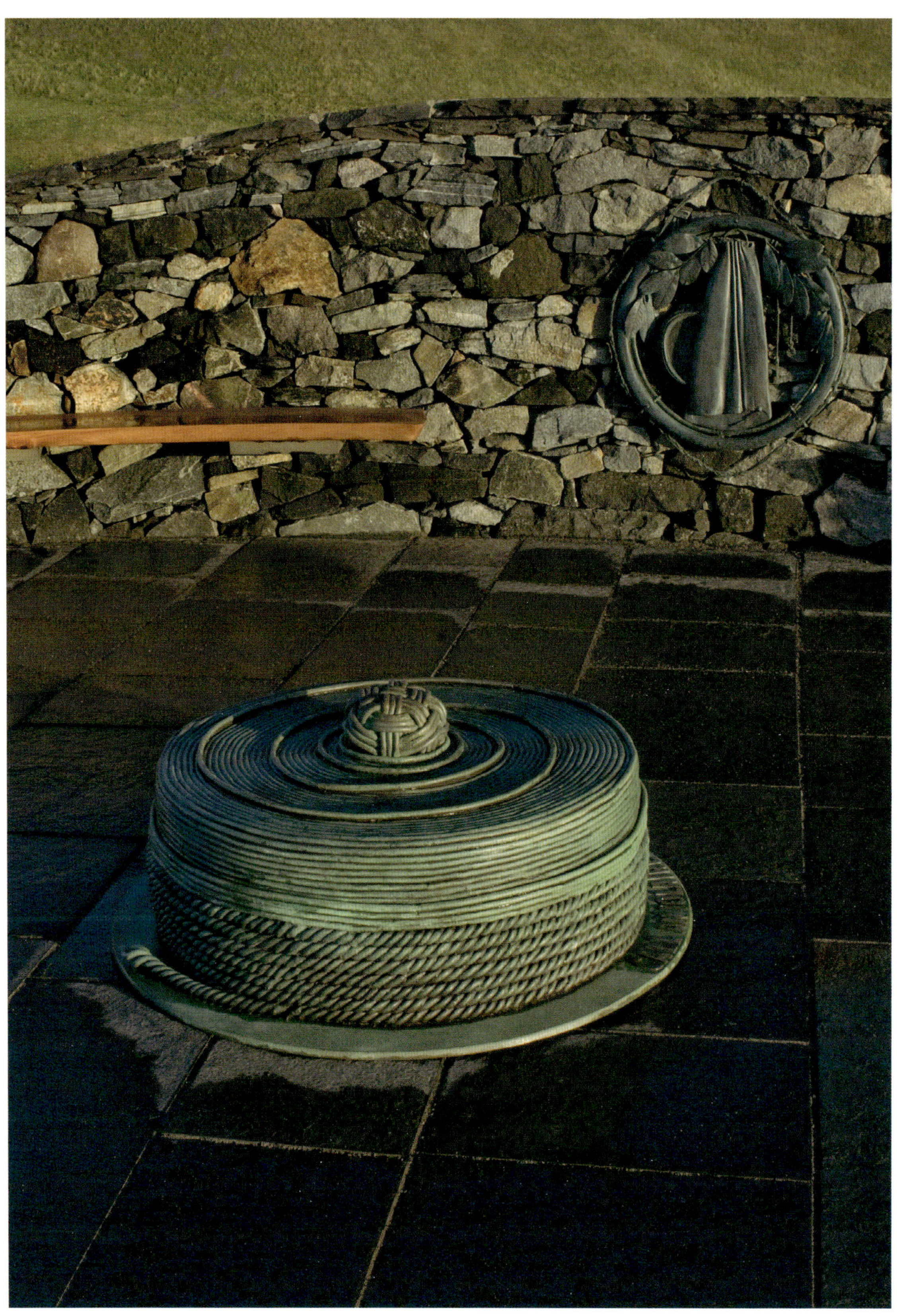

The design of this memorial is intriguing. It occupies a site to the south of the small extant obelisk. Rather than being a standing monument, it is a landscaped space taking the form of a three-dimensional ellipsoidal structure. The whole setting creates an open-air sanctuary. Viewed from above it looks like a human eye. The north wall is built of stone, quarried from the conjoining island of Harris, and curves around a central bronze sculpture. Its curve is echoed in the Caithness stone floor that delineates the southernmost border of the artwork. The arcs do not meet. Open at one end to allow access to the landscaped ambit, the space is open at the other end, giving access to the original monument. The north wall, some one and a half metres high and tapered on its landward side, shelters an arena that opens towards the sea where the marker of the *Iolaire* disaster is clearly visible. Two wooden benches are built into the wall, enabling the visitor to pause for thought and to consider the scene, or to study the bronze arcs of raised lettering carefully arranged with links to the parishes, citing the names of all those who perished.

Two other elements add to the symbolic narrative of the space. Between the benches, Maclean's bronze sculpture is attached to the wall. Circular in form, it resembles a lifebuoy; however, embellished by laurel leaves, the work becomes a wreath. Closer study reveals objects and shapes that reference ropes, a kitbag, a rating's hat – the simple but essential items belonging to the men who drowned. The sculpture is a visual poem; a paean to the unspeakable tragedy and specifically to the individual victims. It is complemented by Arthur Watson's bronze sculpture, which sits at the heart of the memorial in the form of a coiled rope. The knotted head refers to the leaded 'monkey fist' of the thinner heaving line, while the rope refers to the one miraculously carried to shore by John Finlay MacLeod and used to rescue 40 survivors.

Altogether, 'The Loss of the *Iolaire*' is a highly innovative memorial, created to remember the dead, to engage the community, and to pay homage to the nature of island life. As a space, it is self-contained and ethereal. Visitors will find themselves anchored in the stone and the structural motifs of the Western Isles. Within the memorial they will encounter imagery that narrates the tragedy of the *Iolaire*. Sitting or walking in the site offers views of the sea, and everywhere the visitor is able to visualise the historic episode.

This 'remembering' is discreetly symbolised in the overall shape of the memorial. The ellipsoidal structure, with the circular coiled rope sculpture at its centre, connotes the human eye with the central sculpture as its 'iris' – an echoing reference to *An Sùileachan*. In the subtlest of senses the memorial itself becomes a 'witness', an embodiment of remembrance. Equally, it recalls the remains of Viking longships, sometimes encountered in the archaeology of the Western Highlands. Those remnants of wooden hulls, found preserved in the shorelines and strands around the coast, present a shadow outline of burial ships and this, too, is mirrored in the *Iolaire* memorial, connecting the disaster to the earlier history of the island and its

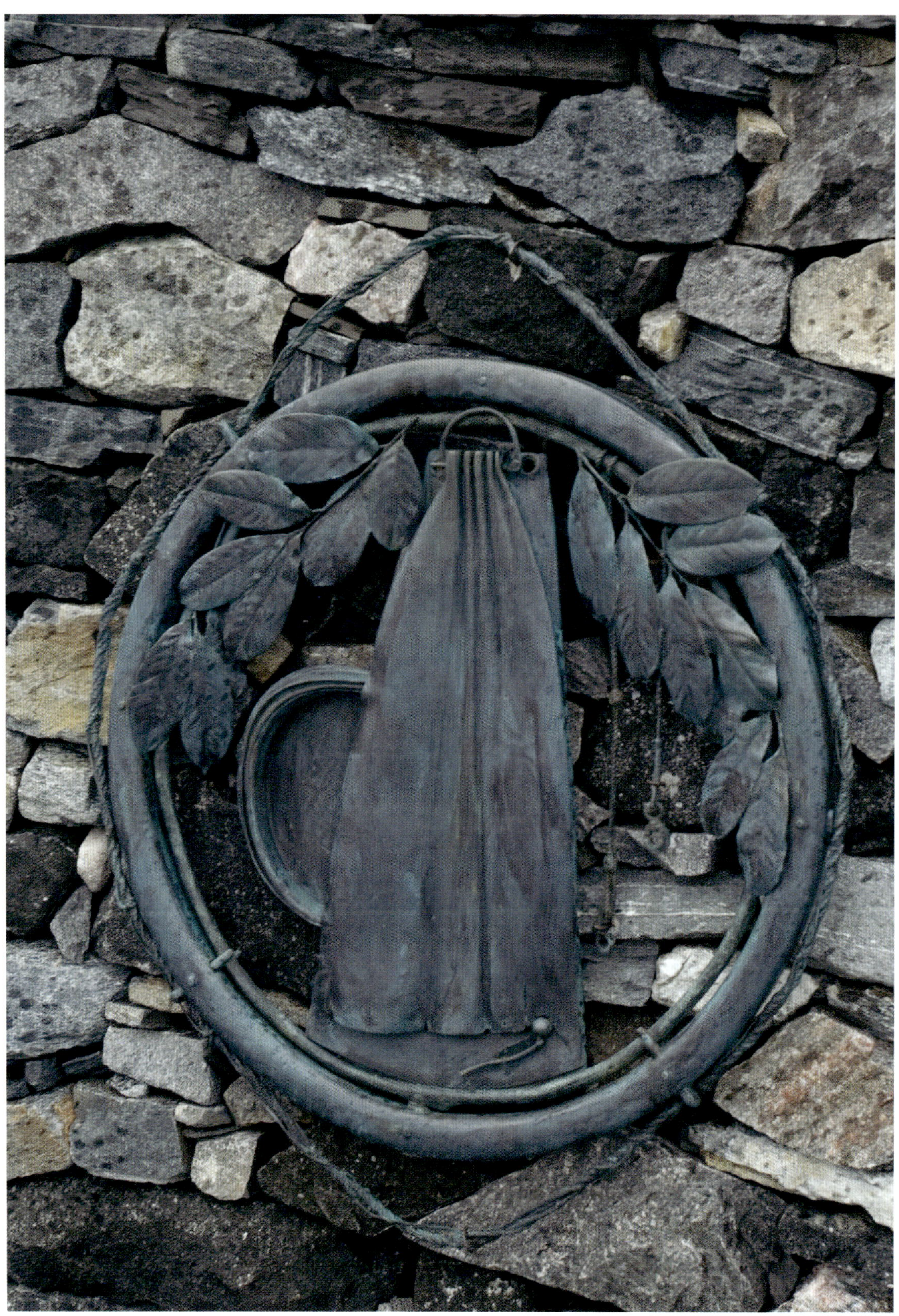

seafaring inhabitants. These alllusions combine to create a dedicated, respectful and resonant place of memory.

The appearance of *Call na h-'Iolaire'* chimes broadly with the earlier land monuments across the island. However, with the Pàirc Memorial cairn, the Aignish memorial and the Gress memorial, Maclean has given expression to the pain and anger of the people of Lewis in respect of their tragic history of ancestral struggle. More enigmatically, with *An Sùileachan* and *Call na h-'Iolaire'* this sense of anger has been tempered by a mood of rapprochement. It should be recognised that this has been achieved consciously, purposefully, for while remembering may invoke feelings of anger, a sense of injustice and a recognition of hurts that remain acute, remembering can also be a kind of healing. That is to say, to recollect, to reflect and to envisage, allows for catharsis and release.

In cultural terms, memorials acknowledge the courage and sacrifice of others, honour their fortitude and sometimes honour their demise. Remembering, then, is much more than nostalgia. It is a kind of 'knowing' that touches on notions of a chronicle, a commemoration and a dedication to the spirit of those who gave for others. Remembering can be a collective devotion and as such it cries out to be marked by individuals and by communities.[11]

As if to accentuate these various qualities, Maclean's three earlier memorial cairns not only helped to recover the buried history of the island's community and the crofters' suffering, but they also articulate a sense of injustice. *An Sùileachan* and the *Iolaire* memorials attain a different tone. Certainly, they pay homage to the crofters' riots and to the Iolaire disaster – this is written into their respective narratives – but each of these monuments is also a communal and a meditational site. They are created in order to memorialise and to heal. They offer places where the commonweal is remembered and refreshed. They are works of art that simultaneously recollect the past and signal a belief in the future. This is their power, and their rare dignity.

Iolaire memorial bronze wreath showing a lifebelt, laurel leaves, rating's hat, kitbag, bosun's whistle and lanyard

1. For a brief biography of Angus Macleod, and a record of his archive, see *The Angus Macleod Archive*,
    the Island Book Trust, Ness, 2004

2. For the fullest, and most accomplished, narrative of this history see Joni Buchanan, *The Lewis Land Struggle:
    Na Gaisgich*, Acair, Stornoway, 1996

3. A discussion of some of these issues may be found in Iain J. M. Robertson, 'Memory, Politics, and the Micropolitics
    of Memorialization: Commemorating the Heroes of the Land Struggle', in Ewan A. Cameron (ed.), *Recovering from
    the Clearances: Land Struggle, Resettlement, and Community Ownership in the Hebrides*, the Islands Book Trust,
    Kershader, 2013, p.161

4. The stonemason, James Crawford, gives the dimensions of this monument as 3.9m high, 4.29m at the base,
    and tapering to 2.8m at the top; James Crawford, letter to the author, 30 July 2015

5. James Crawford indicates that the dimensions of these structures are: 4.7m high, nearly 1.6m wide and 1.3m deep.
    They are separated from each other by a distance of land of more than 2 metres; *ibid.*

6. Again, James Crawford supplies an account of the scale of the component parts, giving the dimensions of the two
    buttresses as 3.0 x 1.0 x 0.6m, and the central column as 3.5 x 1.0 x 0.6m; *ibid.*

7. Indeed, James Crawford indicates that the topmost 0.3m of the central column has been made in beach stone
    'to represent Leverhulme's top hat'; *ibid.*

8. For a full discussion of this event, and related theses, see Tom Normand, 'All Is lithogenesis', from 'Contemporary
    Memorials on the Isle of Lewis', in *Visual Culture in the Northern British Archipelago: Imagining Islands*, eds Y. Holt,
    D. Martin-Jones and O. Jones, Ashgate, London, 2018, pp.83 – 100

9. The artists themselves have spoken of these qualities; see 'Will Maclean and Marian Leven Interview', Janet McKenzie,
    Studio International: Visual Arts, Design and Architecture, September 2014,
    http://www.studiointernational.com/index.php/will-maclean-marian-leven-interview-an-suileachan-isle-of-lewis-scotland

10. Malcolm Macdonald and Donald John MacLeod, *Call na h-'Iolaire'. The Darkest Dawn: The Story of the 'Iolaire' Tragedy*,
    Acair, Stornoway, 2018

11. Some theorisation of these themes may be found in Pierre Nora's landmark publication *Realms of Memory*
    (orig. *Les Lieux de mémoire*), Columbia University Press, New York, 1998. It is relevant, in this island context, that
    Nora has noted that 'the quest for memory in the contemporary world is nothing more than an attempt to master
    the perceived loss of one's history' (pp.xii, xiii), and later adds: 'Memory is rooted in the concrete: in space, gesture,
    image and object' (p.3)

OPPOSITE Arthur Watson's bronze *Iolaire* floor piece seen from the north-west

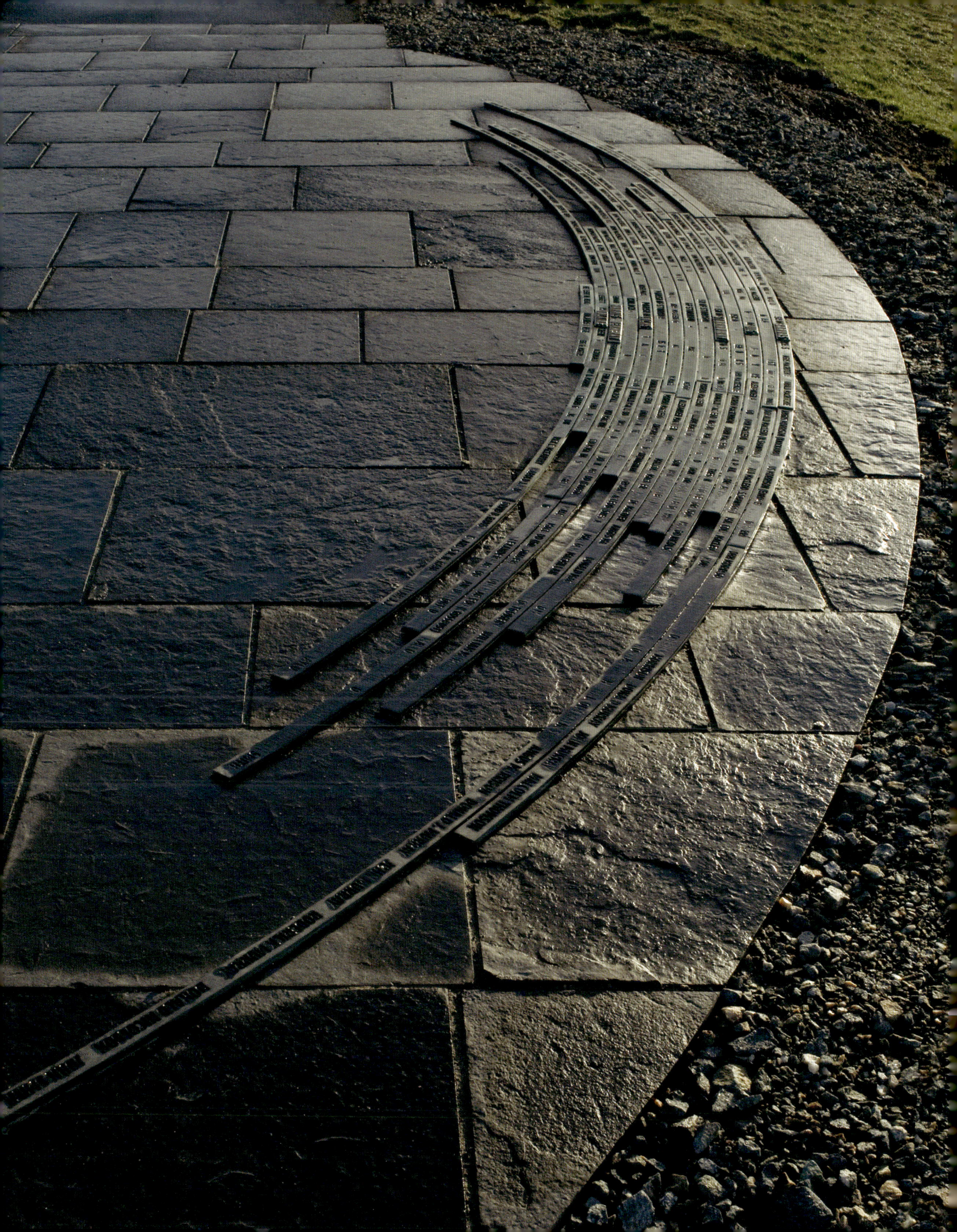

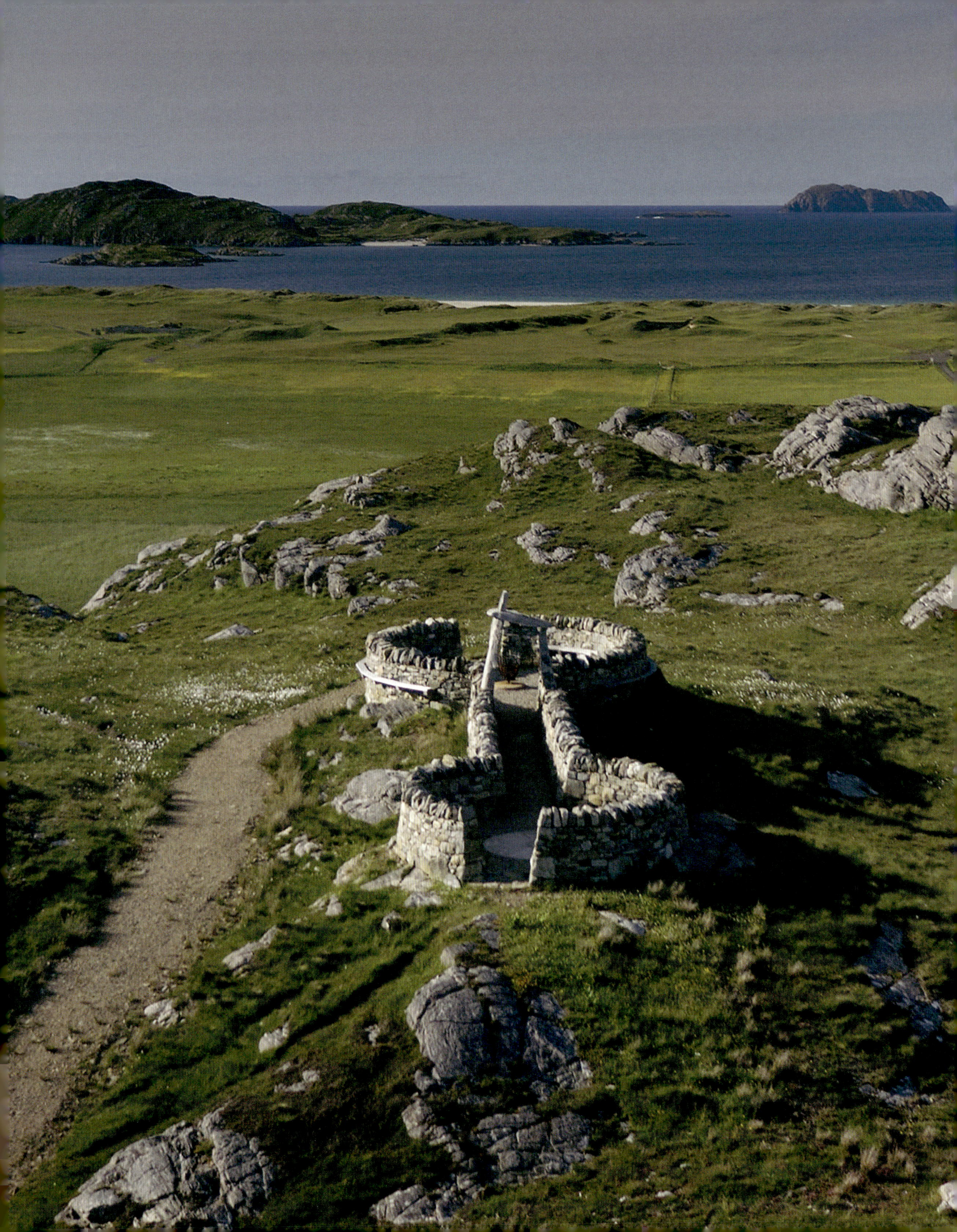

Sentinels of Stone

Lindsay Blair

Each of the five Lewis land monuments discussed in this book forms a different lens or 'seeing eye' upon the past. The form of the *Iolaire* installation in Stornoway, the stone archway of *An Sùileachan* at Reef, the name *An Sùileachan* itself, the 'watchtower' at Pàirc, Balallan – they all refer to the eye, and they all ask us to reflect upon the past. These distinctive structures are also a part of the landscape of Lewis now and in times to come, breathing with something of the terrain from which they arise. They function as sculptural lookout posts or sentinels on the coastal fringes of the island between the land and the sea, between the temporal and the infinite. The discussion which follows considers the pieces in relation to historical events, their geophysical location and as they are representative of a 'vision from within' which reflects both the ideas of 'voices from below' or 'heteroglossia', as articulated by Russian theorist Mikhail Bakhtin, and the implications of the concept of the 'spatial turn' from within contemporary discourse.[1]

The final page of Ian Finlay's book *Art in Scotland*, published in 1948, expresses the author's hope that one day a transformation might take place in Scottish education:
> For generations now the Scots from their school-book days have looked at their country from south of Hadrian's wall, have been coerced in their minds to side with the legions and deplore the threat of Pictish tribes and laugh at their woad. It is time the Scots child realized he belongs not with the legions, but with the tribes. It is time he realized the feet of his forebears trod not the mosaic pavements of Roman baths but the earth floors of the brochs.[2]

The exhibition *As an Fhearann/From the Land: Clearance, Conflict and Crofting* – mounted by An Lanntair in Stornoway and The Third Eye Centre in Glasgow in 1986 to mark the centenary of the Crofting Tenure Act of 1886 – had demonstrated how the representations that had been foisted upon the Highlands and Islands of Scotland had somehow become accepted.[3] An establishment view of self and other/centre and periphery had become an accepted and acceptable perspective. That exhibition and the essays accompanying the exhibition changed all of that. The sculptural commemorative cairns on Lewis are a significant part of the project to ensure that children from the islands can look out onto their own culture and feel positive about their own cultural identity.

 Aerial view of *An Sùileachan*

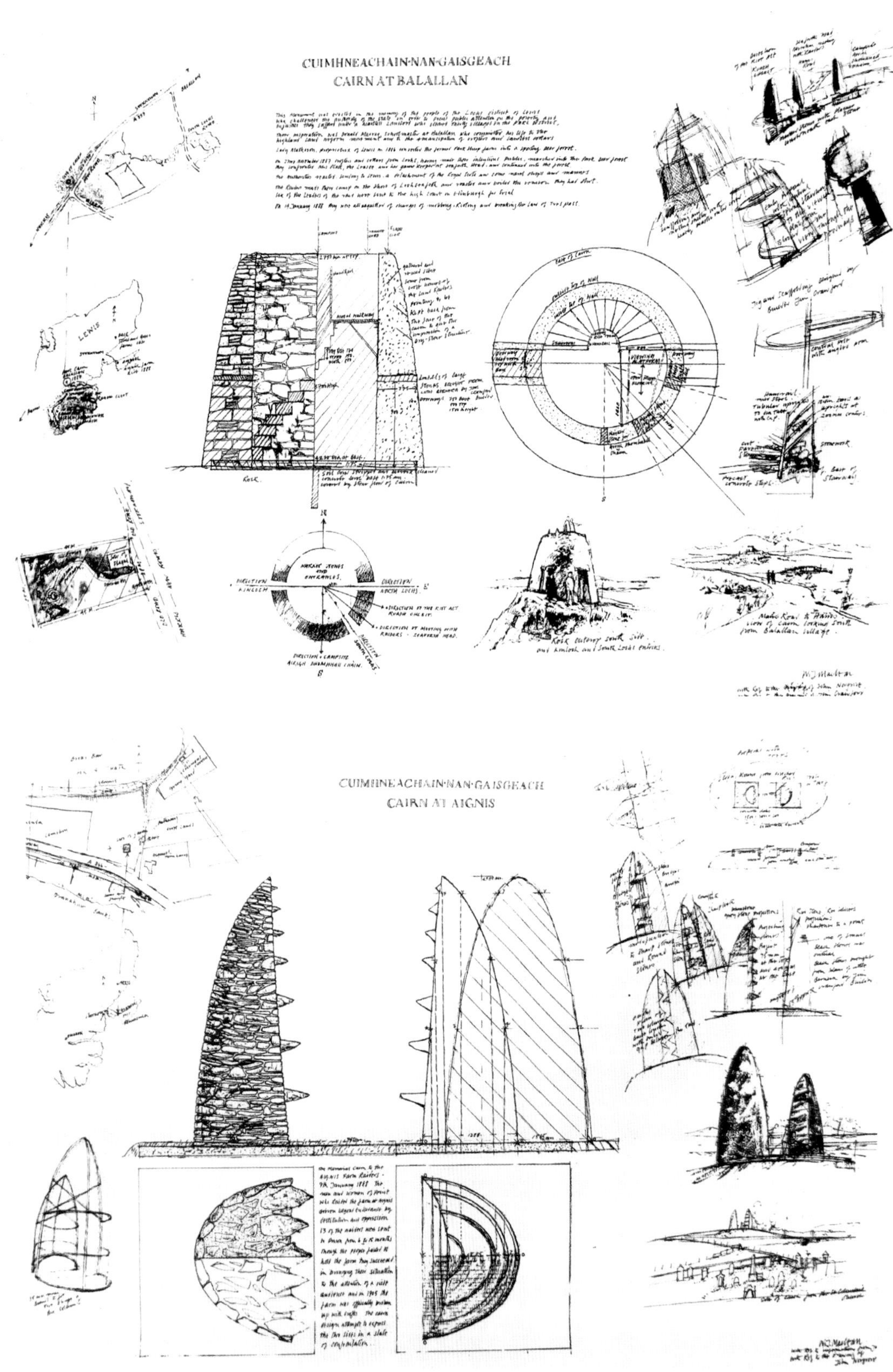

Will Maclean's 1994 pen and ink drawings on Arches paper.
TOP Pàirc memorial cairn; BOTTOM Aignish memorial cairn;
OPPOSITE Gress memorial cairn (see Notes to Illustrations)

The Pàirc monument at Balallan is a circular construction overlooking the township with
a view of the landscape of south Lewis. Maclean's preparatory drawings indicate his multi-
dimensional response to the commission: to the historical in its reference to the events which
comprise the raid itself; to the geophysical in the relationship between the memorial and the
surrounding landscape; to the material in its deliberate use of the stone from the local townships in the structure of the memorial; to the formal in the way that the tower 'looks out' onto
the locations where significant narrative points of the raid were enacted; and, finally, in the
structure/sculpture itself as metaphor – not only as memorial but as symbol of resistance.

The drawings for the memorial structures at Gress and at Aignish show the same scrupu-
lous attention to the multi-dimensional aspect of each commission. The diagrams of the
site at Gress River indicate Maclean's sensitivity to the location both for its historical significance – the site is just next to the Tolsta Bridge where Lord Leverhulme's vision was rejected
by the assembled crofters – and in the way that the contours of the construction sit in
relation to the surrounding landscape features; the construction makes use of different
kinds of finish to reflect the conflict and the trench references the First World War background of those returning to Lewis in 1919. The Aignish structure is again the result of
historical research, community involvement and Maclean's multi-dimensional preparatory
drawings. The culmination of these forces is the dramatic two-part stone construction at
Aignish Farm, which symbolises the antagonistic confrontation between crofters and
Marines in January 1888.

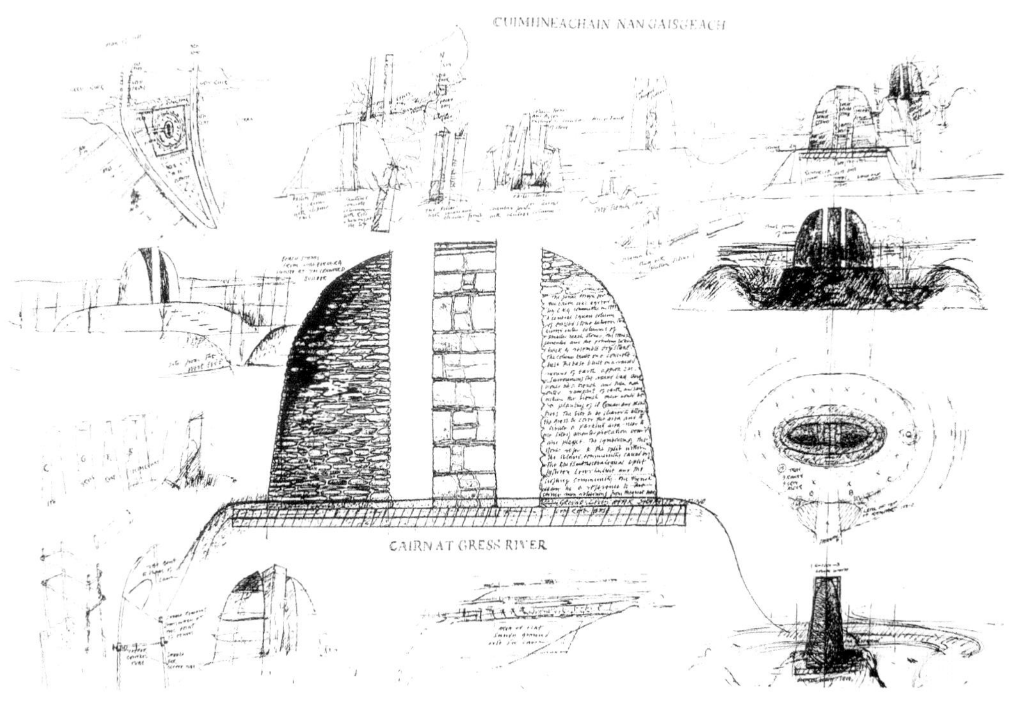

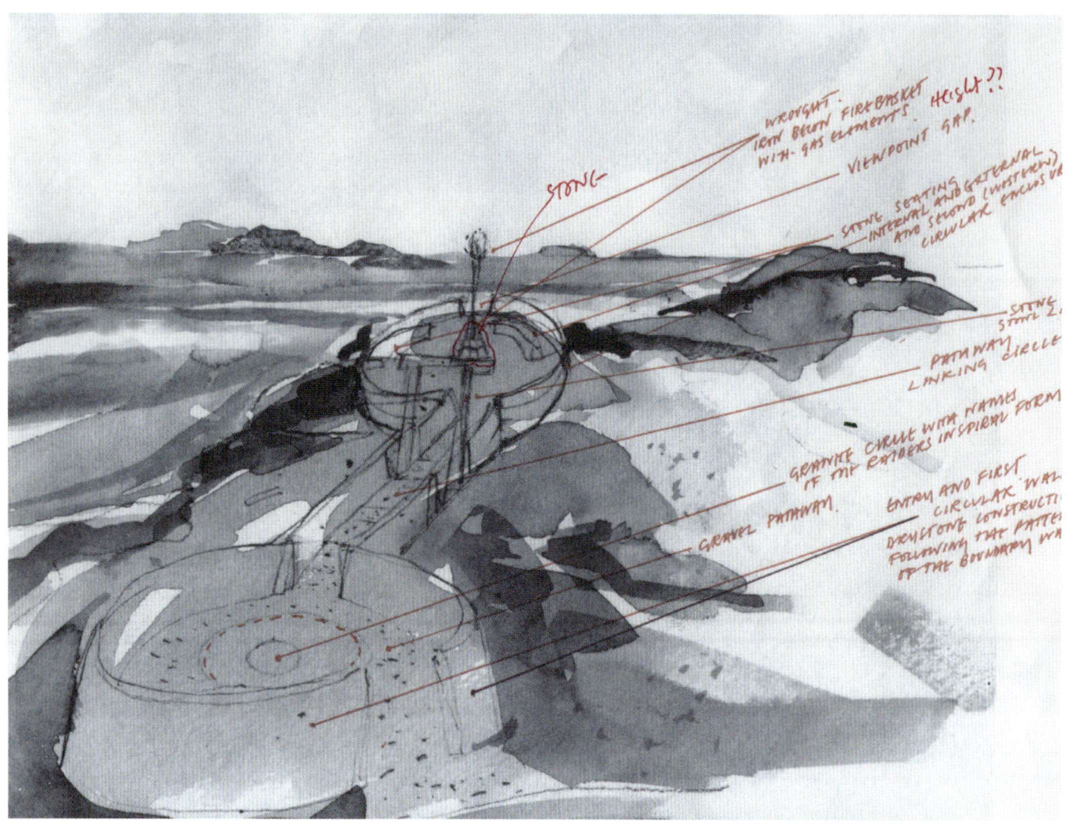

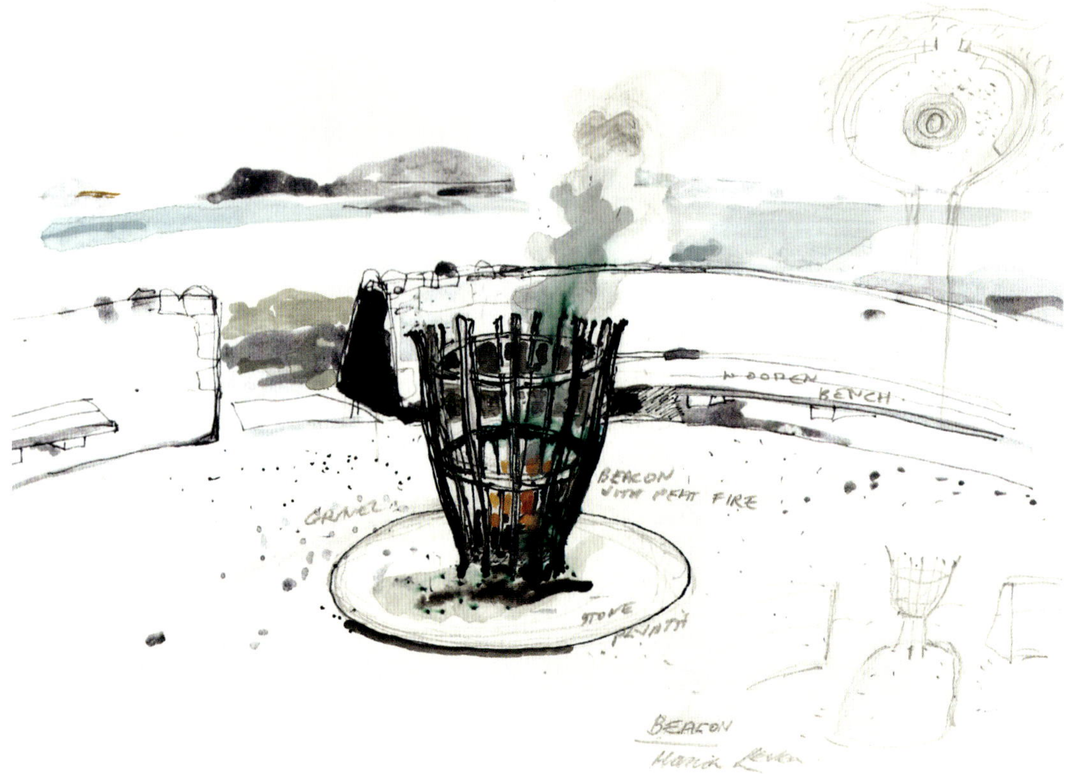

Pen and wash drawings by Marian Leven for *An Sùileachan* (see Notes to Illustrations)

The structure at Bhaltos, *An Sùileachan*, was conceived by Will Maclean together with Marian Leven, to commemorate the actions of the Reef Raiders. A number of massive, submerged stones found near the site (at the low watermark on the Island of Vuia Beag) by Lewis historian and master mason, James Crawford, were used to form an arch, whilst stone donated by crofters from the surrounding townships was reused in the construction of the walls. The names of the raiders are inscribed on the Raiders' Wheel at the centre of the Eastern Circle. The distinctive shape of *An Sùileachan* is based on the decision to adapt a Pictish 'double-disc' design in response to the two rocky outcrops at the allocated site.

The stone-centred culture of a northern island landscape does not lead, necessarily, to a comfortable encounter. Finlay laments the legacy of a centrist perspective: 'So "educated" away from northern impulses and traditions have we been that when we stand before such monuments as the cross of St Martin or the Hilton of Cadboll stone we feel a profound intervening gulf.'[4] The education system that has gradually colonised the North from the South has resulted in a sense of self-alienation amongst the northern peoples. Finlay writes of the paradox that 'we understand better the vision of the catacomb artists, the builders of basilicas, Giotto. The northern world is remote, obscure, protean, in fact barbaric. And yet our roots go down into obscurity.[5] There is now a growing acknowledgement that the perspective through which a culture is viewed is crucial to an understanding of it; the memorials need to be read in relation to their environment.

Designed to commemorate the struggles of the people of the crofting communities in Lewis, the monuments are prominent signifiers in the landscape. They resonate because they embody essential elements of the culture – they are of a piece with a cultural aesthetic which emanates from within. The stone monuments echo the tradition and the features of the geophysical world in which they are located; the Royal Commission on the Ancient and Historical Monuments of Scotland lists 215 scheduled monuments in Na h'Eileanan Siar [the Western Isles] – castles; chapels; brochs; duns; burial cairns; chambered cairns; souterrains; stone circles; standing stones; beehive shielings. Maclean and Leven's monuments take their places within this 'cultural landscape'. Historian Neal Ascherson writes most movingly when he examines his relationship with the landscape of Argyll.[6] He describes his several visits to the cup and ring markings at Poltalloch in mid-Argyll; how in his visits he would try to see them in a way which might have been the rediscovery of a very old way: that is, in learning to see them as part of a 'cultural landscape'. He writes about a tendency amongst anthropologists and archaeologists to regard art, first of all, as art on rock – in other words to see only what is within the frame. His own revelation came with the realisation that art and frame are inherently connected, that 'they are a single context'. It is not just the art, or the art and the rock, but, more than that, the art and the environment: 'the context is not just the sheet of rock, but the landscape itself'.[7]

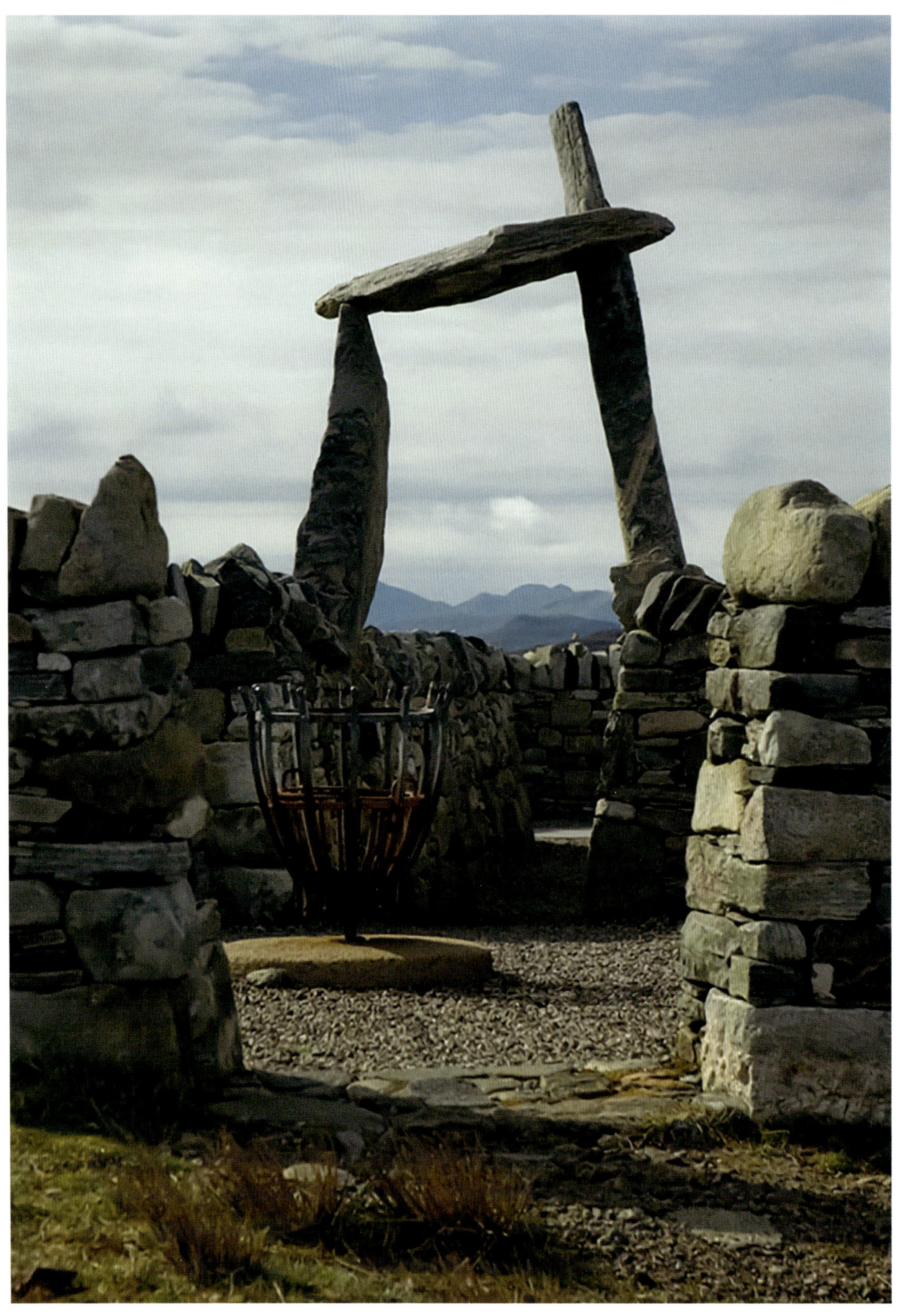

An Sùileachan, with the iron basket on the millstone (see Notes to Illustrations)

In the introduction to his essay 'Lapidification', on the presence of stone on the Island of Lewis, Pàdraig MacAoidh adroitly juxtaposes the material and the psychological:
> Lewis, where I am from, is a constant balancing of stone and water; the moor is medium, mediator and outcome of this straining. The whole island is 'eadar a' chlach 's an sgrath', in the Gaelic phrase: 'between the stone and the turf' or, as English has it, 'in two minds'.[8]

The essay probes the question of a 'cultural landscape' but links it to a sense of the haptic and the phenomenological. Of the landscape surrounding his home, he writes:
> On the hill above the loch is Stein-a-Cleit, a stone circle, or series of circles, dolmens silent and blank in their deep history, 'cast from the dread bosom of the unknown past'. In my lifetime this has been labelled (by an endless succession of government heritage bodies) steading, a chambered cairn, a settlement, an enclosure. It has never been excavated, only surveyed, one of the hundreds of sites on Lewis that keep their meanings to themselves, compacted within.[9]

What is revealed here is doubt: doubt about classifications, terminology, language, the order of things: 'We still don't have enough words for stones, still get nowhere near their pith. Hugh MacDiarmid in *On a Raised Beach*, comes closest, but only serves to break the English language.'[10] Describing his own experience of learning to build a wall, using the stone from a tumbled-down lot wall, MacAoidh uses the expression anastylosis, which comes from the Greek, meaning to 'erect again'. He writes, 'no words can help you know the thisness, the heccecity of a stone as well as working your fingers underneath its heft'.[11] As with Maclean's cairns, MacAoidh's writing exemplifies the 'vision from within'.

The insights in MacAoidh's essay combine with insights drawn from other strands in contemporary research. Developments in Postcolonial studies, Transnationalisms, Diasporic studies, Literary Geographies, Geopoetics, Northern studies and Arctic and Atlantic Archipelago studies have continued to interrogate the notion of centre and periphery. The whole issue of where cultures are seen from underlies contemporary research, and the problematisation of the control of space (including its representations) has become as important as the more conventional control of time (through history). One of the most fertile strands of enquiry has focused on the links between peripheral/marginalised peoples and cultures. The significance of a 'new' and 'postmodern' geography has had a most pronounced effect here, as is clearly indicated in the introduction to *Across the Margins: Cultural Identity and Change in the Atlantic Archipelago*:
> The last decades of the twentieth century witnessed the emergence of what we might call the 'spatial imagination' and the growing realisation of its absolute centrality to human experience (Soja 1989). This development is not only connected with the growth of widespread scepticism towards history in general and institutionalised

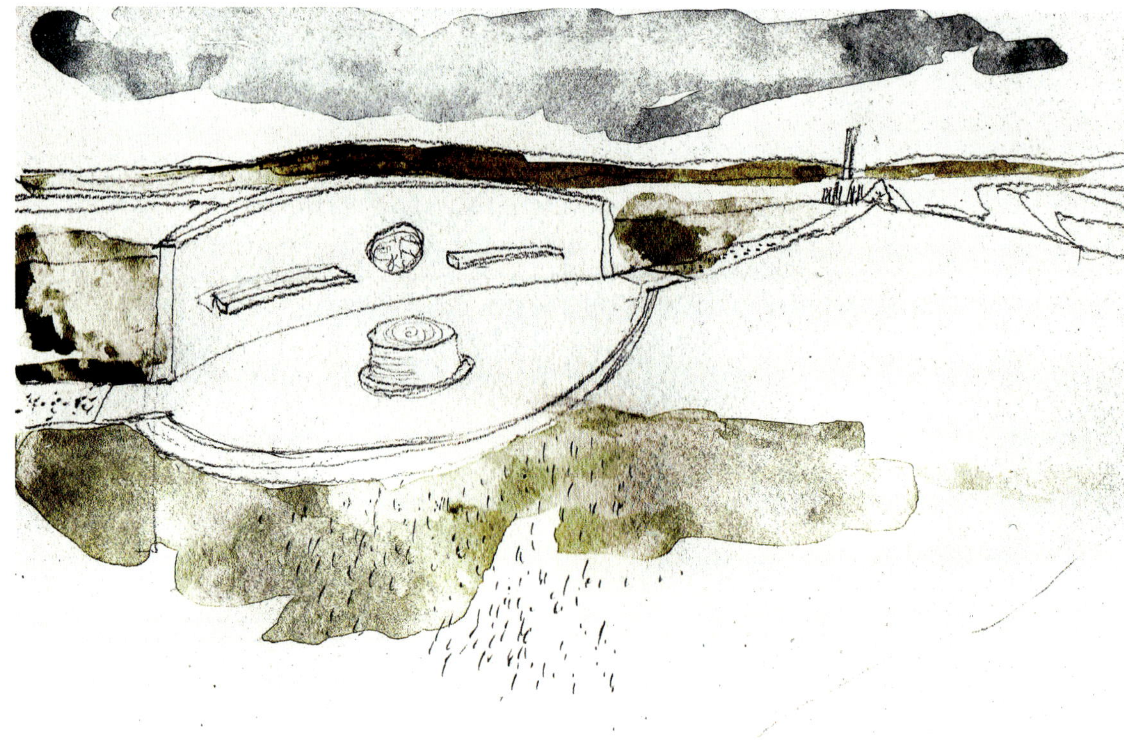
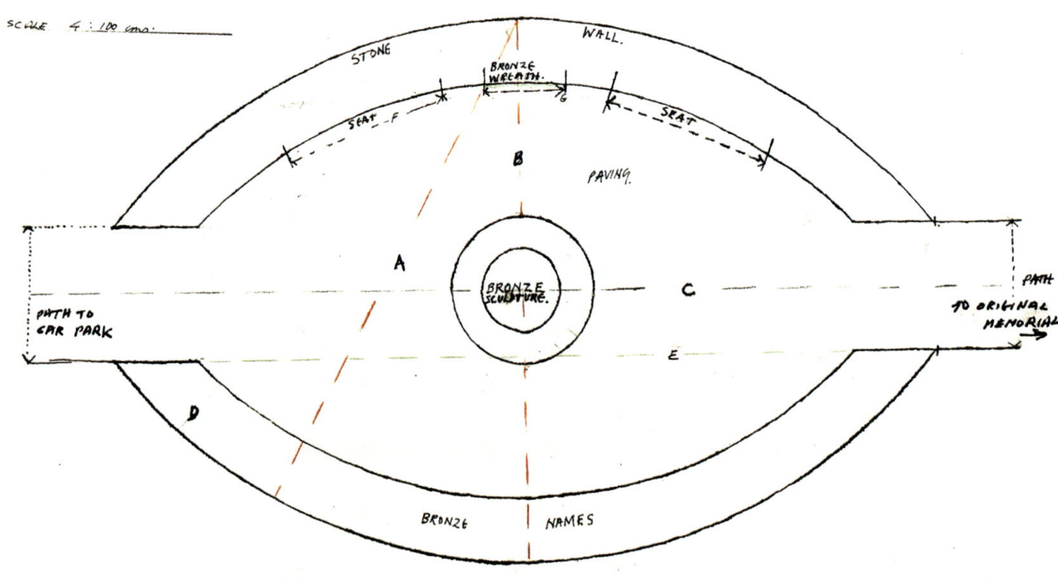

Preparatory watercolour sketch and ground plan by Marian Leven for the *Iolaire* memorial (see Notes to Illustrations)

historiography in particular, but also with a number of factors which have combined to put pressure on the historicism which has dominated western critical/cultural institutions since the nineteenth century.[12]

Maclean's interest in the 'spatial imagination' has been a characteristic of a way of thinking throughout his working life – tracing connections, identifying congruities, matching forms and materials from indigenous Inuit peoples in the Arctic North with his own Highland cultural heritage. Inuit carvings, Newfoundland cod-jiggers, fishing boats and gear, totems, charms, sea-markers, tools and equipment related to exploration, boatbuilding, wayfinding, fishing and whaling, as well as feathered slippers, birds' eggs, vessels for oil, or constructed altars from coastal cultures across a wide geographic range, provide Maclean with a dense and multifaceted vocabulary of forms. One of the best illustrations of the impulse to 'transcend historical precision' by incorporating elements of a 'spatial imagination' is seen in the Inuit arch incorporated into the memorial structure *An Sùileachan*. The arch, which reflects the shared vision of Maclean and Leven, functions architecturally to mark the boundary between one space and another and metaphorically to mark the threshold between the temporal and the spiritual. Yet it also relates vertically through Gaelic culture to that third dimension which John Lorne Campbell defined as the 'everpresent sense of the reality and existence of the other world of spiritual and psychic experience'.[13]

The lives of people from the crofting community and the use of materials and skills which belong to that world are the abiding concerns in almost all of Maclean's work. A hallowed respect for the lifetime of skills accrued by the tradesman, the crofter, the seaman, is a constant element underlying Maclean's own artistic practice. One of the clearest illustrations of this element is revealed in his description of the background to two artworks which were inspired by the epic Atlantic voyage in an open boat, the *James Caird*, undertaken by Ernest Shackleton and five crewmen in 1916 in their desperate attempt to rescue the survivors of the main expedition stranded on Elephant Island:

> A team of six men carried out an open boat journey of 800 miles from Elephant Island to South Georgia. They survived a hurricane and landed on the unoccupied southern shores. Three of the men then crossed the island climbing through glaciers and mountainous terrain to reach the whaling station on the northern shore. One man, Harry McNish, a man from Dundee, a boat's carpenter, had made critical changes to the boat's structure before they had left Elephant Island: he took the tacks out of their boots, gathered up all the tacks and used them to nail down a makeshift deck or cover for the open boat which is what enabled them to survive the journey and eventually send a rescue ship to Elephant Island.[14]

Maclean's admiration for these kinds of qualities and skills have led to a lifetime of collecting – collecting items of equipment, tools, materials and objects which provide him with the essential elements or content for his works.

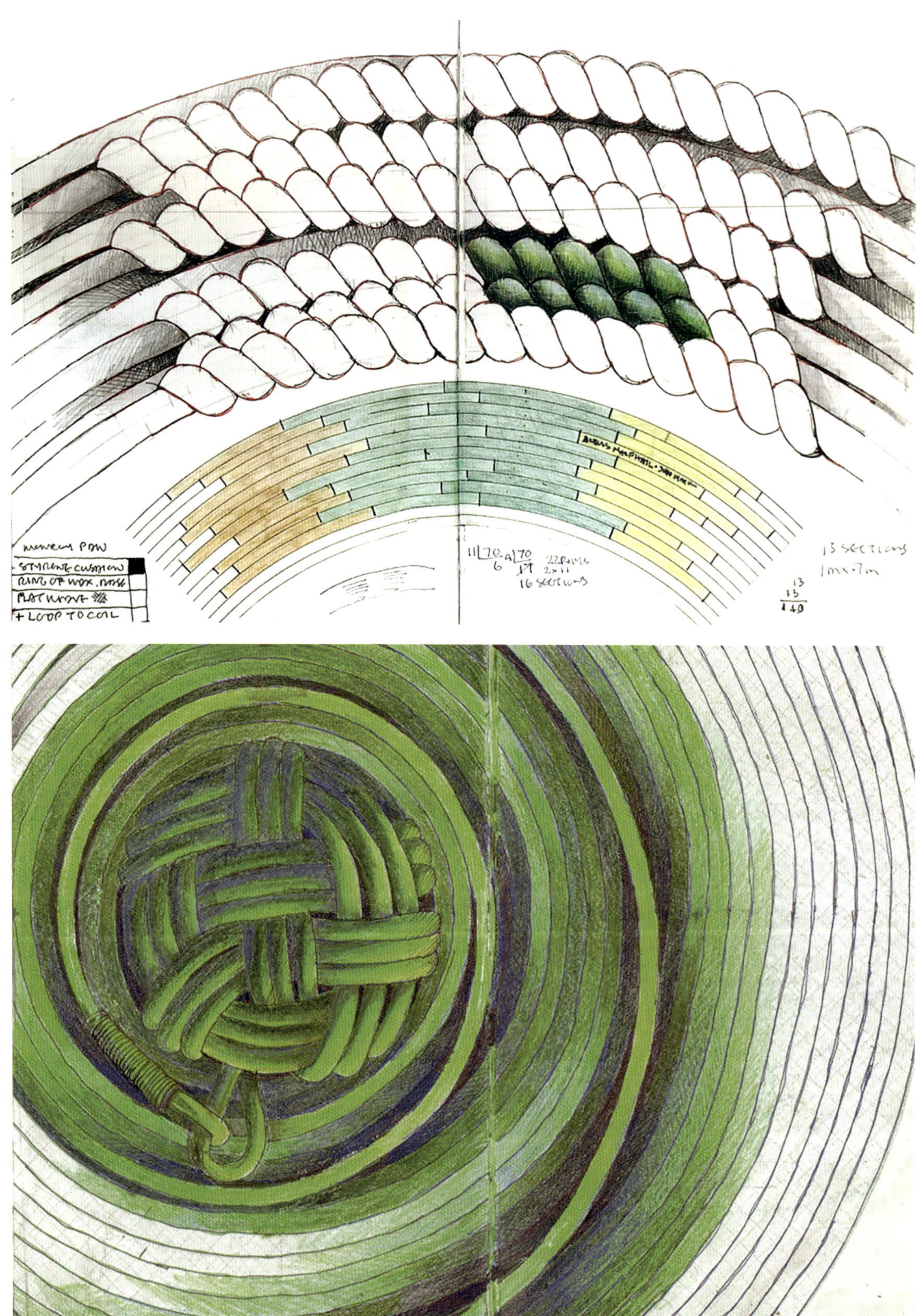

MEMORY PDN
STYRENE CUSHION
RING OF WAX . BASE
FLAT WEAVE
+ LOOP TO COIL
11/70-a/70
6   17   22 ROWS
2x11
16 SECTIONS
13 SECTIONS
1m x .7m
13
13
140

These objects or forms have then to be allied, throughout, with a sense of the symbolic – that is, the search for the visual metaphor that will transform the real into the poetic–and this is what connects Maclean to the Highland poetic tradition. Derick Thomson, the very fine poet from Bayble in Lewis, is wary of images which conceal the truth. For him, it is the way that heather grows on the slopes, hiding – to the unwary eye – the wounds of the Clearances, or the image of a smothering of snow covering the country, where he warns 'though it is white do not believe in its whiteness'.[15] Donald MacAulay, likewise, articulates the need for a 'vision from within', but one which can articulate the meaning:

> [T]hat unless we have our condition
> Clearly depicted in our words
> Unless we have the words
> To state the meaning of our condition
> We will not apprehend it:
> We will not build a poem that concerns us.[16]

I have argued above about the way that representation was foisted upon the Highlands from outwith and that these kinds of representation (of moors and glens empty of people as a supposedly 'natural' landscape) were examples of representation as concealment. However, what we have here in these Lewis memorials of Maclean and Leven is a sense of revelation. As though they are rising from the land itself, the memorials break through the concealments of history, the 'fug o' fame/An' history's hazelraw' as MacDiarmid would have it.[17] The concerns of the artists have been to restore to history the unheard voices: the voices of the lost, the subjugated and the disinherited. The purpose behind these memorial pieces on the Island of Lewis is a dialogical one – that is, the insertion into the historical narrative of the perspective of the dispossessed. They are memorials, certainly, but they are by no means tokens only: the monuments bestride the horizontals of the Lewis peatlands, bodying forth the obdurate defiance of a people to the relentless pressure of capitalist exploitation.

The bronze wreath sculpture located at Holm is part of the HMY *Iolaire* commemorative installation commission awarded to Maclean, Leven and Watson by An Lanntair, the art centre in Stornoway. The testimonies gathered to mark the centenary of the catastrophic foundering of the HMY *Iolaire* bear witness to the ongoing sense of loss felt throughout the island from that night in January 1919 when 201 men lost their lives within metres of the shore. The wreath blends into the stone wall on which it is mounted, creating a place of reflection. The wall, designed by Leven, frames Watson's heaving line and the bronze roll call of names, and points towards the location where the ship went down. Maclean's preliminary drawings for the wreath reveal the way the artist works with symbolic objects

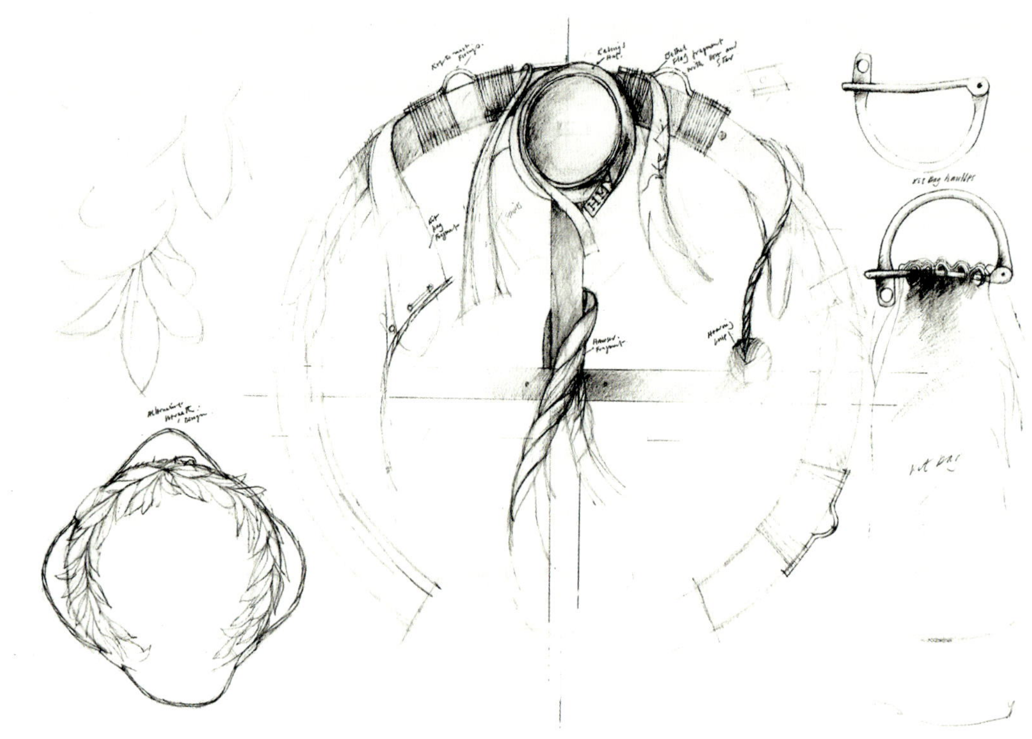

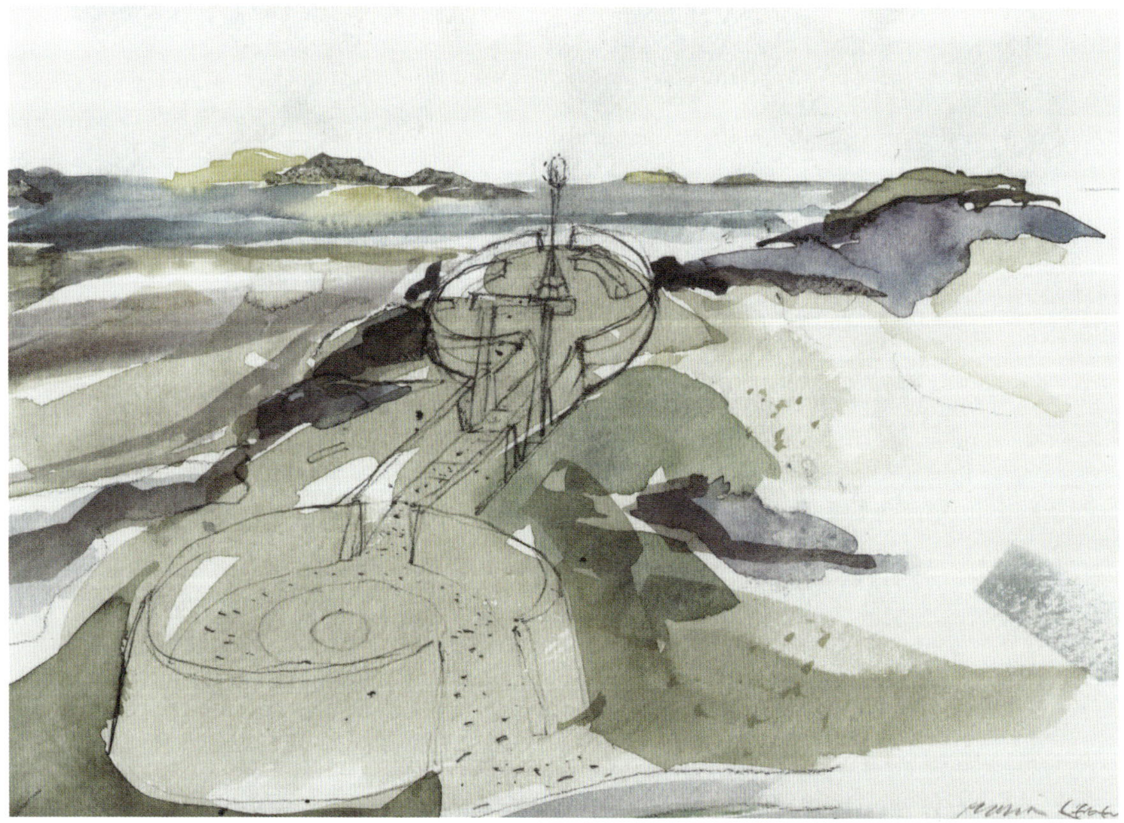

and analogical rhythms, but always in relation to content. The circular external form refers, primarily, to lifebelts and the artist has used old herring fishing line to represent the four loops of cord which were attached so as to allow a group of people to cling to the one belt. The inner ring was made of green willow, referring to the value placed upon the willow, which was grown in stone enclosures on the island and used for making creels and baskets. Within the ring, the artist has deconstructed a rating's hat in reference to the fact that eye-witnesses had recalled the number of hats floating on the sea in the days following the tragedy. It is tucked below a softwood carving of a kitbag laced at the top and ripped at the base. There is also a casting of a bosun's pipe on a lanyard. All these elements were familiar to the men on board the ship. The circular external form finds rhythmical echoes in the rope splice and the drawstring of the kitbag as well as in the shape of the hat and the embellished edge made up of laurel leaves. The sculpture, though, represents so much more. The placing of the kitbag, drawstring, marine shackles and hat within the circular wreath transforms the simple elements into a reliquary – the most ordinary essentials of the Royal Naval Reservist are become precious and sacred. The details concentrated in the fastidious drawings and the assembly of materials are a study in themselves of the way that precision may be employed in leading us to a sense of the hieratic: the very humble elements become the most moving symbols of the lives which had been so tragically lost in the disaster.

When we consider Maclean and Leven's commemorative installation for the *Iolaire*, and the other four monuments on the Island of Lewis, we need to be able to see the forms of these works in relation to underlying truths. When we look at the narrative, which suggests the inexorable march away from a primitive agrarian peasant community towards a private middle-class, ownership-orientated society, we need to see the memorials on Lewis as offering to this march a significant counter-narrative. We read, in the words of philosophers Michel Foucault, Mikhail Bakhtin and members of the Frankfurt School, something of the theoretical thrust behind such resistance, much of which derives from Gramsci's writings on 'manufactured consent' or 'hegemony'. There is no question but that the monuments represent a significant oppositional perspective to the 'manufactured consent' which allowed for the clearing of people from the land and the official sanction of the inferiorisation of the language and the culture of the Highland people. Bakhtin devoted most of his politically-charged writings to the novel, to the potential within the novel to question and overturn dominant, hegemonic voices by the inclusion of the voices of the non-integrated other or the 'voices from below'. The term that he used was 'heteroglossia' and it is this sense of the 'voices from below' that reverberates through the works on Lewis. The reinsertion of the voices of the people allows for a rereading of history, and the way that the monuments reverberate in the form of a contemporary discourse ensures that a minoritarian voice becomes part of a dialogue within a much broader world debate on memorialisation.

OPPOSITE TOP Will Maclean's pencil drawing (56 x 76 cm) showing details of the *Iolaire* memorial wreath
OPPOSITE BOTTOM A preparatory pencil and wash drawing by Marian Leven for the *Iolaire* memorial

1. M. M. Bakhtin, *The Dialogic Imagination*, University of Texas Press, Austin, 2014 [1981]

2. Ian Finlay, *Art in Scotland*, Oxford University Press, London, 1948, p.174

3. Malcolm MacLean and Christopher Carrell, *As An Fhearann/From the Land*, Mainstream Publishing, Edinburgh, 1986

4. *ibid.*, p.21

5. *ibid.*

6. Neal Ascherson, *Stone Voices: The Search for Scotland*, revised ed., Granta Books, London, 2003

7. *ibid.*, pp.217 – 8

8. Pàdraig MacAoidh, 'Lapidification', *Archipelago*, 11 (Winter), Clutag Press, 2016, p.50

9. *ibid.*, p.51

10. *ibid.*, p.53

11. *ibid.* p.54. Note that 'heccecity' is often spelt 'haecceity'

12. Glenda Norquay and Gerry Smyth, *Across the Margins: Cultural Identity and Change in the Atlantic Archipelago*, Manchester University Press, Manchester, 2002, p.5

13. Ronald Black, 'Introduction', in *An Tuil: Anthology of 20th Century Scottish Gaelic Verse*, Polygon, Edinburgh, 1999, p.xxiii

14. Will Maclean, interview with the author, 2011

15. Derick Thomson, George Campbell Hay, Donald MacAulay and Sorley Maclean, 'Ruraidh MacThómais/ Derick Thomson', in *Nua-Bhardachd Ghaidhlig/Modern Scottish Gaelic Poems*, Canongate, Edinburgh, 1987 [1976], pp.154 – 5

16. Donald MacAulay, quoted in Iain Crichton Smith, 'The Modest Doctor: The Poetry of Donald MacAulay', in *Towards the Human*, MacDonald Publishers, Edinburgh, 1986, p.117

17. Hugh MacDiarmid, *Hugh MacDiarmid: Selected Poems*, Penguin Books Ltd., Harmondsworth, 1970

OPPOSITE *An Sùileachan* looking westwards through the passageway connecting the two 'discs', towards the sea

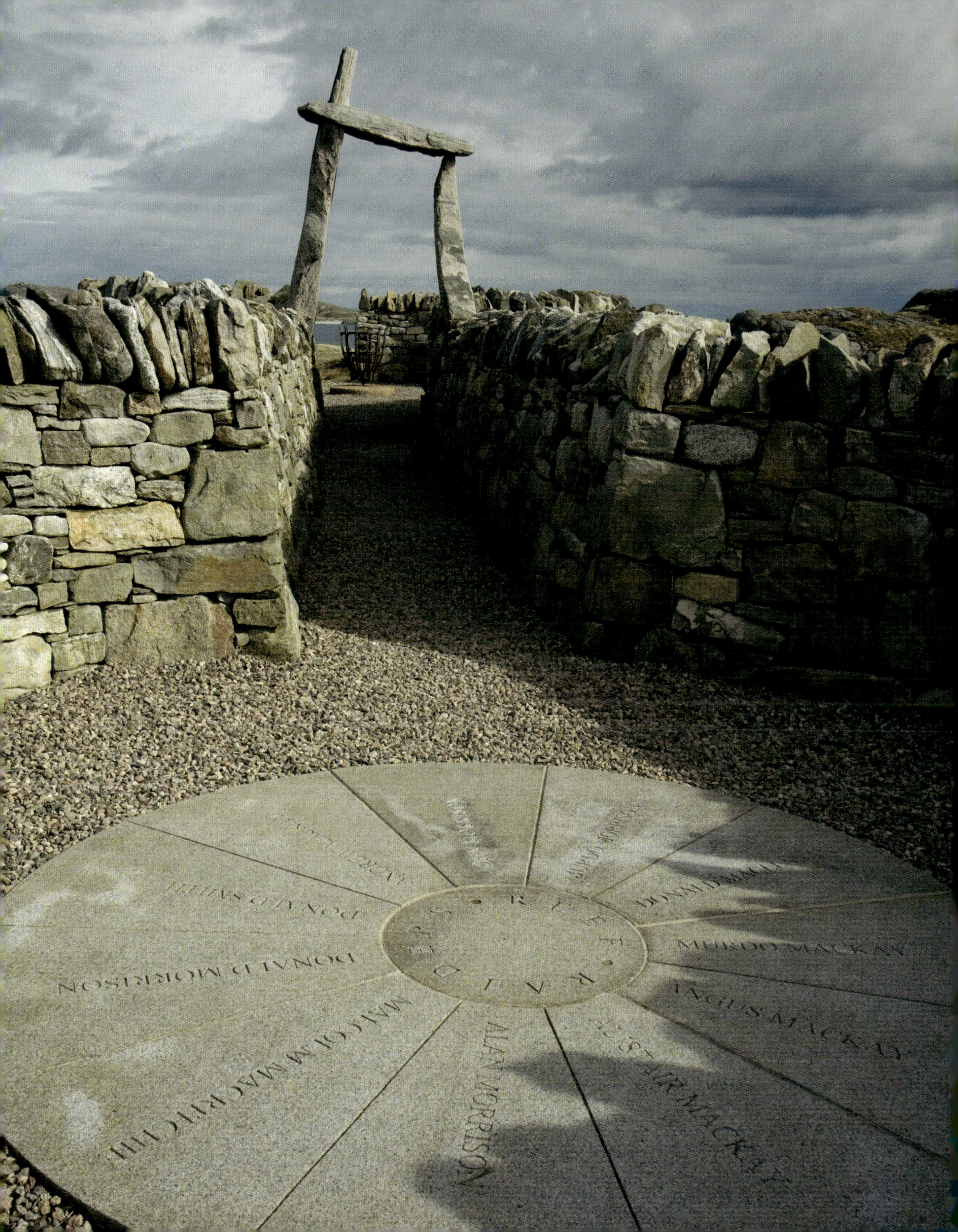

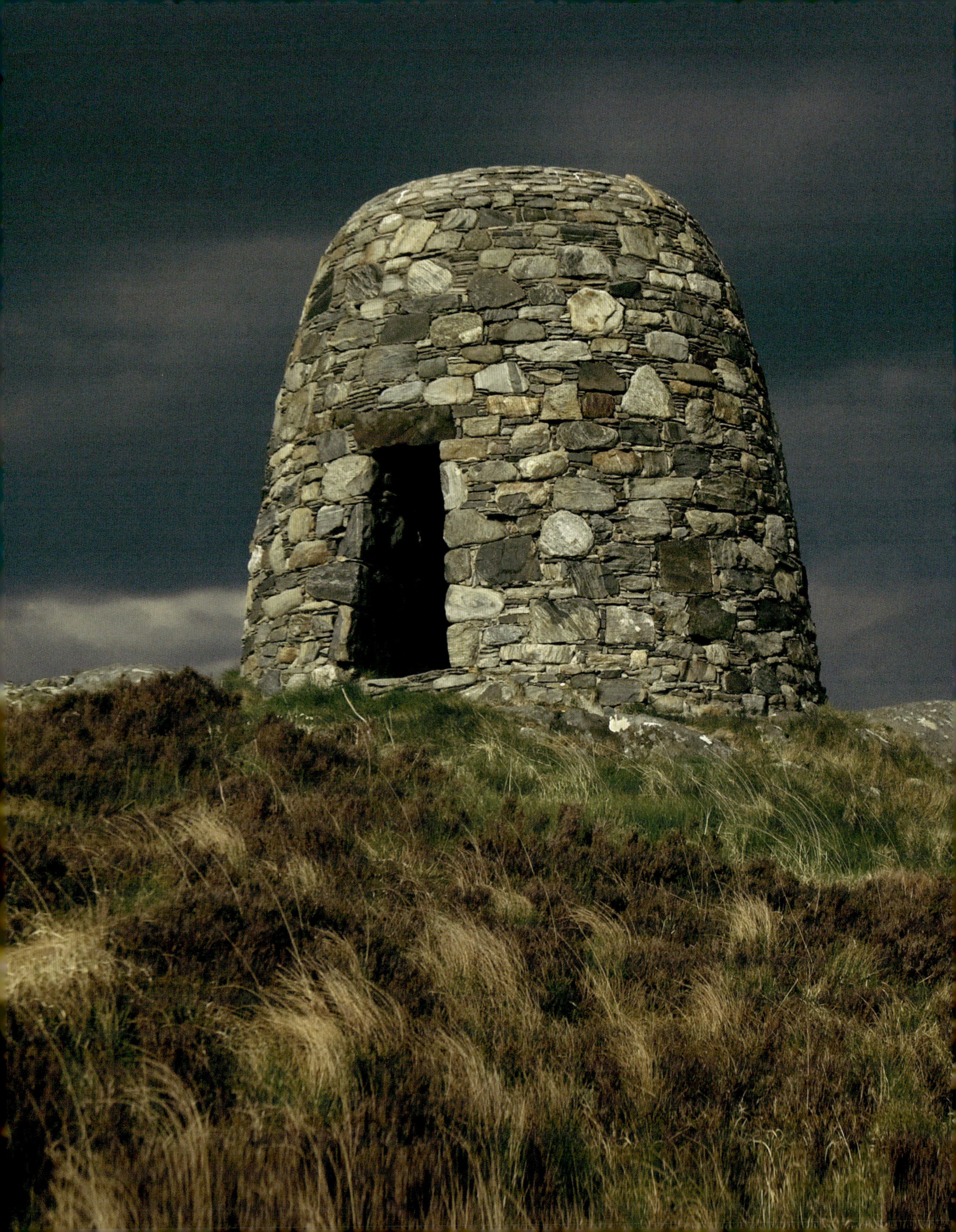

Teacsan Gàidhlig le Joni Bhochanan & Eilidh Ghreumach

Eachdraidh Charraighean-cuimhne
Strì an Fhearann

Air an cuairteachadh le mòinteach riabhach Leòdhais, tha ceithir carraighean-cuimhne air an dealbhachadh leis an neach-ealain Will MacIllEathain.[1] Gach tè mar shàmhla air eachdraidh shònraichte anns an dearbh àite far a bheil iad nan seasamh, iad cuideachd a' sònrachadh gach fear 's tè a sheas an aghaidh an ana-cheartais a thachair anns na coimhearsnachdan seo air iomall na Roinn Eòrpa. Tha daoine beò annta fhathast air sgàth na h-oidhirp eachdraidheil a chaidh a dhèanamh.

San t-seachdamh 's san ochdamh linn deug bha cuid de dhùthchannan ri taobh an Iar na Roinn Eòrpa a' gabhail ris an t-siostam ùr chalapachais agus a' cur an cùl ris an t-seann dòigh beatha sòsio-eaconamach. A reir MhicAonghais[2] chaidh a' Ghàidhealtachd agus na h-Eileanan; 'a ghluasad bho cho-chomunn traidiseanta gu siostam maileartach, ann an dòigh bhuaireasach agus le làimhseachadh làidir'. Chaidh cur às do sheann dòigh-beatha nan cinn-cinnidh agus a-nis na h-uachdarain a' togail màl bhon t-sluagh, iad a' sireadh na prothaid a bu mhotha agus a' cumail smachd air iarrtas agus sòlar.

Ann an Leòdhas, stèidhich Morair Shìophort a' chiad ìre den dòigh ùr am fearrann a roinn. Thug e earannan mòra den mhòintich a-mach à croitearachd agus roinn e an talamh àiteach sna bailtean nan lotaichean beaga. Bha a' mhòinteach a-nis air a cur gu feum mar thuathanas chaorach agus airson sealgaireachd. Còmhla ri seo chaidh na croitearan fhastadh aig gnìomhachas na ceilp (a' toirt Alcalaidhn à feamainn). Cha do sheas an gnìomhachas fada ach chaidh airgead mòr a chosnadh leis na h-uachdarain – leithid Sìophort. Bha am màl agus na cìsean a chaidh a bhuilleadh air na croitearan leis an oighreachd furasta gu leòr a phàigheadh fhad 's a bha obair na ceilp soirbheachail ach uair 's gun do chrìon e, thàinig fiachan orra, gun dòigh sam bith am pàigheadh. Leis an t-saothair a bha an luib obair na feamainn cha robh tìde ann airson obair àiteachais agus leis mar a bha iad a' beathachadh an crodh air a' phiòs beag de thalamh a chaidh fhàgail aca, cha robh e fada gus an robh iad an urra ris a' bhuntàta a-mhàin airson a bhith beò.[3]

Tràth san naoidheamh linn deug bha am buntàta loit anns an talamh, obair na ceilp air fàiligeadh agus an sluagh air an sguabadh a-mach gu gach ceàrnaidh. Dh'fhalbh an fheadhainn a b' urrainn gu dùthchannan eile. Thug na dòighean seo buaidh mhòr air na ginealaichean a thàinig às an dèidh.[4]

Thòisichear le fuadaichean ann an sgìre na Pàirc mu 1819, chaidh mu thrithead baile fhàgail gun duine beò. Anns na h-ochdadan, aig àm creachadh na Pàirc (far a bheil a' chiad obair-shnaighte aig MacIllEathainn) chaidh 70,000 acairean a thoirt a-mach à croitearachd. Chùm na fuadaichean a' dol le Seumas MacMhathain a cheannaich an t-eilean ann an 1884.

Bha MacMhathain, a chaidh a thogail an Cataibh, na cheannard air a' chompanaidh Jardine Matheson, a bha ri gnìomhachas san àite a bha air aithneachadh mar an Orient. Bha iad a' reic an leithid sìoda agus tì ach b' e opium am bathar a bha gu h-àraidh soirbheachail dhaibh.

Mus tàinig meadhan an naoidheamh linn deug bha dithis às gach còignear (còrr 's mìle duine) air an sgiùrsadh a-mach à Ùig air Taobh Siar Leòdhais (far a bheil an càrn, *An Sùileachan* na sheasamh). Ann an 1870 bha 40,000 acairean den fhearann ann an làmhan seachd tuathanaich, trì nan oighreachdan sealgaireachd. Air los an ìre bheag de dh'fhearann a bh' aig daoine bha na bailtean beaga a' cur thairis, aig amannan trì teaghlaichean beò air aon lot –aon chroitear agus dà theaghlach às aonais fearann dhaibh fhèin. Nan aghaidh gu mòr bha dìth tèarainteachd agus nach robh dòigh laghail sam bith ann an còraichean a sheasamh. Cha robh càil a mhath a bhith a' gearan no dheigheadh peanas 's cìsean a bhuaileadh orra. 'S e toiseach tòiseachaidh a bh' ann an aimhreit Bheàrnaraigh 1874, aimhreit a dh'eirich bho 56 teaghlaichean rabhadh fhaighinn teicheadh far an fhearainn. Bha an aimhreit seo a' sealltainn nach robh an sluagh dol a sheasamh ris an àmhghar tuilleadh. Dhà no trì bhliadhnaichean às dèidh seo – ann an 1882, dhiùlt croitearan a' Bhràigh san Eilean Sgitheanach am màl a phàigheadh agus sheas iad an aghaidh an rabhadh gus gluasad a-mach às na dachaighean – a' leanntain an aon dòigh ris na h-Èireannaich a bha a' sabaid airson còraichean fearainn cuideachd. Air sgàth 's na h-aimhreit, chaidh aire an Riaghaltais a thogail don ghnothach agus stèidhich iad an Coimisean Rìoghail. Cha robh iad air gnothach a ghabhail bho 1840 nuair a rinn iad cobhair 's a' bhochdainn ann. Chaidh aithisg fhoillseachadh ann an 1884 agus chaidh a dhearbhadh gun robh cus dhaoine beò còmhla, gun robh bochdainn air sìor fhàs agus gun robh ana-ceartais ann a thaobh làimhseachadh làidir nan uachdaran.

Anns an Fhaoilleach 1886 chaidh ceathrar a thaghadh nam Buill Pàrlaimaid le uallach airson croitearachd. Chaidh Achd nan Croitearan a chur air bhonn leis na Libearalaich, Achd a ghabh a-steach tèarainteachd fearainn, airgead airson leasachadh agus cuideachd a chuir Comisean nan Croitearan air bhonn, seòrsa de chùirt fearainn. Bha seo na cheum mòr dha na croitearan ach dha tug seo còraichean sam bith dha na coitearan, cha tug e a bharrachd am fearann a chailleadh air ais. Bha draghan agus buaireadh ann fhathast. Tha ìomhaigh chumhachdail an Aignis san Rubha, Leòdhas, an càrn a dhealbhaich MacIllEathain a' sònrachadh na h-aimhreit ann an 1888 eadar na croitearan a bha ag iarraidh an fhearainn air ais agus na Royal Marines a chaidh a thoirt a-steach gus an t-sìth a chumail. Chaidh oidhirpean a dhèanamh agus fhuaireadh ceum air adhart ach thàinig stad air cùisean nuair a bhris An Cogadh Mòr a-mach.

Bha gnothaichean fhathast rin rèiteachadh nuair a thill na fir às a' chogadh. Cha robh am Morair Leverhulme, a bha air an t-eilean a cheannach, idir deònach talamh a thoirt dhaibh agus bha aca ri sealbh a ghabhail air an fhearann iad fhèin. Tha an ceathramh càrn mar chuimhneachan air an t-strì eadar Leverhulme agus na croitearan aig drochaid Ghriais ann an 1919.

Còmhla, tha na carraighean-cuimhne mar shamhla air eachdraidh shònraichte, eachdraidh a thug buaidh air dòigh-beatha ann an Leòdhas agus tha a' bhuaidh sin follaiseach sìos chun an latha an-diugh.

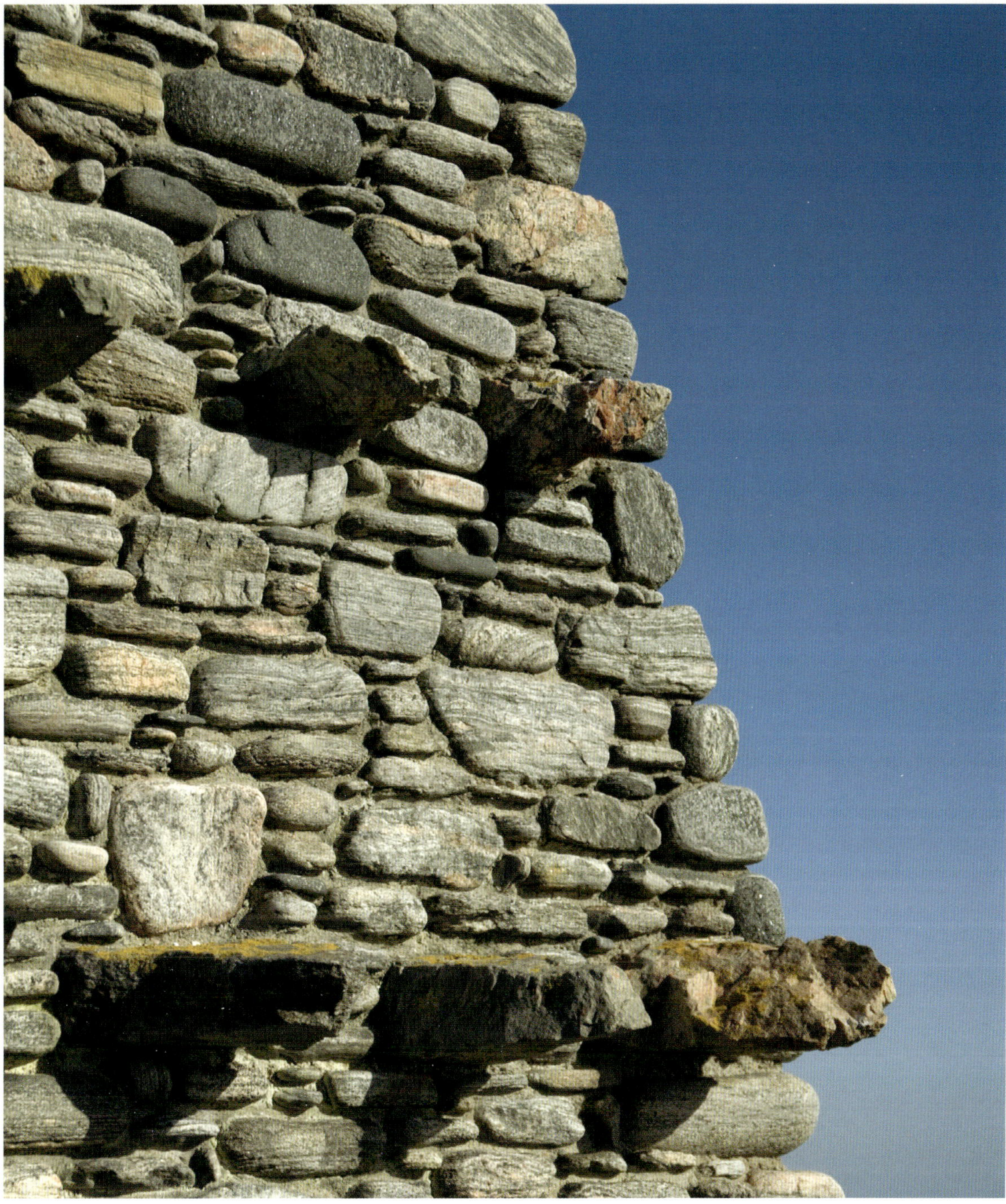

Mionaideachd nan clachan a tha a' tighinn a-mach à càrn cuimhneachaidh Aignis

---

1. An ceathramh ìomhaigh-shnaighte, *An Sùileachan*, chaidh a cho-dhealbhadh le Will MacIllEathain agus Marian Leven
2. MacAonghais, A I, *Clanship, Commerce and the House of Stewart, 1603–1788,* Tuckwell Press, Linton an Ear, 1996.
3. Aithisg Sir John MacNeill, 1851
4. *Aithisg Coimisean Napier*, 1884, le coimisean sgrùdaidh air staid chroitearan is choitearan ann an Gàidhealtachd agus Eileanan na h-Alba (a chaidh a chur air bhonn ann an 1883 le Morair Napier sa Chathair)

   Faic cuideachd, Buchanan, J. (1996) *The Lewis Land Struggle: Na Gaisgich*, Acair, Steòrnabhagh

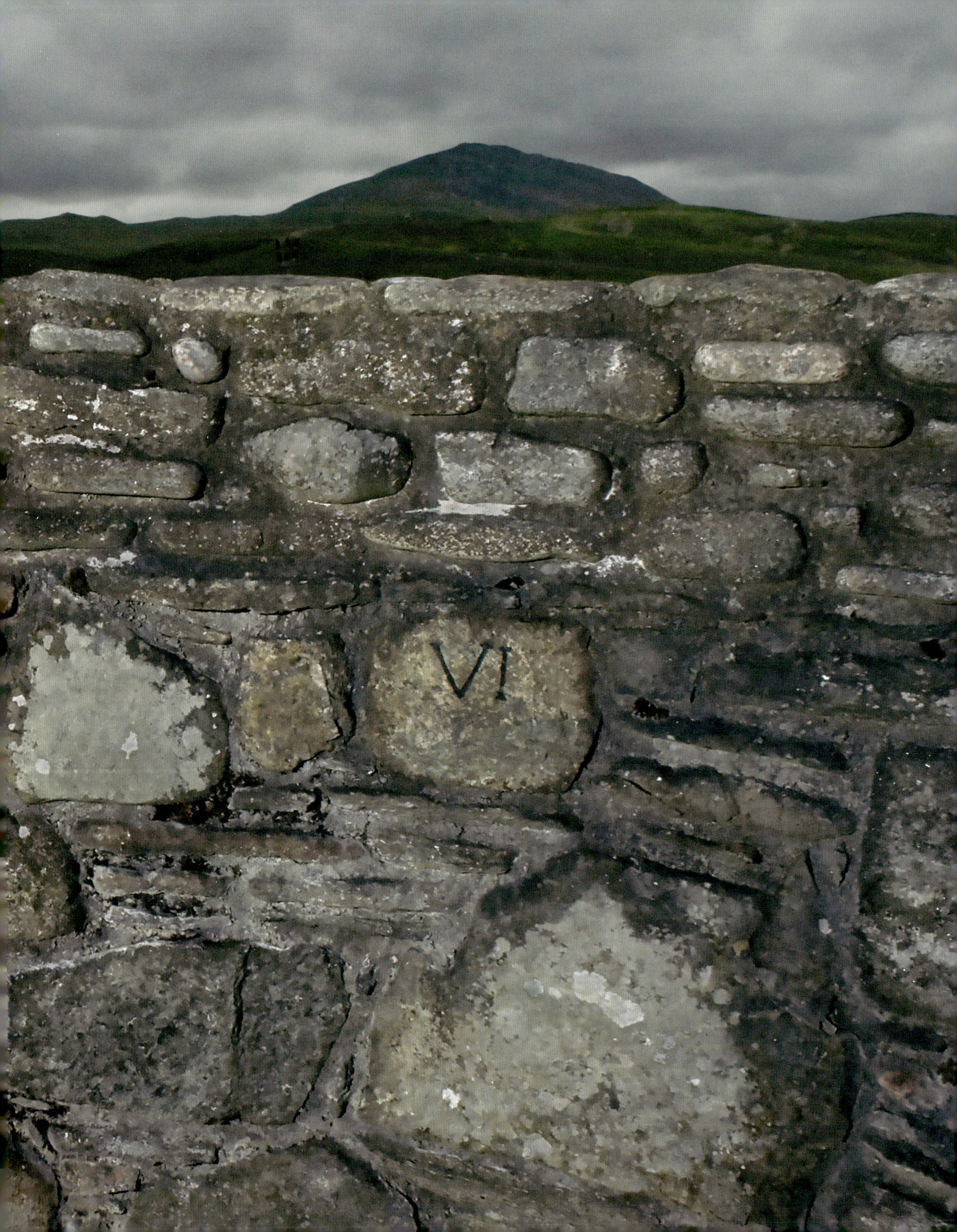

VI

Rèid na Pàirce 1887

'Talamh torach, am monadh agus bàghan brèagha na Pàirce. Air a dhealbhadh dha mac
an duine gus cofhurtachd fhaotainn mar dhìoladh airson a shaothair. Ochd air fhichead
baile air an sguabadh a-mach, an cothrom a thoirt bhuapa, an cuid àmhghar agus bròn
air a chunntadh mar rud suarach, na caoraich 's na fèidh ag ionaltradh nam machrach
's a mhòinteach a chaidh a ruagadh agus na h-uachdaran a' faighinn toileachas às.'
Coimisean Napier, Vol 2, p.1139, Dùn Èideann, 1884

Bha Iain Mac a' Ghobhainn à Bail' Ailein ann an sgìre nan Loch, ochd bliadhna a dh'aois nuair
a chaidh e fhèin 's a theaghlach a ruagadh às a' Phàirc. 'S ann mu 1820 a dh'fhàg sean agus
òg na bailtean, iad fo bhròn 's iad air an tilgeadh a-mach às an dachaighean, iad a-nis nan
sluagh às aonais àite dhaibh fhèin, gach nì a bha prìseil nam beatha air an cùlaibh. Bha
cuimhne mhath aig Iain Mac a' Ghobhainn air na thachair. Na sheann aois thug e fianais
seachad dha Coimisean Napier, thuirt e gun robh iad, 'Mar chaoraich air an cruinneachadh
dhan fhaing le na coin'. Bha cuid air an sgiùrsadh a dh'Aimeireaga agus cuid eile air an sadail
an siud 's an seo le pìosan beaga, bochd de thalamh air a thoirt dhaibh.

Chum na fuadaichean sa Phàirc a' dol airson dà fhichead bliadhna eile. An fheadhainn nach
deach a sgiùrsadh a dh'Aimeireaga, chaidh an cur gu bailtean beaga, truagh, an aghaidh an
toil. Ro 1880, ann an sgìre nan Loch air fad, bha faisg air dà mhìle duine beò air muin a chèile
ann an naoi bailtean, mu dhà fhichead dhiubh nan coitearan, le 181 lotaichean mu aon acair
gach fear air a roinn eatarra.

Ann an 1888 bha aonta fearainn airson tuathanas chaorach na Pairce ri ùrachadh. Dà uair,
chaidh iarraidh air a' bhanntrach NicMhathain talamh a thoirt dha na croitearan. 'Mura
faigh sinn barrachd fearainn feumaidh sinn an t-àite fhàgail no a bhith nar n-uallach air an
oighreachd.' Cha tàinig freagairt sam bith bhon tè uasal a bha os cionn na h-oighreachd.
Thuirt na croitearan rithe nach robh dòigh às ach an aon slighe ri cuid de chroitearan eile san
dùthaich a ghabhail, gus an còraichean a sheasamh. Dhiùlt i gach tagradh agus a bharrachd
air an sin bha i den bheachd gum b' e iad fhèin a bu choireach airson na staing anns an robh
iad. Leig i tuathanas na Pàirc (26,000 aicearan) a-mach air mhàl agus a' choille (42,000
aicearan) dha Eòsaph Platt airson nam fèidh. Cha deach aon phìos talmhainn a thoirt do
mhuinntir an àite.

Lean tachartas sònraichte bhon t-suidheachadh seo a tha air a chomharrachadh le obair-
shnaighte Will MhicIllEathain, an càrn seo na sheasamh os cionn sgìre na Pàirce. Am measg
nan iomadh cloich a chaidh a chleachdadh sa chuimhnneachan mhaireannach, tha taghadh
prìseil de chlachan bho dhachaighean nam fir 's nam mnathan a thug aire na rìoghachd don
t-suidheachadh uabhasach anns an robh iad.

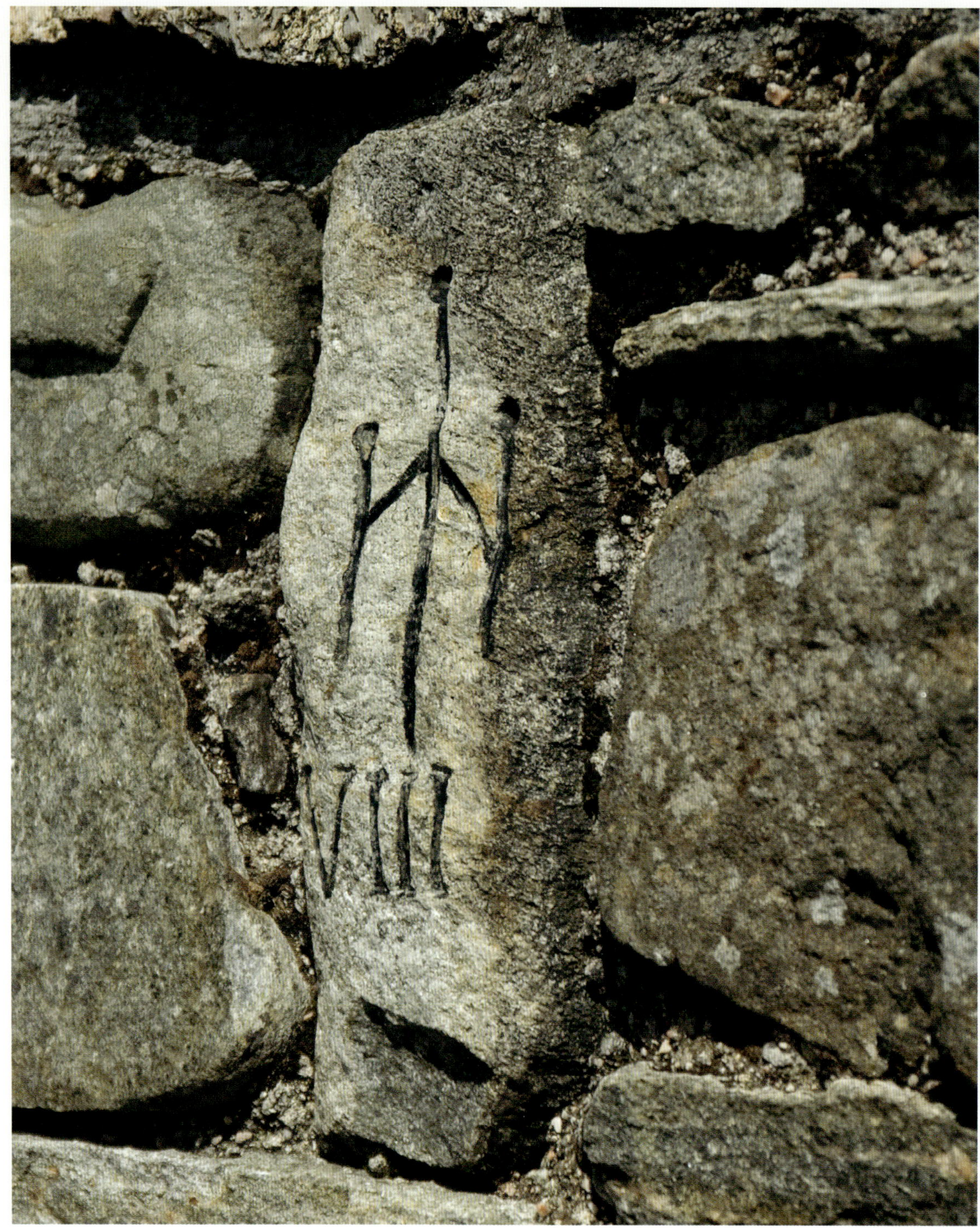

Gu fàbharach, no a rèir cuid aig an àm 'b' e obair freastail' a thug Dòmhnall MacRath à Alanais a Bhail' Ailein na mhaighstir-sgoile, fear a bha an sàs gu mòr ann an strì an fhearainn gu ruige siud. Bha MacRath a' tuigsinn nan robh iad gu bhith soirbheachail le bhith a' toirt aire dhaoine don chùis gum feumadh iad slighe phoilitigeach a bha rianal a ghabhail.

As t-Fhoghar 1887, dh'aontaich MacRath 's na croitearan ri plana, plana a chuireadh iad air bhonn air 22mh dhen t-Sultain a' bhliadhna sin. Chaidh gabhail ris, na croitearan agus gu h-àraidh na coitearan a thoirt còmhla agus gun gabhadh iad a-mach gu coille na Pàirce gus na fèidh a bh' innte a mharbhadh no an sgiùrsadh a-mach don mhuir. Air an latha, dh'fhalbh dà cheud neach dhan choille, biadh nan cois agus pìobaire aig an ceann. Bha na boireannaich, an cuid chloinne agus na bodaich, aig oir an rathaid gam brosnachadh gus cumail orra.

Chaidh teileagram ann an cabhaig bhon t-Siorraidh ann an Steòrnabhagh gu Dover House 'aca cumail orra gun tèid gach beathach a mharbhadh agus chan èist iad ri comhairle sam bith'. Anns a' bhad chaidh na Royal Marines à Barags Cnoc Moire ann an Glaschu a ghairm gus seòladh a Steòrnabhagh. 'A' cur ceòl air feadh na fìdhle' chuir bean Eòsaph Platt fios gu Oifis na h-Alba 'na dèan dàil 's a' chùis cunnartach'.

Bha MacRath airson 's gum biodh an naidheachd air a sgaoileadh fad 's farsaing. Chuir e fios gu na pàipearan-naidheachd agus cuideachd nochd fianaisean sna pàipearan nàiseanta bho fheadhainn a bha thall 's a chunnaic. Thàinig fear-naidheachd *An Scotsman* air eathar gu coille na Pàirc, dìreach ceud slat bhon champa. Dh'aithris e, 'Bha an sealladh cumhachdail agus cha robh fuaim ri chluinntinn ach na ràimh a' plubraich sa bhùrn. Timcheall an rubha thàinig solas an teine gu m' aire. Aig àirigh Dhòmhnaill Chaim, bha teanta air a togail le fiodh agus air a chòmhdach le canabhas. Bha pìobairean a' cluich, teintean beaga a' gabhail agus biadh air ullachadh'. Chaidh iarraidh air an luchd-naidheachd 'biadh a ghabhail còmhla ris na croitearan agus eisteachd ris an sgeulachd mu na thug orra an cuid biadh a shealg'.

An ath-latha thàinig an Siorradh Friseal, agus anns a' Ghàidhlig dh'iarr e air na creachadair-ean a dhol dhachaigh. Nuair a dhiùlt iad, leugh e an Rabhadh agus le eagal gun rachadh an cur an grèim, dh'aontaich iad a' choille fhàgail. Mus tàinig an oidhche bha a' choille falamh agus na croitearan air an suidheachadh a thoirt gu aire a' mhòr-shluaigh ann an dòigh shìtheil, èifeachdach.

Chum am Morair Tagraidh a' dol leis an ullachadh gus an t-arm a thoirt a-steach. 'Bhiodh e gòrach cùisean atharrachadh gus an tèid fuasgladh fhaighinn a thaobh an lagh agus cuid a chur an grèim.' Chaidh sia deug neach a chur fo chasaid gun do chruinnich iad gràisg agus gun do thog iad buaireadh agus àimhreit. Cha deach ach sianar a thoirt gu cùirt mu dheireadh. Ann an Ard-chùirt Dhùn Èideann air 14mh dhen Fhaoilleach thòisich a' chùis-lagha le Morair a' Cheartais Moncreiff, am Morair MacLabhrain agus am Morair Lee os cionn chùisean. An dèidh nam fianaisean cha tug an diùraidh ach leth-uair a thìde gus neoichiontach air gach chasaid a bhuilleadh air na croitearan.

B' e moladh mòr a chluinneadh sa chùirt nuair a thàinig an co-dhùnadh. Chaidh Dòmhnall MacRath a thogail air gualnean bhon chùirt gu Àrd-eaglais Naomh Giles, thug e an sin taing dhan t-sluagh. Thuirt e nach do chosg a' chùirt càil dhaibh. 'Bha sinn air dìon agus air ar riochdachadh le luchd-lagha a bha dìcheallach agus comasach agus a bha air deagh chliù a chosnadh ann an roinn sam bith de dh'eachdraidh na h-Alba.'

Bha buannachd mhòr ann an latha ud ach bha sabaid ri dhèanamh fhathast.

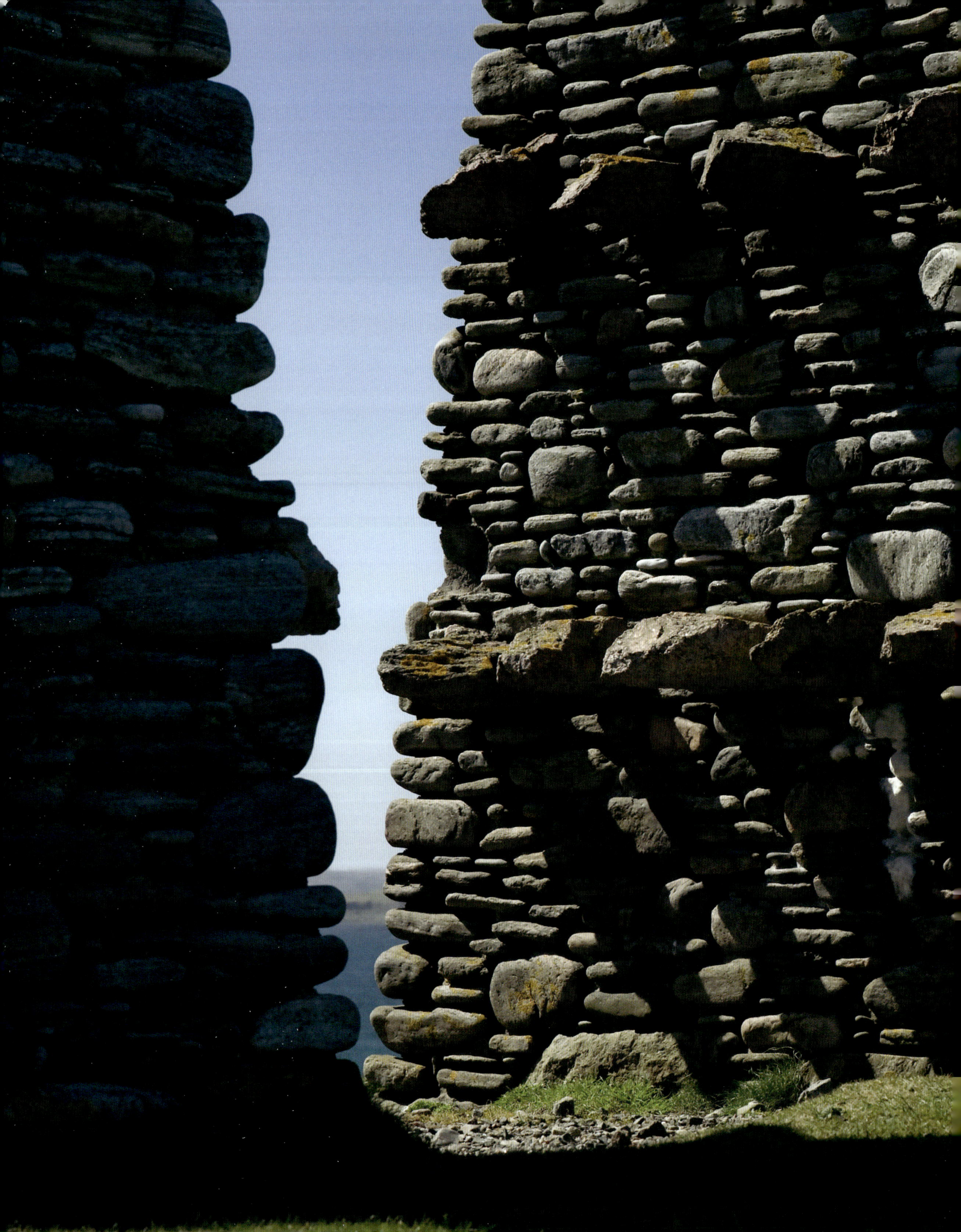

Aignis 1888

'Bithear ag ràdh gur e àite fiadhaich tha ann an Rubha na h-Adhairce. Nis tha an t-àite seo far a bheil mise a' fuireach fosgailte ri gaoithean bhon ear às a' Chairbh agus à Rubha Robhanais on tuath – dà àite tha a' cheart cho fiadhaich ri Rubha na h-Adhairce. Tha na cladaichean cho fosgailte, agus ged a gheibh sinn air obair ceart gu leòr aig muir, glè thric chan eil e comasach dhuinn ar bàtaichean agus uaireanan ar beatha a shàbhaladh nuair a ruigeas sinn tìr. Nam biodh laimrig againn ann an seo, for gu bheil sinn cho math air ar n-obair, gheibheadh sinn bith-beò às an iasgach, cho math ri àite eile an Alba.'
Coimisean Rìoghail Rannsachaidh air staid Chroitearan agus Choitearan sa Gàidhealtachd agus na h-Eileanan Albanach, Vol.ii, d.1051, Dùn Èideann,1884.

Thairis air an fhichead bliadhna is an còrr eadar 1860 agus 1886, bha sia tubaistean mara ann an sgìre an Rubha an Leòdhas. Leis gach bàthadh chaidh an sgioba gu lèir a chall, mar is tric sianar fhir. Nuair a thug Iain Stiùbhart à Pabail fianais mu choinneamh Coimisean Napier thuirt e 'Chaill sinn ar mac fhèin agus ceathrar eile nuair a chaidh an eathar fodha dìreach mu choinneamh an taighe'. Bha na laimrigean fosgailte agus cunnartach. Coitearan às aonais fearainn a bha sa mhòr-chuid de na h-iasgairean, am bith-beò an urra gu tur ris an iasgach. Thuirt Iain Stiùbhart 'Tha mise a' toirt mo chuid bith-beò às a' mhuir, na bheir mi às an lot cha chumadh sin an teaghlach fiu 's aon seachdain'. Cha robh rian aig an dà chuid, cunnartan aig muir agus dìth fearainn, ach a bhith neo-sheasmhach agus eu-dòchasach.

A bharrachd air an sin, nan deigheadh iad an aghaidh sònrachaidhean na h-oighreachd bhathas a' bagairt an cur a-mach às an dachaigh agus bhon fhearann. Thuirt Coinneach MacLeòid à Garrabost ri Coimisean Napier 'Tha sinn cho ìosal is gu bheil eagal làn-chumhachd na h-oighreachd air ar misneachd a thoirt bhuainn'. Mar a bha fìor do chroitearan eile air an eilean, aig an àm, cha robh sealbh aca air an fhearann agus bha am màl a bhathas ag iarraidh orra tòrr a bharrachd air na b' fhiach na feannagan beaga a bhathas ag àiteach.

Aig an àm seo cuideachd bha an aon suidheachadh cunnartach agus eu-dòchasail a' gabhail aite air feadh na Gàidhealtachd. Bha barrachd 's barrachd a' seasamh an aghaidh eucoir agus aintighearnas nan uachdaran. Bha bàillidh ainmeil an Leòdhas, Dòmhnall Rothach, esan dhen fheadhainn a bu miosa a thaobh làimhseachadh làidir nan croitearan.

Sgrìobh Iain MacArtair, nach maireann, anns an leabhar *Na Gaisgich* 'Dè an t-iongnadh a-rèiste ged a leanadh mallachd an t-sluaigh an Rothach (an seann bhàillidh) chun na crìche is nach tugadh iad urram a' bhàis fhèin dha. 'S e theireadh na croitearan, a' dùnadh na h-uaghach aige 'Cuiribh air, cuiribh air; chuireadh e fhèin oirrne'.

Chan e dìth-mhisneachd nan daoine a-mhàin a tha ìomhaigh-shnaighte Will MhicIllEathain a' comharrachadh. Tha strì agus àmhghar gaisgich a bha sgìth dhem beatha chruaidh air a shnìomh innte cuideachd. Tha an dà cholbh nan seasamh mu choinneamh a chèile air taobh an ear cladh na h-Aoidh, aig 'oisean a Ghàrraidh Ghil', àite cumhang eadar dà ghàrradh àrd aig ceann a' Bhràighe. Tha iad air an dealbachadh le clachadaireachd dùthchasach eireachdail. Chruthaich Will MacIllEathain na cuilbh mar gum biodh iad a' crùbadh a-steach air a chèile, 's iad fo chorraich mhòir. Tha pìosan de chlachan biorach an siud 's an seo, mar dà cholbh de bheugaileidean a' cuimseachadh an aghaidh a chèile, dìreach mar a thachair.

Thàinig na duilgheadasan, aig muir agus air tìr, uile gu ceann aig deireadh 1887. Ann an iomadach dòigh 's e slighe iomchaidh a ghabh na croitearan an seo. Bha rèidearan na Pàirce air aithne dhaoine a thogail don ana-cheartas a bha a' leudachadh air feadh Leòdhais. Aig fìor dheireadh na bliadhna chaidh dà choinneamh a chur air dòigh ann an Eaglais Gharraboist. Dh'aontaich iad buidheann de dh'fhir an àite a chur gu taca Aignis gus na gàrraidhean a thoirt às a chèile agus an sprèidh a sgiùrsadh bhon tuathanas.

Ruig blas dhen chòmhradh sin cluasan bàillidh an fhearainn agus an Siorram Friseal an Steòrnabhagh. Chuir iadsan dà Chonastabal sìos, air faire, chun na taca, nan cois bha fear-naidheachd bhon phàipear-naidheachd, *An Scotsman*. Mu mheadhan-oidhche, Oidhche na Bliadhna Ùire, nochd na fir agus chaidh gàrraidhean na taca a leagail gu talamh. Leum na poilis orra agus ghlac iad aon dhiubh, ruith an còrr air falbh dhan dorchadas.

Bha a' chuis na bu mhiosa buileach a-nis agus cha robh seo ach blas de na bha ri thighinn leis an Aimhreit mhòr air an t-seachdamh latha den Fhaoilleach 1888. Chunnacas an dà thaobh a' tighinn còmhla, a h-uile càil a' tighinn gu ceann agus an tachartas air a chomharrachadh gu h-èifeachdach le ìomhaigh-shnaighte Will MhicIllEathain. Chruinnich mu chòig cheud duine, fir is mnathan, aig beul na maidne, air leathad os cionn na taca gus an sprèidh sgiùrsadh.

Ach bha na h-ùghdarrasan an Steòrnabhagh air a bhith ag ullachdadh cuideachd, bha iad deiseil airson stad a chur air aimhreit sam bith a dh'èireadh. Bha buidheann de na Maraich-ean Rìoghail stèidhichte ann an Steòrnabhagh agus chaidh fios a chur orrasan agus air suas ri fichead Conastabal dèanamh air Mealbost an oidhche ron sin agus iad fhèin a dheisealachadh. Bha na Maraichean Rìoghail air an neartachadh anns a' mhadainn le fir às a' Chabhlaich Rìoghail a bha air falach ann an toglaichean an tuathanais. Tha teagamh ann an robh iad a' tuigsinn cò mheud duine a bhiodh a' feitheamh riutha agus cho laidir 's a bha an iomairt.

Chaidh Achd na h-Aimhreite a leughadh leis an t-Siorram Friseal, ann am Beurla agus ann an Gàidhlig barrachd air aon uair (a rèir *An Scotsman*) ach chum an sluagh a' dol ag èigheachd 'Tha ar teaglaichean leis an acras agus feumaidh sinn am fearann'. An taobh a-staigh uair a thìde bha mìle duine air an taca. Sgrìobh fear-naidheachd *An Scotsman* 'Cha do dh'eist iad aon uair ri na Maraichean Rìoghail . . . Cha do stad iad gus an robh a h-uile beathach air an sgiùrsadh bhon taca'.

Chaidh cuid a chur an grèim, agus 's ann an uair sin a thòisich an t-sabaid gu ceart. Sheas na Maraichean Rìoghail sìos le eagal gum biodh fuil air a dòrtadh. Chuir iad fios a Steòrnabhagh airson taic bho na h-Albannaich Rìoghail. Mu dheireadh dh'fhalbh iad leis an fheadhainn a bh' aca an grèim, an sluagh a' sadail pìosan cheap, clachan agus maidean orra.'

'S e adhbhar feirge am measg chuid a bha san ìochdalachd a chaidh a shealltainn do rèidearan na Pàirce ann an Àrd-chùirt Dhùn Èideann. Air sgàth 's seo chaidh am Morair Graighill, fear a bha gu math cruaidh le bheachdan, a chur os cionn chùisean. Bhuail esan binn eadar sia agus còig mìosan deug air na sia deug phrìosanaich a bha mu choinneamh. Dh'aithris *An Scotsman* 'dh'adhbhraich naidheachd na binn mòran feirge agus ghuidhe am measg nan daoine' nuair a nochd e air uinneagan nam bùitean ann an Steòrnabhagh. Mhol am buidheann 'Strì an Fhearainn' iad cumail orra le an iomairt. B' e Aimhreit Aignis ceum cudromach eile air an t-slighe, leantainneach, dhuilich a dh'ionnsaigh ceartas agus ath-leasachadh an fhearainn.

Mar a cho-dhùin Iain MacArtair anns an leabhar *Na Gaisgich* 'Is math dh'fhaoidte nach robh mòran èifeachd aig an àm anns na rinn iad, ach thug iad aire a' mhòr-shluaigh às ùr gu suidheachadh bochd nan eilean, is chun chrannchur, is rinn iad oidhirp air an saorsa is an còraichean dligheach a ghlacadh. Bu bhuaidh sin fhèin. Rinn iadsan am measradh, ach b' e na h-àil a lean iad a bhlais air an ìm'

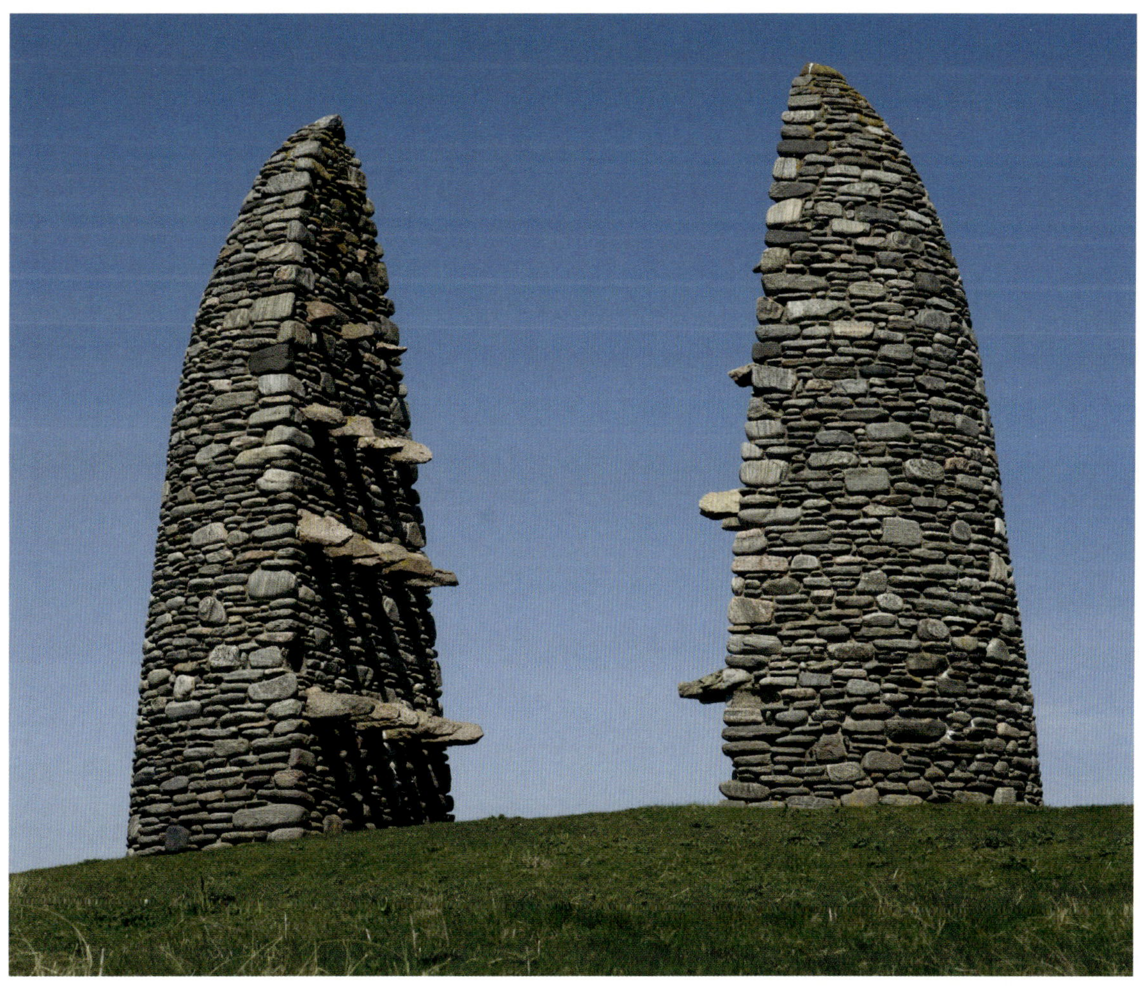

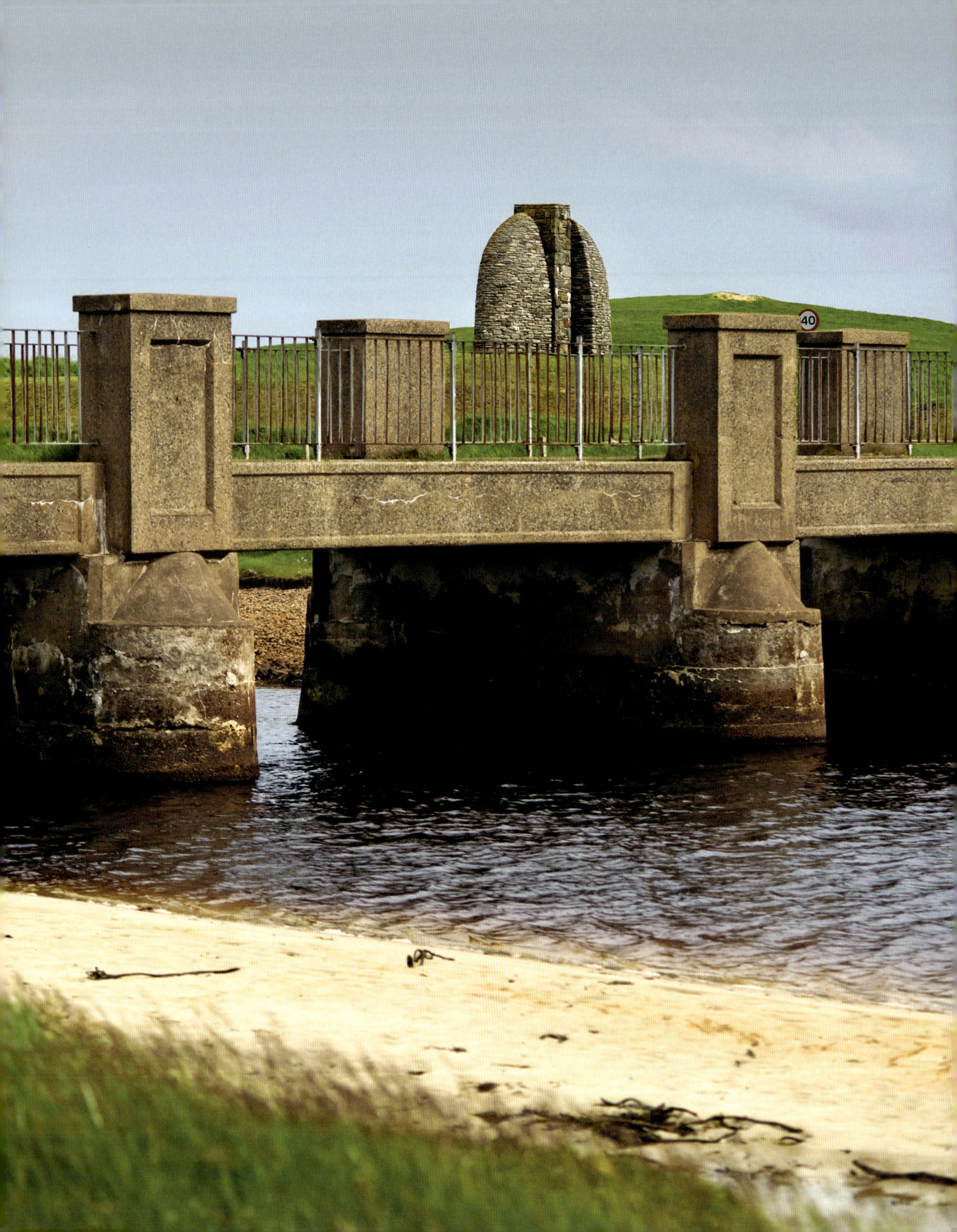

Col agus Griais 1919

Tha smuaintean 's faireachdainn a' ruith mar shnàithleanan tro cholbhan na seann creige agus tron talamh timcheall air obair-shnaighte Will MhicIllEathain aig drochaid Ghriais. An talamh mar shamhla air na trainnsean às an tàinig na saighdearan bho chionn ùine ghoirid. An colbh sa mheadhan mar shamhla air a' Mhorair Leverhulme, a cheannaich an t-eilean ann an 1918, fear a bha os cionn gnìomhachas mòr cumhachdail Lever Brothers; an colbh na sheasamh dìreach 's daingeann. Air an taobh a-muigh, dà cholbh mar shamhla air an t-sluagh, iad a' gabhail fasgadh bhon ghaoith 's ag èisteachd, air an sàrachadadh ach a cheart cho daingeann. Am beàrn eadar an colbh sa mheadhan 's an dà cholbh air an taobh a-muigh a' sònrachadh a' bheàirn eadar feallsanachd Leverhulme agus dòigh smaoineachaidh nan croitearan.

Chaidh tagradh gu Cùirt an Fhearainn bho Bhòrd an Fhearainn san Iuchar 1914. Iarrtas gus tac Ghriais a bhriseadh an àirde. Bhathas a' sùileachadh dà fhichead lot às ùr a chruthachadh. Chaidh dàil air a' chùis air sgàth 's nach robh oighreachd MhicMhathain agus Bòrd an Fhearainn rèidh. Leis gun robh an cogadh a' dol fhathast cha robh am Bòrd airson airgead a chosg air cùis lagha. Dh'aontaich iad mu dheireadh, 'casg a chur air na sgeamaichean rèiteachaidh fearainn; airson greis co-dhiù'.

Bha am Bòrd a' beachdachadh a-rithist air na sgeamaichean mus tàinig crìoch air a' chogadh. Anns an t-Sultain 1917 bhuail iad òrdugh èigneachail air tacan Leòdhais. Bha gnothaichean eile air togail ceann a bheireadh buaidh air cùisean, bha teaghlach MhicMhathain a' sùileachadh an t-eilean a reic ri William Hesketh Lever, a stèidhich a' chompanaidh, Lever Brothers. Sa Chèitean 1918, nuair a ghabh e sealbh air an eilean thuirt Leverhulme, 'Chan e gnìomhachas a tha san amharc dhomh le Leòdhas ach gun dèan mi dachaigh chofhurtail ann an eilean àlainn am measg dhaoine uasal'

A dh'aindeoin 's na thuirt e' b' e fear gnothachais a bh' ann a bha air airgead a chosnadh dha fhèin agus cha robh malairt fada bho inntinn. As t-Fhoghar 1918, chaidh planaichean a dhealbhadh airson baile Steòrnabhaigh, bhathas a' dol a chruthachadh a' bhaile as bòidhche an taobh an iar Alba. Anns an amharc bha gnìomhachasan ùra, loidhne-rèile agus taighean ùra dhan luchd-obrach. Bha na planaichean seo gu math feumail aig an àm, leis mar a bha an eaconamaidh a' crìonadh air los a' chogaidh.

Bha am fearann agus rèiteachadh fearainn air feadh an eilein na phrìomh chuspair deasbaid aig na taghaidhean ann an 1918, bha an triùir thagraichean mothachail air an fheum a bh' aig an eaconamaidh air gnìomhachas coltach ri planaichean Lever ach bha iad gu mòr den bheachd gun obraicheadh an dà chuid, croitearachd agus gnìomhachas, còmhla. Goirid ro na taghaidhean, agus mar thomhas air cho èiginneach 's bha a' chùis, sgrìobh coitearan às aonais fearann à Col agus Griais gu Bòrd an Fhearainn ag iarraidh orra, 'roinneamh a-mach

Griais cho aithghearr is a ghabhas, ro àm an Earraich gus am faigh sinn ar dachaighean a thogail fhad 's tha an aimsir math', a' fàilligeadh sin, thuirt iad, 'gabhaidh sinn an làgh nar làmhan fhèin'.

Tràth latha na Bliadhna Ùire 1919, dhùisg muinntir Leòdhais gu buille ghoirt, an tubaist uabhasach, call na h-Iolaire, 's thàinig àmhghar 's cràdh don eilean nach gabh innse. 'S ann sna seachdainean an dèidh a' chall uabhasach a thòisicheadh le sgeamaichean obrach Leverhulme. Thug seo beagan dòchais do na h-eileanaich nuair a bha droch fheum air leis na bha iad a' fulang.

Cha robh e fada ge-tà gun do thuig daoine gun robh Leverhulme gu mòr an aghaidh croitearachd mar shiostam àitich, ann an litir chun a' Bhùird thuirt e gur e croitearachd, '… an dòigh as miosa fearann a roinn agus duilgheadasan a bharrachd 's tuilleadh bochdainn ri thighinn le bhith a' leudachadh siostam a tha do-dhèante mar thà'. Dh'iarr e air Bòrd an Fhearainn bacadh a chur air na sgeamaichean airson 'grunn bhliadhnaichean'.

Airson a' chiad uair ann an eachdraidh bha an lagh air taobh nan croitearan. Bha Raibeart Rothach, Rùnaire na Stàite airson Alba a' toirt taic dhaibh agus le Achd Rèiteachaidh an Fhearainn (Alba) 1919 thàinig barrachd maoineachaidh gus talamh a cheannach. Thuig an Riaghaltas cuideachd gun robh uallach orra airson 'talamh àiteach do na gaisgich'. Sgrìobh Aonghas Greumach, riochdaire nan croitearan, gu an Rothach. 'Chan eil sinn ag iarraidh càil ach na chaidh a ghealltainn dhuinn nuair a bha sinn a' treabhadh a' chuain agus suas gu ar glùineann sna trainnsean aig Flander.'

Tha obair-shnaighte Will MhicIllEathain aig drochaid Ghriais a' sònrachadh a' chiad chòmhstri eadar Leverhulme 's na rèidearan air an dàrna latha deug den Mhàrt 1919. Sheas Leverhulme air baraill an teis-meadhan nam mìle duine a bha san luchd-èisteachd. Seo na bh' aige ri ràdh, 'Tha uidhir de spèis agamsa do Leòdhas agus dhuibhse gu bheil mi an dùil airgead mòr a chosg air leasachadh iasgaich agus stòrasan. Gheall e còig millean not a chosg air bàtaichean iasgaich, factaraidh èisg agus air a' bhaile fhèin'.

Bha Leverhulme a' dèiligeadh ge-tà, ri daoine foghlaimte. Chuir Ailean Màrtainn, duine gaisgeil, stad air agus bhruidhinn e ris an t-sluagh sa Ghàidhlig, chaidh eadar-theangachadh a dhèanamh le fear de luchd-obrach Leverhulme. 'Seo, seo fhearaibh! Cha dèan seo an gnothaich! Bheir am bodach mil-bheulach tha 'n sin a chreidsinn ort gu bheil dubh geal 's geal dubh. Ciod e dhuinn am bruadar aige, a thig no nach tig? 'S e am fearann tha sinn ag iarraidh. Agus 's e tha mise a' faighneachd an toir thu dhuinn am fearann?'

Cha robh Leverhulme ach cinnteach na bheachd fhein, fhreagair e, 'Cha toir mi dhuibh am fearann, chan e gu bheil mi an aghaidh nam beachdan agaibh … Tha mi a' creids nan èisteadh sibh rium, nan toireadh sibh cothrom dhomh le na sgeamaichean bhiodh sibh nas fheàrr dheth agus bhiodh toileachas ann an Leòdhas'.

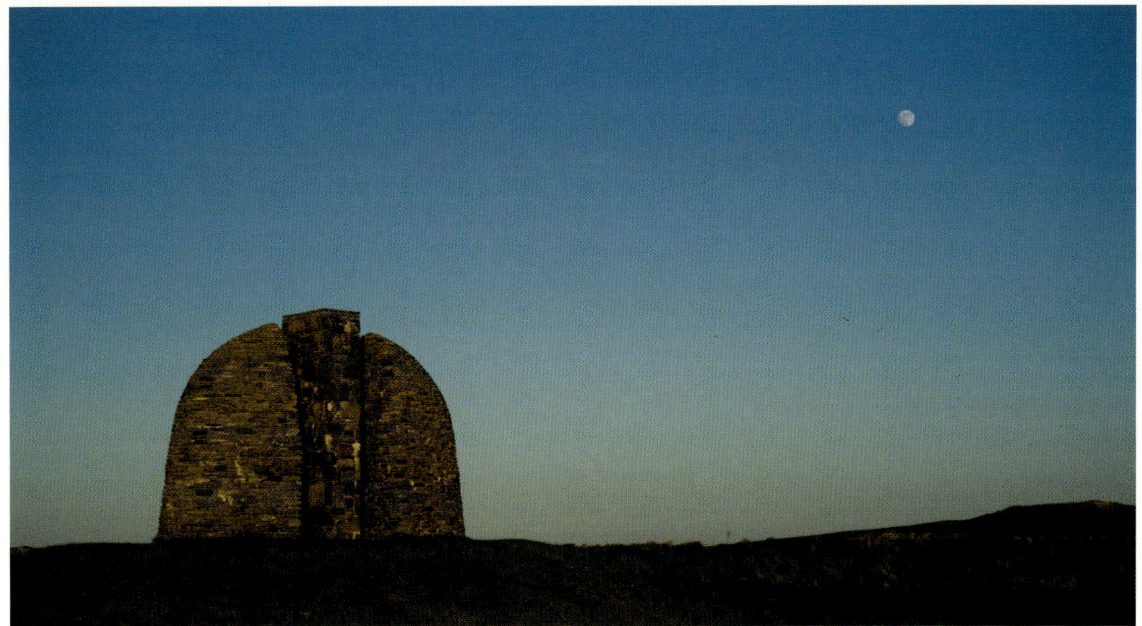

Chaidh stad a chur air a-rithist, ann am Beurla an uair seo, 'Chan eil sinn an aghaidh nan sgeamaichean obrach agad, chan eil sinn ach an aghaidh nach toir thu dhuinn am fearann agus seasaidh sinn nad aghaidh gu daingeann air an sin. Tha thu air an t-eilean a cheannach ach chan eil prìs oirrne agus cha bhi sinn nar tràillean aig duine sam bith. Tha sinn airson a bhith beò anns an dòigh againn fhìn, às aonais nan nithean a thèid a cheannach ach saor bho ghlag na factaraidh, bidh ur beatha sona'.

Bha dùil a-nis ri còmhstri leantainneach. Chaidh na tacan a rèideadh trì tursan, sheas Lever-hulme nan aghaidh agus chuir e a h-uile bacadh a b' urrainn orra gus sgaradh a dhèanamh. Cha leigeadh e dha na rèidearan obair a dhèanamh agus chuir e stad air an obair gus an teich-eadh iad bhon fhearann. Nuair a theich iad cha do chuir e na sgeamaichean air dòigh a-rithist. Anns an Fhaoilleach 1921 bha na ruaigearan air na tacan fhàgail agus bha an Riaghaltas air gabhail ri iarrtas Leverhulme airson deich bliadhna de bhacadh a chur air rèiteachadh fearainn agus nan gabhadh iad ris chuireadh esan na sgeamaichean obrach air bhonn uair eile.

Aig an àm seo nochd duilgheadasan a thaobh airgead air Lever Brothers air sgàth 's nan gnothaichean a bh' aca air taobh an Ear Afraga agus aig an aon àm bha an eaconamaidh dhùthchail a' crìonadh gu mòr. Thug seo air Leverhulme tarraing à Leòdhas agus cha deach an còrr obrach a dhèanamh a thaobh nan sgeamaichean aige. Tràth ann an 1922 ghabh Bòrd an Fhearainn a-null tac Ghriais agus tac Chuil, tac Tholasta bho Thuath agus Orasaigh cuideachd. Chruthaich iad 180 lotaichean ùra agus thug iad barrachd talmhainn dha 81 aig an robh lot mar-thà.

Bha sgeamaichean Leverhulme a-nis mar obair na mac-meanma a dh'fhalbh ann am prioba na sùla.

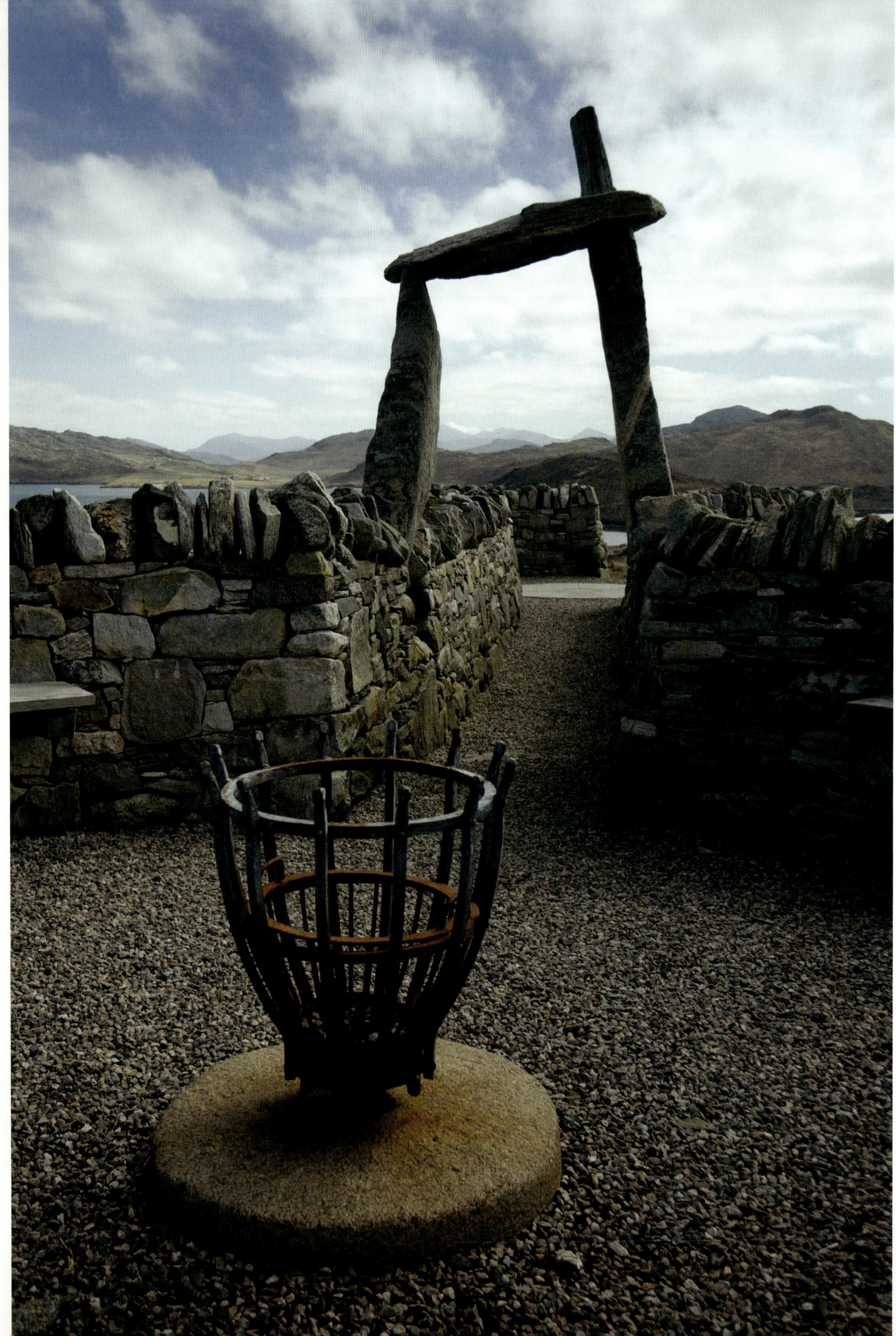

Rèid na Riobhadh 1919

Shuas air mullach Eicleat Bheag, cnoc beag creagadh an teis-meadhan baile na Riobhadh,
tha *An Sùileachan*, an ceathramh carragh-cuimhne a bha air a choimiseanadh gus urram
a thoirt dhan fheadhainn a sheas an aghaidh làn-chumhachd nan uachdaran agus a fhuair
sealbh air an fhearann dha teaghlaichean à Bhaltos agus an Cnìp a bha às aonais talamh.

Tha *An Sùileachan*, a chaidh a dhealbhadh le Will MacIllEathain agus a bhean Marian Leven,
mar shamhla air slighe tro thìm. Thathas gar tarraing air ais gu fuadaichean 1850 agus a' toirt
aithne do na gaisgich a fhuair sealbh air an fhearann. Air taobh dheas a' charragh-chuimhne
tha fosglan air a chruthachadh le leacan eireachdail de sheann chreag Leòdhais, gar gluasad
nar n-inntinn bho àm a dh'fhalbh gun latha an-diugh agus a' toirt oirrne sùil a thoirt air an
àrainneachd timcheall oirnn, sinn a' beachdachadh air na tha fa-near don àite shàmhach
seo san àm ri teachd, àite a tha a-nis ann an làmhan na coimhearsnachd fhèin.

Thug suas ri deich air fhichead teaghlach a bhuineadh do sheann bhaile na Riobhadh,
trì bliadhna a' seasamh gu sìtheil an aghaidh oidhirpean oighreachd An Ridire Seumas Mhic-
Mhathain, an cur às an fhearann. Ach, ann an 1850, chaidh an ruagadh a-mach à tìr an sinnsir.
Chaidh cuid a sgapadh air feadh Leòdhais agus cuid eile a chur thar a' chuain a dh'Ameireaga.
Nuair a thug Niall MacIlleathain à Brèascleit, fianais mu choinneamh Choimisean Napier,
thuirt e 'An fheadhainn againn a thàinig ann an seo (gu mòinteach Bhrèascleit), thug sinn leinn
mullach ar taighean, dh'fhàg an còrr a h-uile nì agus chaidh e gun fheum'.[1] An ath bhliadhna,
chaidh ceithir-deug teaghlach a ruagadh à Bhaltos agus bhon Chnìp.

Ro dheireadh na 19mh linne, bha an sluagh a bh' air fhàgail anns a' cheàrnaidh a bha air
aithneachadh mar sgìre 'na Ceithir Peighinn Deug' air an dinneadh ann an dà bhaile gun
chead cas a chur air an talamh mun cuairt orra a bha a-nis na phàirt de na tacan mòra. Nam
measg, bha a h-aon deug air fhichead teaghlach de choitearan a bha às aonais fearainn.

Thar na h-ùine seo chaidh còrr air 40,000 acraichean de dh'fhearann Ùig a thoirt a-mach
à croitearachd agus a thoirt dha seachdnar thuathanach agus do oighreachdan sealgaireachd
mòra. 'S e toiseach-tòiseachaidh a bh' ann an aimhreit Bheàrnaraigh ann an 1874, aimhreit
a dh'èirich bho 56 teaghlaichean rabhadh fhaighinn teicheadh bhon fhearann. Bha an aimhreit
na comharra air seasamh nas làidire an aghaidh ana-ceartas.

Thòisich naidheachd na strì an taobh a deas Ùig a' nochadh ro dheireadh an naoidheamh linn
deug. Ann an 1884 thàinig HMS *Assistance*, le mu cheud saighdear-mara air bòrd, a-steach
do Loch an Ròg gus ochd fir à Bhaltos a chur an grèim agus iad fo chasaid stoc a chur air na
h-eileanan beaga gun chead, fiachan màl agus brath a thoirt air Oifigearan an t-Siorraim. Chaidh
an toirt air beulaibh Cùirt an t-Seisein an Dún Èideann agus fhuair iad am prìosan car ùine.

An ath bhliadhna, chaidh càin air deichnear fhir agus seachdnar mhnathan airson gnìomhan den aon seòrsa, na mnathan fo chasaid gràisgidh, aramach agus briseadh na sìth. Phàigh meur Lunnainn de Chomann Gàidhealach ath-leasachaidh Lagh an Fhearainn a' chàin, 5/- an tè.[2]

Ann an 1891 agus a-rithist ann an 1896, mhol Coimisean Frìth nam Fiadh rèiteachadh fearainn a chur an cèill ann an Riobhadh. Cha do ghabh an oighreachd ri seo. Ann an 1909 dh'aontaich an oighreachd tac na Riobhadh fhàgail airson barantas sìor-mhàil bhon Riaghaltas. Cha do dh'aontaich Bord an Fhearainn ri seo air sgàth 's an ìre iseal de mhàl a ghabhadh a thogail, ceithir fichead not sa bhliadhna. Bha seo a' ciallachadh nach b' urrainn don Riaghaltas am màl a sparradh orra.[3]

Bha an t-eagal air Bòrd an Fhearainn, nan reiceadh iad am fearann ('s còir aig na croitearan a cheannach a rèir Achd nan Gabhaltas beaga agus nan Cuibhreann Talmhainn (Alba) 1911), gun toireadh seo cothrom dha càch agus gum biodh tuilleadh 's a chòir de dh'iarrtasan roimhpe.

Bha coitearan às aonais fearainn ann am Bhaltos agus sa Chnìp dhen bheachd gun robh an Riaghaltas a-nis a' cur chnapan-starra nan aghaidh, agus mar sin dh'aontaich iad an tuathanas a rèideadh. Leig iad fios chun a' Bhùird ag ràdh 'Talamh ar sinnsearach tha seo agus bidh sinn dha àiteach as t-Earrach'.

Sa Gheamhradh 1913 agus dà uair sa bhliadhna ùir, ruaig còig deug de na coitearan an tuathanas. Sgiùrs iad stoc an tuathanaich air falbh bhon taca. Thuirt Alasdair MacAoidh, fear de na ruaigearan, ris a' phoileas 'Bidh prìosanaich gu leòr agaibh a-nis. Chaidh an Riobhadh a ghealltainn dhuinn, tha sinn air a bhith a' feitheamh ro fhada agus tha sinn a-nis a' dol ga ghabhail, ge bith dè thachras dhuinn'.

Anns a' Ghearran 1914, thòisich na croitearan a' tionndadh na talmhainn 's iad a' dol a threabhadh as t-Earrach. Chaidh òrdugh-bacaidh a bhualadh orra le oighreachd MhicMhathain. Cha do ghèill na ruaigearan ris agus chaidh ochd deug dhiubh a chur a Dhùn Èideann far an d' fhuair iad binn sia seachdainean sa phrìosan aig Cùirt an t-Seisein. Dh'adhbhraich seo mòran feirg air feadh Alba agus an ceann ceala-deug, thug iomairt làidir a-mach às a' phrìosan iad.

Thàinig bacadh air cùisean aig an àm chudromach seo air sgàth 's a' Chogaidh Mhòir. Dh'fhalbh a' chuid as motha de na fir agus an fheadhainn a thug am beatha agus bha iad na bu chinntiche buileach gum faigheadh iad 'fearann freagarrach do ghaisgich'. Bha an cogadh uabhasach agus bha an fheum a bha an rìoghachd a' cur air na fir calg-dhìreach an aghaidh am briseadh-dùil a thaobh na chaidh a ghealltainn dhaibh. Suidheachadh nach gabhadh a thuigsinn no gabhail ris.

Sa Ghearran 1920, cha b' urrainn dha na croitearan 's na coitearan feitheamh nas fhaide agus chaidh litir bho a h-aon deug de na ciad ruaigearan gu Rùnaire na Stàite airson Alba ''S e saighdearan agus seòladairean air ar leigeil dheth agus gun chosnadh bhon t-Sultain

a chaidh a th' annainn . . . is fheudar dhuinn tòiseachadh air obair an Earraich air Taca
na Riobhadh. Ma chuireas sibh Comiseanairean nan Tuathanasan Beaga thugainn gus
an taca a roinn a-mach na lotaichean agus sealbh a thoirt dhuinn orra mar a tha sinn ag
earbsa a nì sibh, cuiridh sinn dheth an obair chun a' chiad là den Mhàrt. Mura bi iad an
seo an uair sin, feumaidh sinn tòiseachadh air an obair gus tighinn beò'.

Nuair a thill iad bhon chogadh bha am Morair Leverhulme air an oighreachd a cheannach
agus bha e a' sabaid an aghaidh Oifis na h-Alba, bha e cuideachd a' feuchainn ri tacan
Ùig a leigeil seachad mar dhìoladh gus grèim a chumail air na tacan nas fhaisg air baile
Steòrnabhaigh. Ged a thug e ùine, leig Leverhulme seachad tuathanas Ùig mu dheireadh
thall, agus, ann an 1921, fhuair muinntir Bhaltois an cuid fearainn air ais.

'S ann mar thoradh air an t-strì an aghaidh ana-ceartas a tha baile an seo an-diugh agus
agus seasmhachd ann. Tha *An Sùileachan* na chuimhneachan iongantach air gach strì
a ghabh àite.[4]

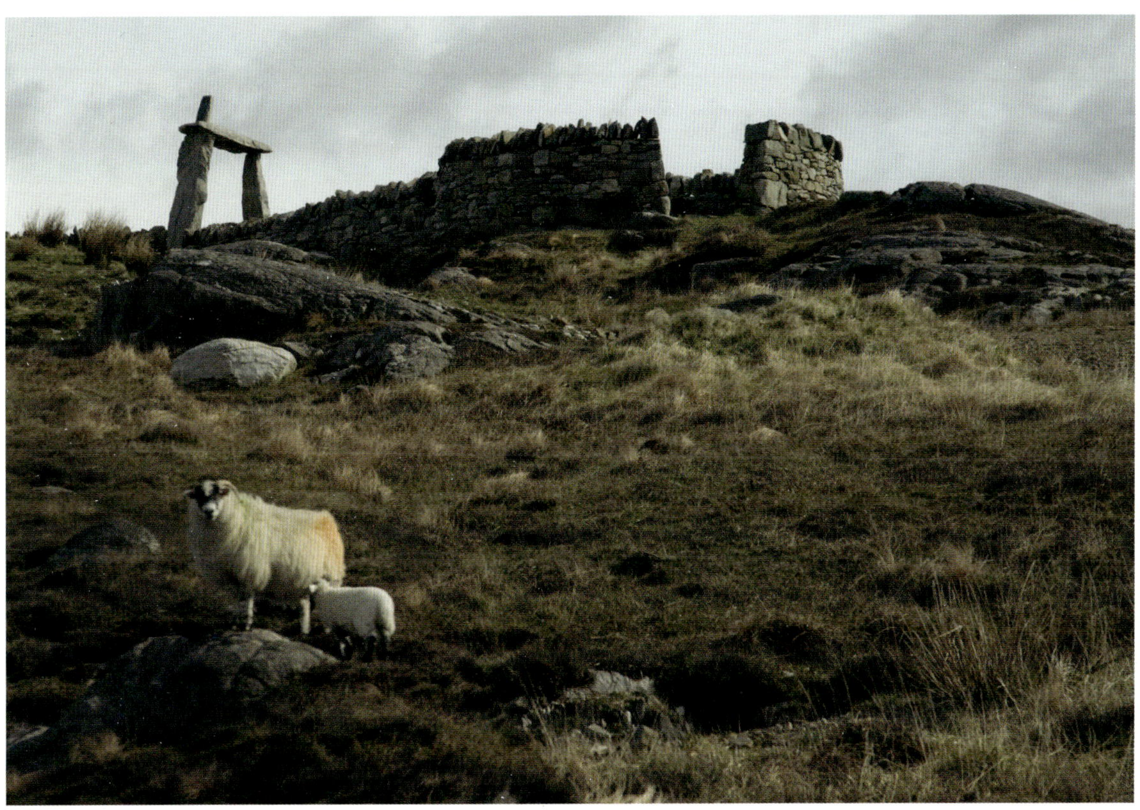

An Sùileachan (Faic notaichean nan Dealbhan, d. 58)

---

1. MacCoinnich, J,M, *Diary 1851*, Acair, Steòrnabhagh, 1994

2. *Aithisg Coimisean Napier*, 1884, le coimisean sgrùdaidh air staid chroitearan is choitearan ann an Gàidhealtachd
   agus Eileanan na h-Alba

3. *Coimisean Sgrùdaidh Rìoghail nam Frìth*, 1892

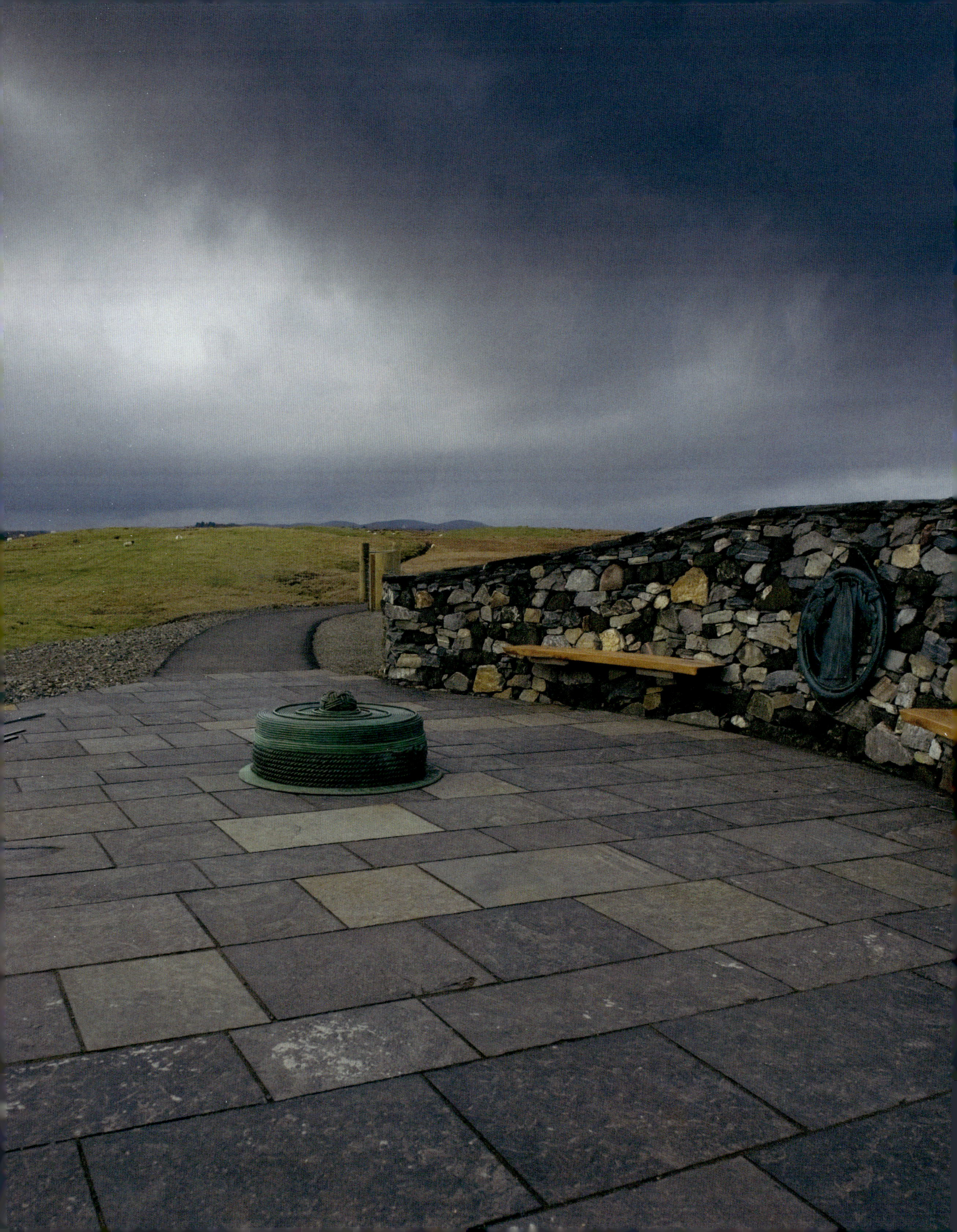

Call n h-*Iolaire* 1918

Thairis air ceithir bliadhna a' Chiad Chogaidh chaidh còrr 's sia mìle fireannach òg à Leòdhas is na Hearadh a thogail dhan nèibhidh 's dhan arm. Cha d' fhuair an còigeamh cuid dhiubh sin às lem beatha. Mhùch ceithir bliadhna de dh'uabhas bith-bhrìgh nan eilean, agus cha robh an call fhathast seachad. Dìreach aig glasadh na sìthe, agus am fianais an dachaigh chaidh còrr 's dà cheud eile, 174 à Leòdhas agus seachdnar às na Hearadh, a bhàthadh nuair a chaidh an *Iolaire* às an rathad air Biastan Huilm. Bhuail an t-uabhas cha mhòr a h-uile baile agus an doilgheas a lean gach sgìre 's gach eileanach, bha an call cho tiamhaidh 's cho do-thuigsinneach.

Mar a chaidh a sgrìobhadh ann an cunntas fhìnealta *Gasaet Steòrnabhaigh* bha an t-eilean còmhdaichte ann an neul duabhal nach gabhadh togail 'Tha eileanaich air a bhith caoineadh mar nach do chaoin iad a-riamh ron seo agus cha ghabh an cofhurtachadh. Tha bàs air a thighinn fa an comhair ann an cùis-mhulaid uabhasach, mì-thròcaireach, brùilleadh is le drùidhteachd searbh'. Is e call na h-*Iolaire* an tubaist-mhara a bu mhiosa ann am muir a' chladaich na rìoghachd thar an fhicheadamh linn. An àite coimhead air adhart ri na seòid a fhuair às a' chogadh lem beatha tilleadh dhachaigh, dh'fhàg an call tuilleadh 's a chòir bhanntraichean òga, clann a' fàs suas gun athair, pàrantan air am briseadh agus leannanan òga às aonais gràdhaiche an cridhe. Lean buaidh na h-*Iolaire* tro ghinealaichean de theaghlaich nam fìr a chaidh às an rathad, ach air taobh a-muigh nan eilean cha robh fios no tuigse aig a' mhòr-shluagh mun chiùrradh a dh'fhàg an call air teaghlaichean agus air a' choimhearsnachd air fad.

Am measg sreath de phròiseactan cuimhneachaidh a' comharrachadh a' cheudamh bliadhna on thachair an call, chaidh carraighean-cuimhne ùr a choimiseanadh on ealanaiche shònraichte, Will MacIlleEathain ARA, Marian Lìobhann ARA, agus Artair MacBhatair ARA. Tha an obair eireachdail aca, air a dhealbhachadh ann an umha agus clach ionadail, a-nis a' coimhead a-mach thar a' phìos ghoirid den chuan gu làrach an uabhais, Biastan Huilm.

Dhealbhaich iad ròpa tarraing agus loidhne taod ann an umha, iad sin nan laighe mar chuartagan air leacan eibhir far a bheil na fìr a chaidh air chall ainmichte. Tha na leacan san ròpa air an cuairteachadh le leth-chearcall de ghàrradh cloiche mar àite sìtheil, smuaineachail is a' crochadh air a' ghàrradh sin tha figheachan umha air an dealbhadh mar chrois-shàbhalaidh. Tha duilleagan labhras, seann mhoitifean de bheatha 's bàs agus stuthan eile am broinn an fhigheachain mar gum biodh e a' cròthadh cuimhneachan is spiorad nam feadhainn a chaidh a bhàthadh agus an dubhas mhaireannach a lean.

Tha na ròpan mar shamhail den cheangal eadar an cuan is muinntir nan eilean, an earbsa, an eagal, an eòlas, an cunnart, còmhradh air ais agus air adhart a bhios a' dol gu sìorraidh. Ach os cionn a h-uile rud tha e mar shamhail air uabhas na h-oidhche. Bràithrean, caraidean is nàbaidhean air an tilgeil bhon t-soitheach gu doimhneachd na fairge. Air an sadadh ri na creagan agus a' chuid mhòr a' dol fodha. Cuid dhiubh a' faighinn air a thighinn gu uachdar, ach bha an sruth nan aghaidh agus gan slaodadh sìos air ais, is dòcha iomadach uair, gus an do chaill iad an lùths a dh'fheumadh iad airson sabaid an aghaidh onfhadh na fairge. Am measg an uabhais eagalaich a bha seo thachair gnìomh dòchais tha dearbhadh ath-leumachd spiorad a' chinne-daonna; leum aonan den bha air bòrd dhan fhairge is greim daingeann aige air an ròp a bha ceangailte mu làimh agus mu òrdag mhòr. Leis an ròp sin shàbhail e beatha dà fhichead de cho-chreutairean.

Nuair a chaidh prògam air sgeul na h-*Iolaire* a dhèanamh le Fred MacAmhlaigh don BhBC ann an 1961 thuirt Iain Fionnlagh MacLeòid, am fear a leum leis an ròpa, gun robh e doirbh dha bruidhinn gu poblach mu na thachair le eagal gun ùr-bheòthaicheadh sin cuimhneachan goirt mu rudan bha air a dhol seachad. Dh'aindeoin sin bha an cunntas a thug e dhan a phrò-gram mu na rinn e an oidhche ud, smuaineachail agus màlda, mar gnàth an duine fhèin.

Thuirt e gun robh an oidhche cho fiadhaich agus cho dorch 's cha mhòr gum faiceadh tu càil. Nuair a chaidh an soitheach ri na creagan chaidh lasair-bhoillsgean a leigeil às, las sin suas na creagan agus rinn e a-mach far an robh iad. Nuair a chunnaic e am peucan thuig e gun robh an soitheach air a dhol ri Biastan Huilm, mar a dh'innse e do Fred:
    Thurchair dhomhsa a bhith nam inntinn an loidhne thoirt leam na mo làimh 's leum
    mi mach air an deireadh airson feuchainn ri faighinn air tìr. Cha robh duil a'm gun robh
    a' chreag cho doirbh 's a bha i. Ach nuair a ràinig mi 'n toiseach bha creag os mo chionn
    's thug sùghadh na mara mach air ais mi. Agus nam bithinn air bualadh ri aghaidh
    na creige cha robh càil air mo shon. 'S chaidh mi an uairsin na b' fhaide air falbh ann
    an sùghadh na mara na bha mi bho thoiseach, agus an uair a chaidh trì sualachan mòra
    seachad – an trìtheamh tè, dh'fhalbh mi roimphe 's bha mi na bàrr gus na chrìochnaich
    i leam air uachdar an stalla, an stalla gus an deach mi bho thoiseach; 's chaidh mo
    bhroilleach a bhualadh suas orra ann an sin. Sin mar a fhuair mis' air tìr agus ghlèidh mi
    loidhne fad na tìde. Agus nuair a fhuair mi suas ann an sin agus am muir seachad, shuidh
    mi ann an sin, gus an tàinig aon cheathar air tìr air an loidhne chaol sin, gus na dh'èigh
    mi gun robh i ro ghoirid 's ro chaol is nach dèanadh i a' chùis, iad ròpa garbh a chur oirre.
    Chaidh ròpa garbh a chur oirre an uair sin. Thàinig an còrr air tìr air an ròpa sin.[1]

Is ann à teaghlach shaoir-eathraichean agus maraichean bha Iain Fhionnlaigh agus bha eòlas na mara a' dol sìos tro na ginealaichean, mhìnich a mhac, Iain Mhurchaidh, dòigh smaoineachaidh athar, a' dearbhadh cho cudromach 's bha eòlas na mara dha mus do roghnaich e falbh leis an treas suail. Thuirt Iain Mhurchaidh:
    Is dòcha gun robh e fortanach gun robh eòlas aige air a' chosta. Bhitheadh e a' dol
    suas an taobh sin ann an geòla malairt bh' aig mo sheanair. Nuair a roghnaich e an
    dòigh air adhart thug e deireadh an loidhne do fhear a bha ri thaobh agus thuirt e ris
    greim daingeann a chumail oirre. Cha do chuir e an ropa timcheall a mheadhan idir,
    ach dà thriop timcheall a làimh chlì agus ghlas e ceann an ròp le òrdag. Leig e e fhèin
    an uairsin sìos dhan fhairge.

Aig a' chiad oidhirp faighinn gu tìr dh'fhalbh an sruth leis. An uairsin rinn e rud a bha gu math iongantach gu h-àraid anns an duilgheadas san robh e. Thug e ealla air a shuidheachadh agus le eòlas na mara thuig e gum biodh cliath, trì tuinn làidir a' tighinn

air sàil fàth an t-seachdamh suail. Roghnaich e falbh air an treas tonn agus thug i sin
gu tìr e. An dèidh ceathrar a thighinn air a' chiad loidhne thuig e nach robh i laidir gu
leòr agus chuir iad airson loidhne-tarraing. Chaidh dà fhichead de na fìr a shàbhaladh
agus bha esan aig ceann na loidhne gus an tàinig am fear mu dheireadh gu tìr.[2]

Chaidh na bàtaichean-teasairginn, an aon dòchas a bh' aca tighinn beo às an uabhas,
a lìonadh le fìr agus a leigeil sìos dhan fhairge, ach mar a dh'aithris Dòmhnall Dòmhnallach
à Cro Mòr bha iad gun fheum, bha an oidhche ro gharbh:

Bha sinn eòlach air mèinnean 's air toirpeadan agus armachd cogaidh ach bhuail seo
feagal nar cridheachan. Bha fios againn gun robh sinn air ar glacadh, cha robh dòigh
againn air teicheadh. Bha pìosan de dh'fhiodh nan eathraichean a' falbh leis a' ghaoith,
gan sadadh os ar cionn. Bha feadhainn a' feuchainn ri dà eathar a leigeil sìos taobh
an-asgaidh 's chrom mi sìos chun nam bàbain gus am faighinn air leum dha aon de
na h-eathraichean. Taing do fhreastal nach d' fhuair mi innte, bha i loma-làn de
bhalaich òg agus chaidh an dà eathar sin a lìonadh làn mara – cha do sheas iad ris
a' mhuir. Chìthinn spotan dubha ann an cop na mara. Chaidh a h-uile duine a bha
sna h-eathraichean, cho fad 's a b' aithne dhomhsa, a bhàthadh.[3]

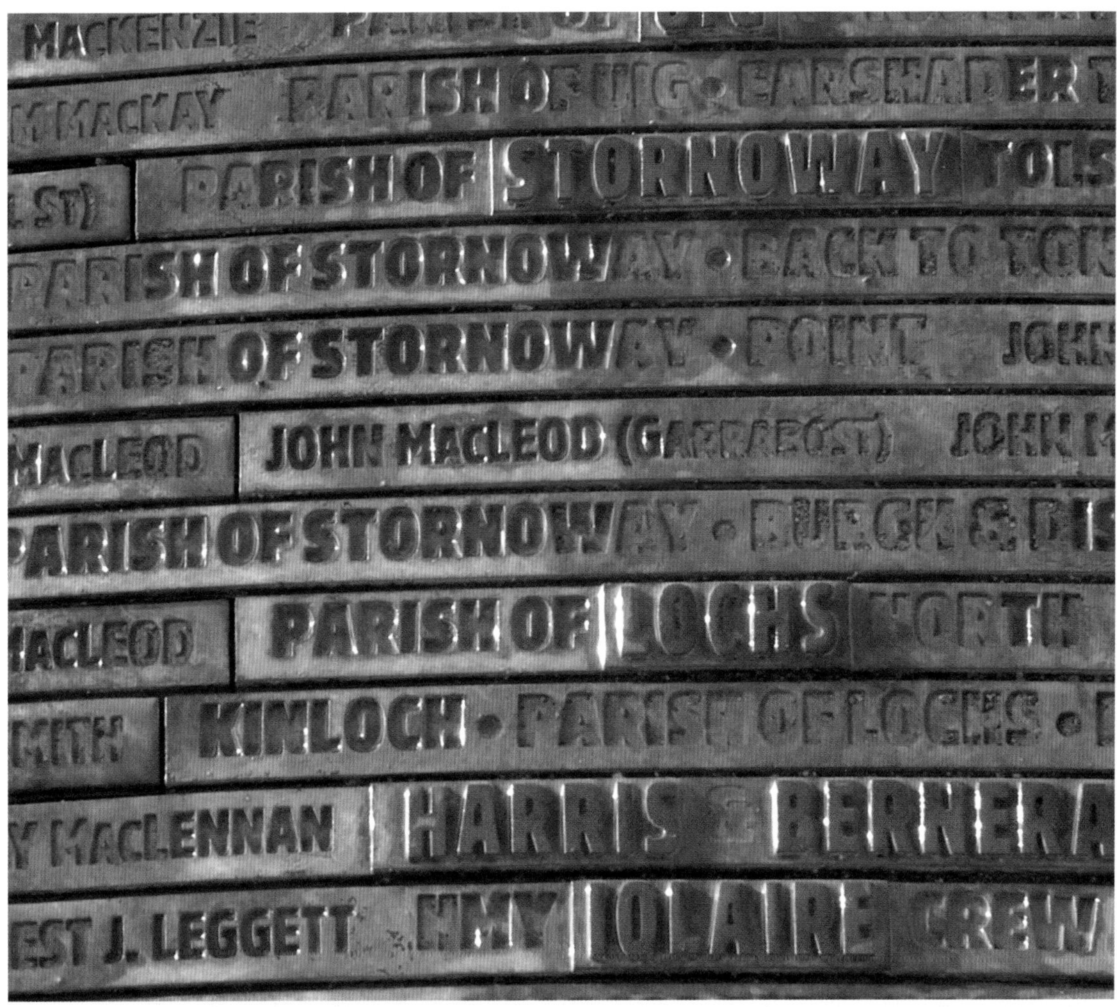

Fiù 's ma fhuair iad air leum dhan fhairge agus greim fhaighinn air an loidhne bhathas gam spìonadh bhon ròp' le cumhachd an t-sruth agus obair an t-soithich. Thòisich i a' drioftadh a-mach agus an uair a thaom i a-mach, tharraing i an ròp' às làmhan nam fir, tòrr aca gam bàthadh. Bha an fhairge na cùis uabhais gan tarraing sìos 's bha na truaghain a' call an lùths agus a' dol fodha. Seo mar a dh'inns Dòmhnall Dòmhnallach à Tolastadh na thachair ris:

> Rud a bu mhiosa dheth 's e mar a bha na tuinn gan spìonadh bhon loidhne, fear an dèidh fear a' falbh le na tuinn. Bha mi a' coimhead sìos cho fada agus ag ràdh rium fhèin nach robh mi a' dol a dh'fhàgail an t-soithich. Ach thòisich mi smaoineachadh nam faighinn air falbh air suail dheidheadh mo thilgeil gu tìr mus deidheadh an t-suail a-mach air ais. Nuair a bha i a' tionndadh bha neart na suaile agus obrachadh nan soithich gan sguabadh bhon ròp'. Cha chreideadh tu neart na mara. Chaill tòrr de na bha a' faicinn na bha tachairt am misneachd ach thurchair mi teansa air beatha no air bàs a ghabhail agus leum mi air an ath shuail a' dol a-steach gu tìr. Fhuair mi greim daingeann air an ròp agus fhuair mi gu tìr. Cha robh m' àm air tighinn.[4]

Anns na lathaichean a lean bha muinntir nan eilean air an tumadh ann am bròn do-labhairt; chaidh làmh thoisgeil a dhèiligeadh orra, an leithid nach fhacas a-riamh roimhe seo. Ann an glasachadh na maidne chunnacas an sgrios. Cuirp dhaoine òga brist 's air an leòn. Luideagan de dheiseachan an Nèibhidh agus an cuideachd, nan èiginn, a' coimhead airson mac, no bràthair, no caraid am measg na feamad, air na creagan is air an tràigh. Bhathas a' toirt nan corp chun a' Bhataraidh, bunait an Nèibhidh ann an Steòrnabhagh. Is e Lt. Frederick Townsend a bha os coinn gnìomhachd ann an sin agus an uair a thog e aithris mun Iolaire àn dèidh làimhe thuirt e:

> A' faicinn càirdean nam fir a chaidh air chall a' lorg an cuid fhèin, càil is tiamhaidh 's a chunnaic mi a-riamh na mo bheatha agus gu h-àraid an uair a dhèidheadh an corp aithneachadh. Anns na mìosan an dèidh làimh chithinn, ann am bruadar, sreath de bhrògan thacaideach an Nèibhidh, le àireamhan (a rèir 's cò às a bhuineadh an duine marbh) air an sgrìobhadh le cailc air sàilean nam bròg.[5]

Anns na bailtean chaidh a h-uile rud a bhathas ag ullachadh airson na seòid tilleadh dhachaigh an dèidh ceithir bliadhna de chogadh a chur air falbh. Dh'fhalbh athraichean, bràithrean is uaireannan màthraichean is peathraichean, le 'n eich 's cairtean a Steòrnabhagh a dh'fhaighinn cuirp an cuid mairbh. Seo an dealbh tiamhaidh a thog Dòmhnall MacPhàil à Bràdhagair nuair a bhruidhinn e ri Fred MacAmhlaigh ann an 1961. Bha e fhèin agus dithis eile air a dhol còmhla ri fear à Siabost a lorg corp a mhic,

> Dh'fhalbh mise a Steòrnabhagh – tha cuimhne agam – 's e deireadh oidhche bh' ann, le cairt 's each, mi fhìn 's gille òg eile, chan eil fìos agam nach robh dithis eile còmhla rium agus athair fear dhe na gilllean a chaidh air chall; agus chaidh sinn sìos dhan Bhataraidh far an robh na cuirp air an cur a-mach ach an aithnicheadh daoine iad, 's tha cuimhne agam gun robh ticead orra – Liùrbost, agus Siabost agus Tolastadh. Agus am fear à Siabost a chaidh a-null còmhla rinn bha mac leis ann, 's tha cuimhne agam, 's cuimhne agam gun robh e cho brèagha 's gun canainn nach robh e marbh idir, am fiamh a bh' air aodann – tha cuimhne agam air an sin cho brèagha fhathast.

Chaidh athair air a ghlùinean ri thaobh agus thòisich e a' toirt litrichean às a phòcaid,
's bha airgead, airgead geal agus airgead pàipeir, am pòcaid a bhriogais; agus bha
e a' coimhead ri litir a bha e air fhaighinn agus na deòir ri tuiteam air corp a mhic,
's bha mi smaoineachadh gur e sealladh cho tiamhaidh 's cho duilich 's a chunnaic
mi riamh; 's cha robh sin ach aonan de mhòran a dh'fhaodadh sinn fhaicinn anns
a' Bhataraidh an latha bh' ann an seo – 's lathaichean às a dhèidh.[6]

Ghiùlainn iad cuirp nam mairbh dhachaigh chun nam bailtean air an tuath. Coiseachd
gu socair, 's cho drùidhteach, sealladh cho duilich 's a chitheadh tu a-riamh. Chuimhnich
Ciorstaidh Nic Gille Mhoire à Lìonal gun robh an sealladh 'cho cianail 's mar gun robh an
t-uabhanta a' dèanamh an coiseachd trom – uabhanta uabhasach. Cogadh an dèidh sgur
's dùil aig a h-uile duine riutha dhachaigh'.

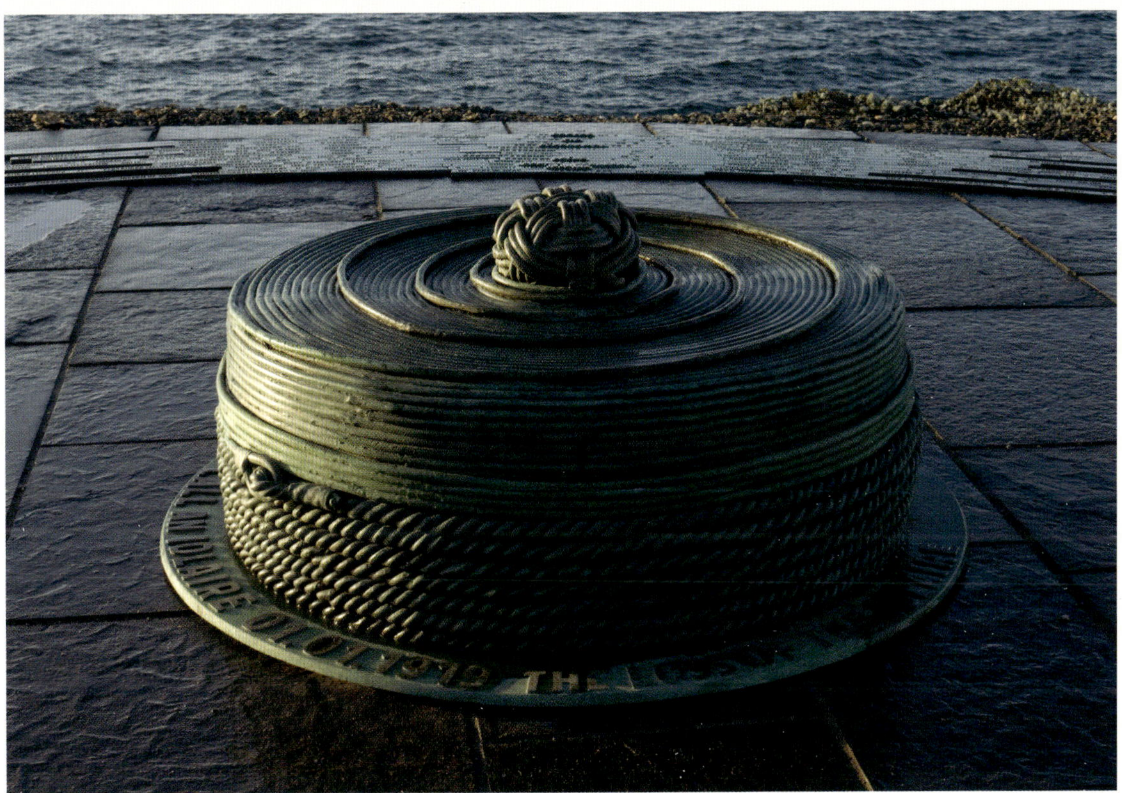

1   Iain Fhionnlaigh MacLeòid, agallamh le Fred MacÀmhlagh, BBC Radio nan Gàidheal, 1961

2   *West Highland Free Press*, Dùbhlachd, 1993

3   Dòmhallach, T C, *Call na h-Iolaire*, Acair, Stornaway, 1978

4   MacDonald, M & Macleod, D J, *The Darkest Dawn, The Story of the Iolaire Disaster*, Acair, Steòrnabhagh, 2018

5   *ibid*

6   Dòmhallach, T C, *Call na h-Iolaire*, Acair, Steòrnabhagh, 1978
     Faic cuideachd: BBC Radio nan Gàidheal, Agallamhan a rinn Fred MacÀmhlaigh: Coinneach MacÌomhair,1986, 1987;
     Jo NicDhòmhnaill,1989; Annella NicLeòid,1999; agus Nan S. NicLeòid,2008). Leabhar Bliadhnail *Eilean an Fhraoich/Gasaet*
     Steòrnabhaigh,1977; Tasglann Comunn Eachdraidh Nis; Macleod, J, *When I Heard the Bell, The Loss of the Iolaire*, Birlinn,
     Dún Èideann, 2009

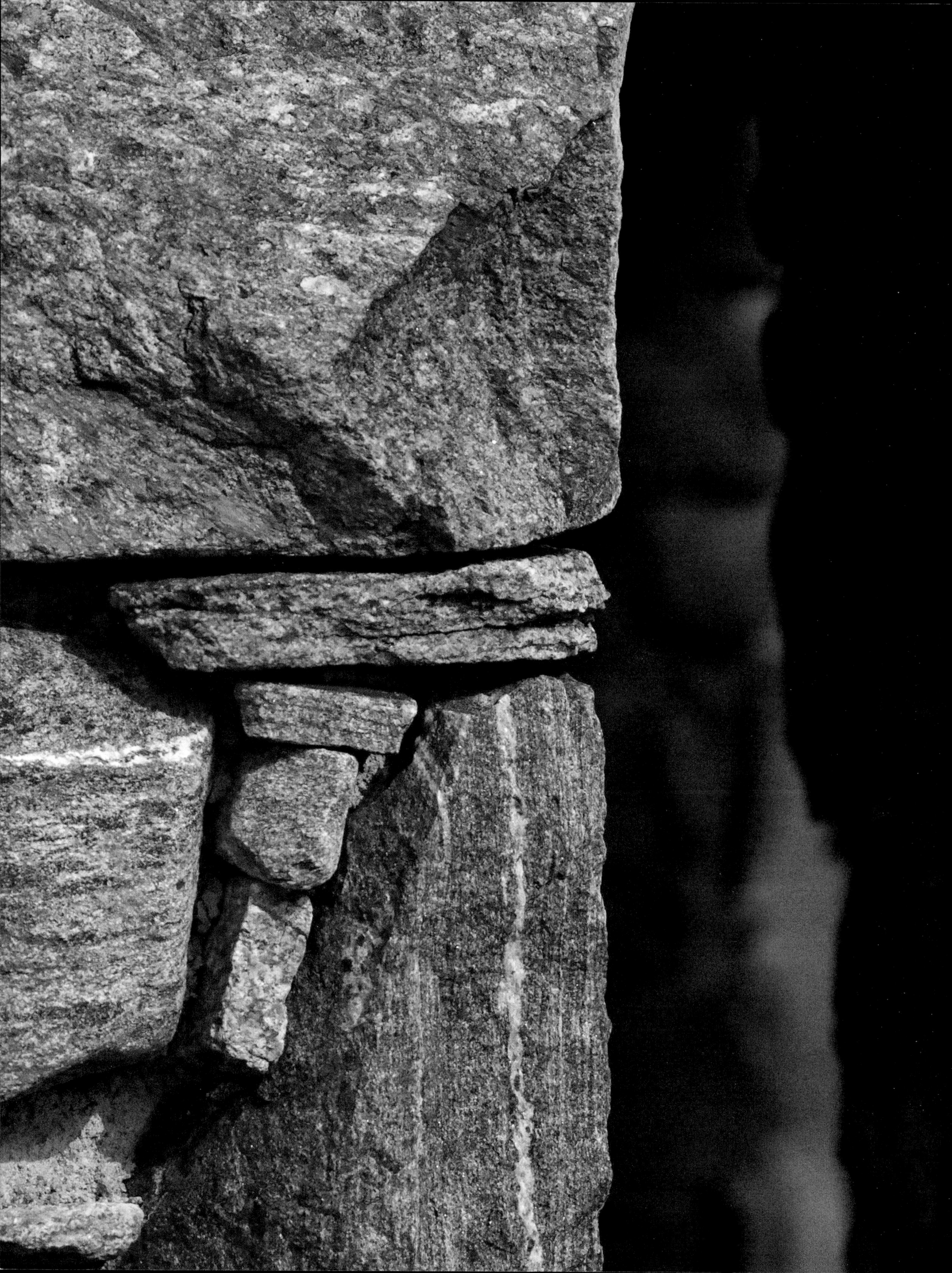

Selected archive photographs

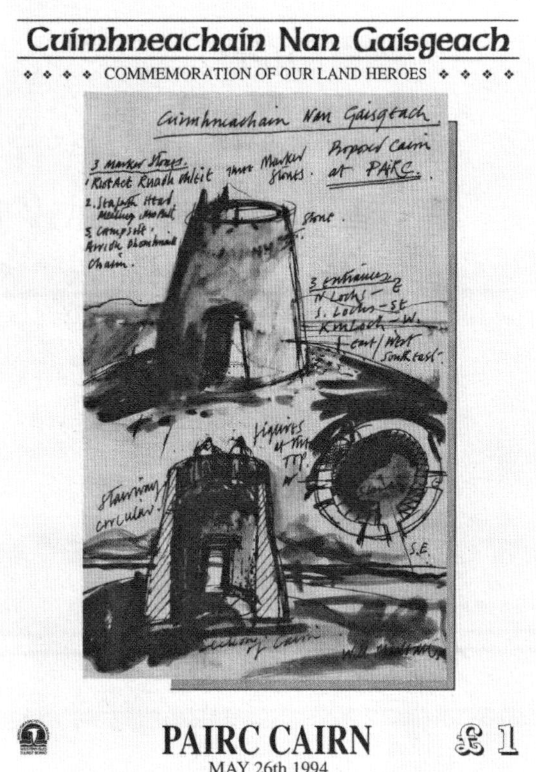

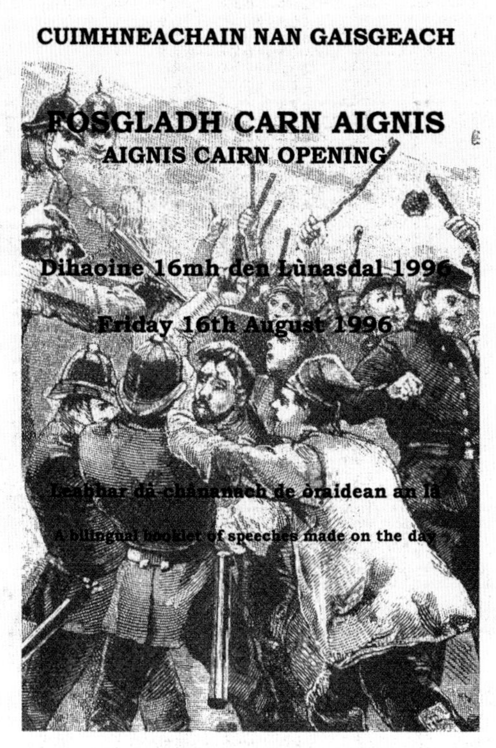

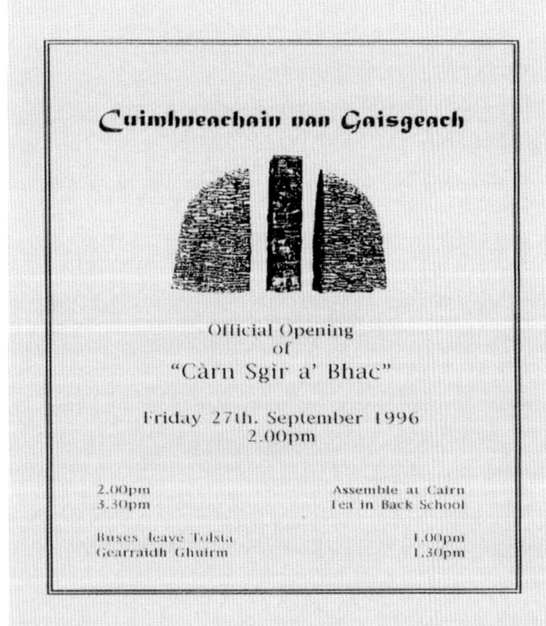

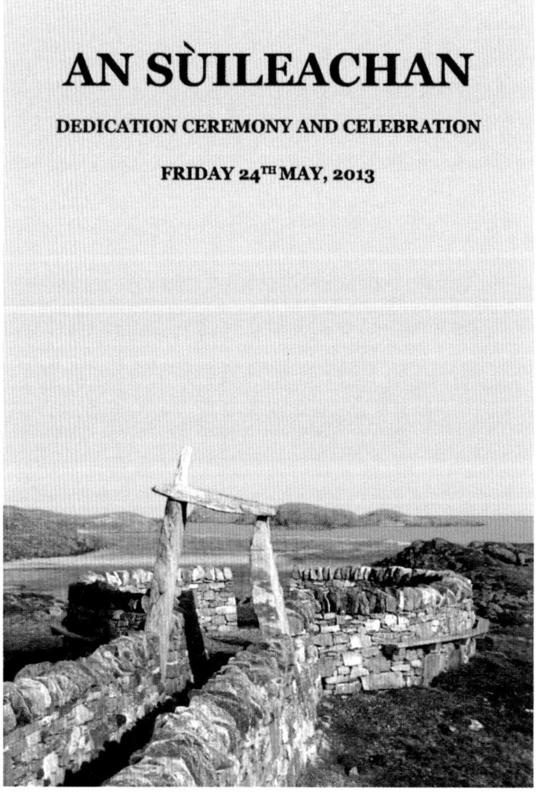

TOP Covers of booklets printed for the openings of the memorials at Balallan and Aignish (see Notes to Illustrations)

BOTTOM LEFT Advertisement for the opening of the Gress cairn

BOTTOM RIGHT Poster for the opening of *An Sùileachan* at Reef

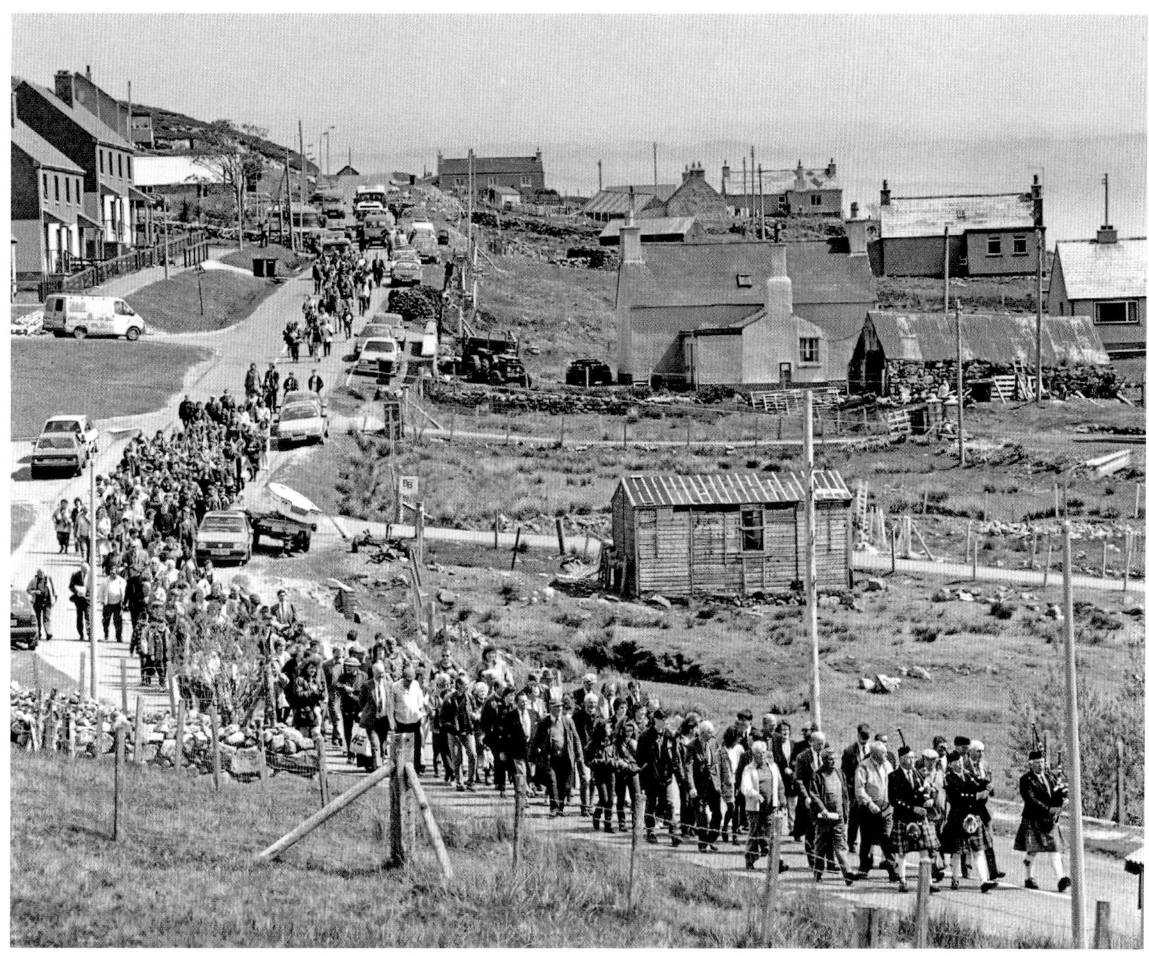

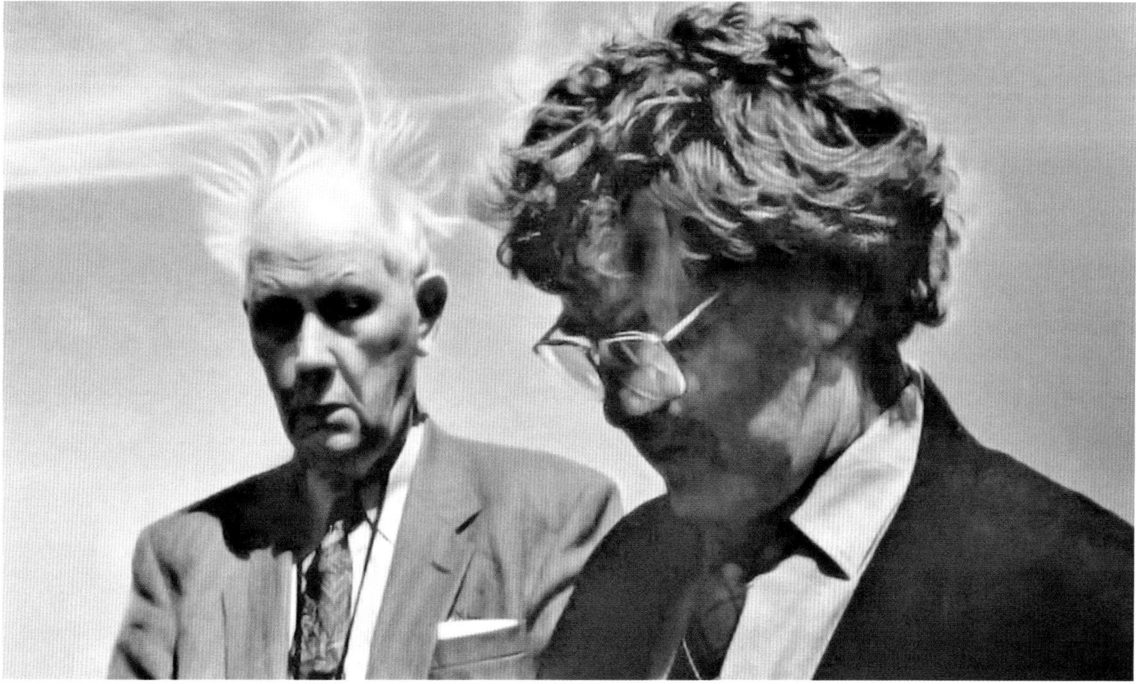

TOP Pipers lead the two-mile march through Balallan to Pàirc memorial cairn for its opening ceremony, 26 May 1994 (see Notes to Illustrations)
BOTTOM Angus 'Ease' Macleod and Will Maclean at the opening of the Pàirc cairn (see Notes to Illustrations)

Will Maclean and James
Crawford on site at Aignish
Photo: Derrick Mackenzie

Dugie MacLean and James Crawford
at the recovery of the Neolithic stones
for *An Sùlichean*

Marian Leven recording the
construction of *An Sùlichean*

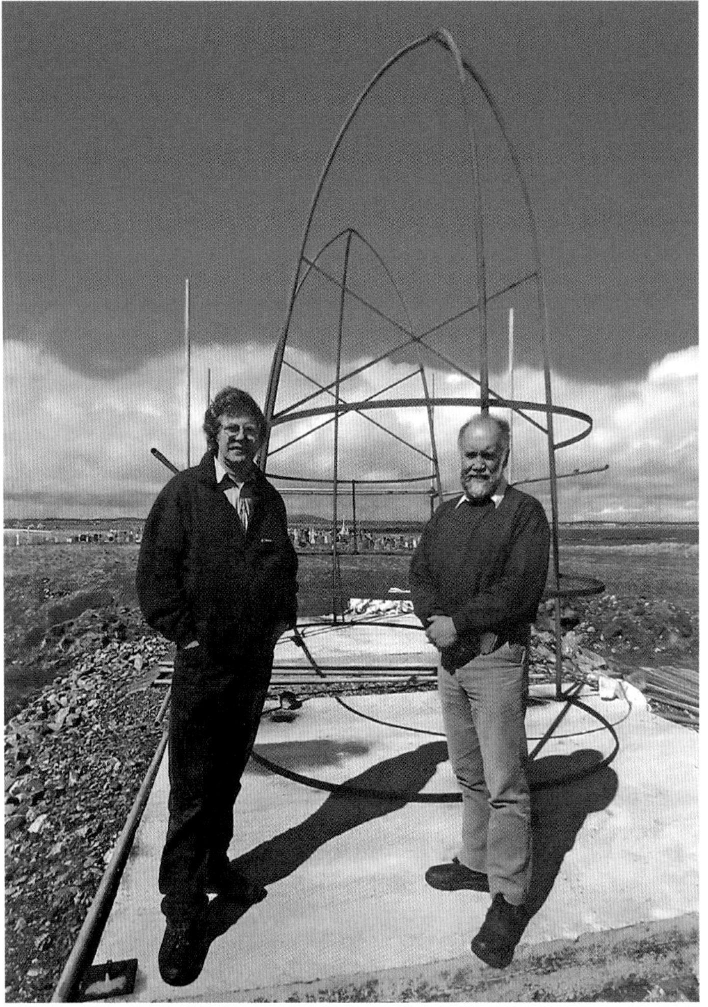

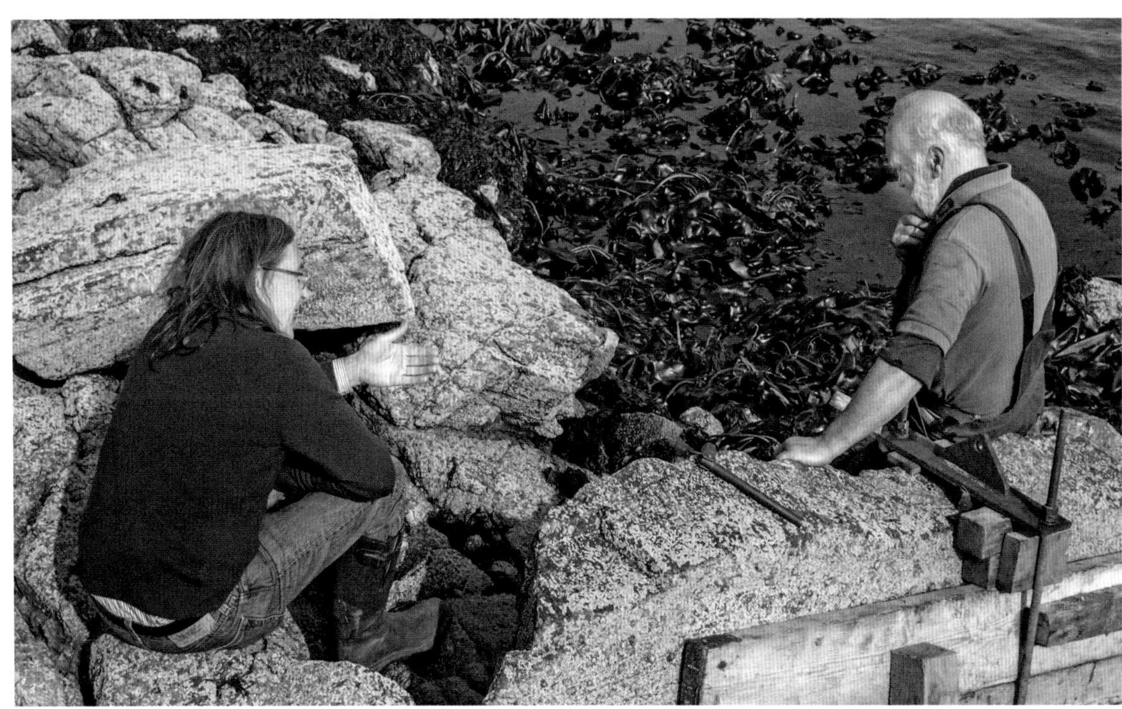

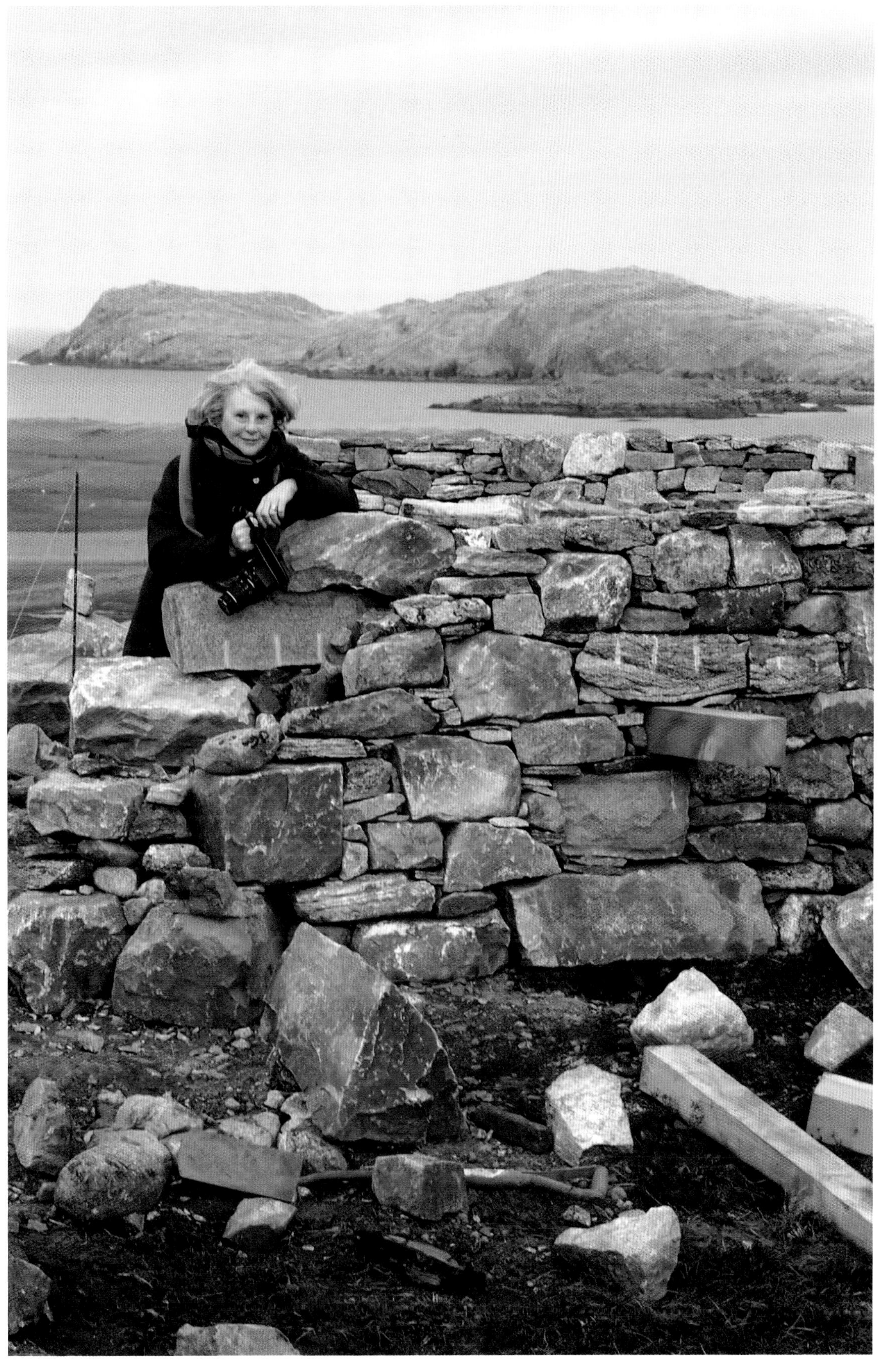

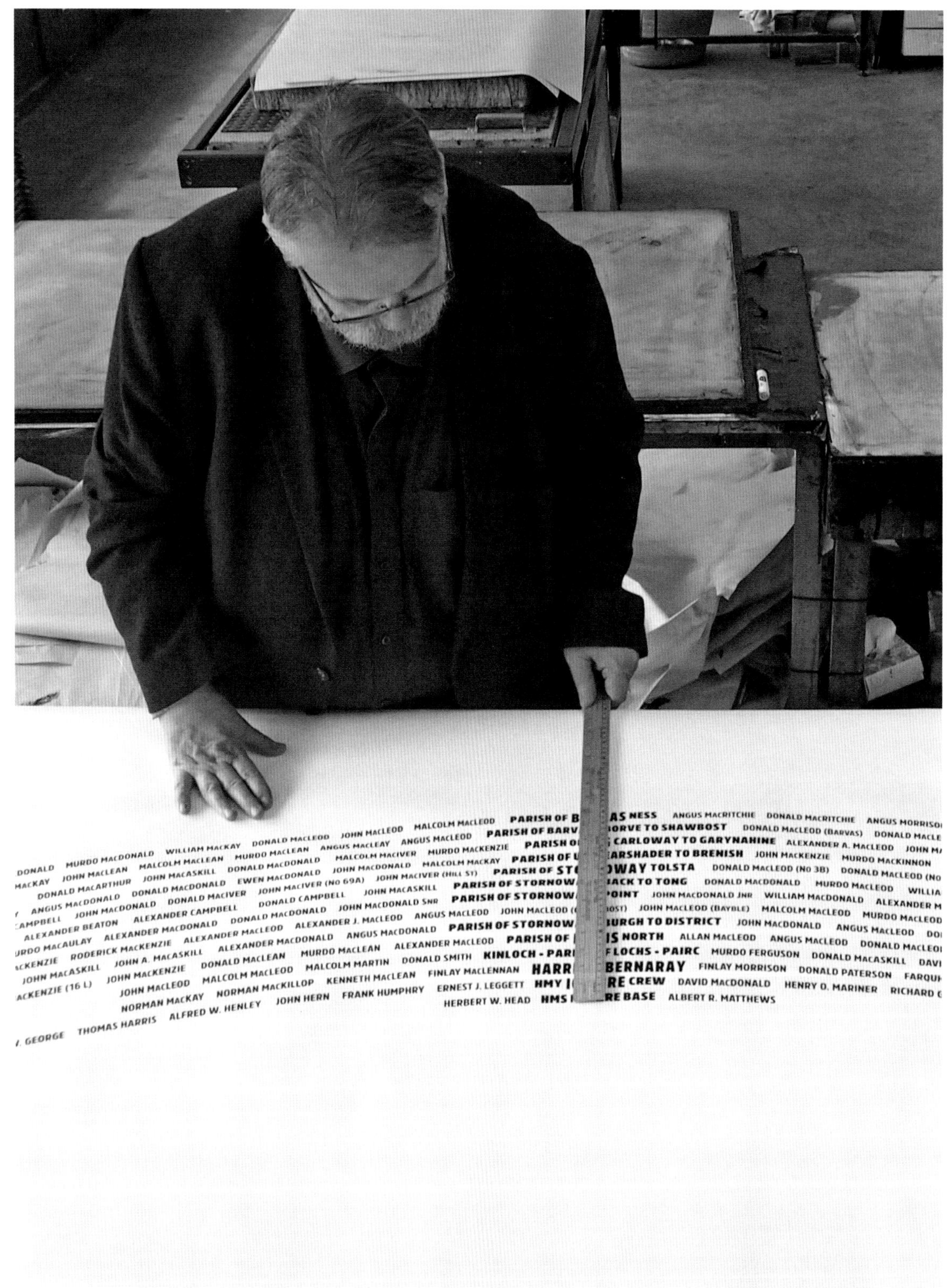

Arthur Watson preparing for the *Iolaire* names to be cast in bronze

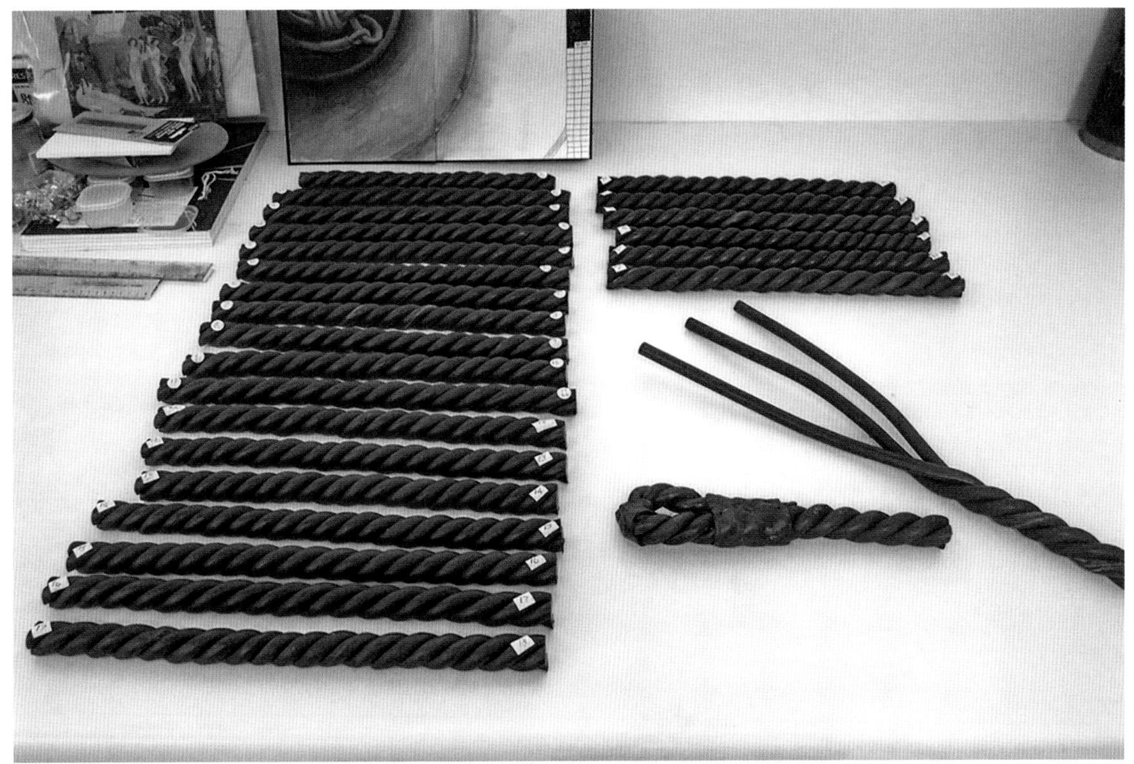

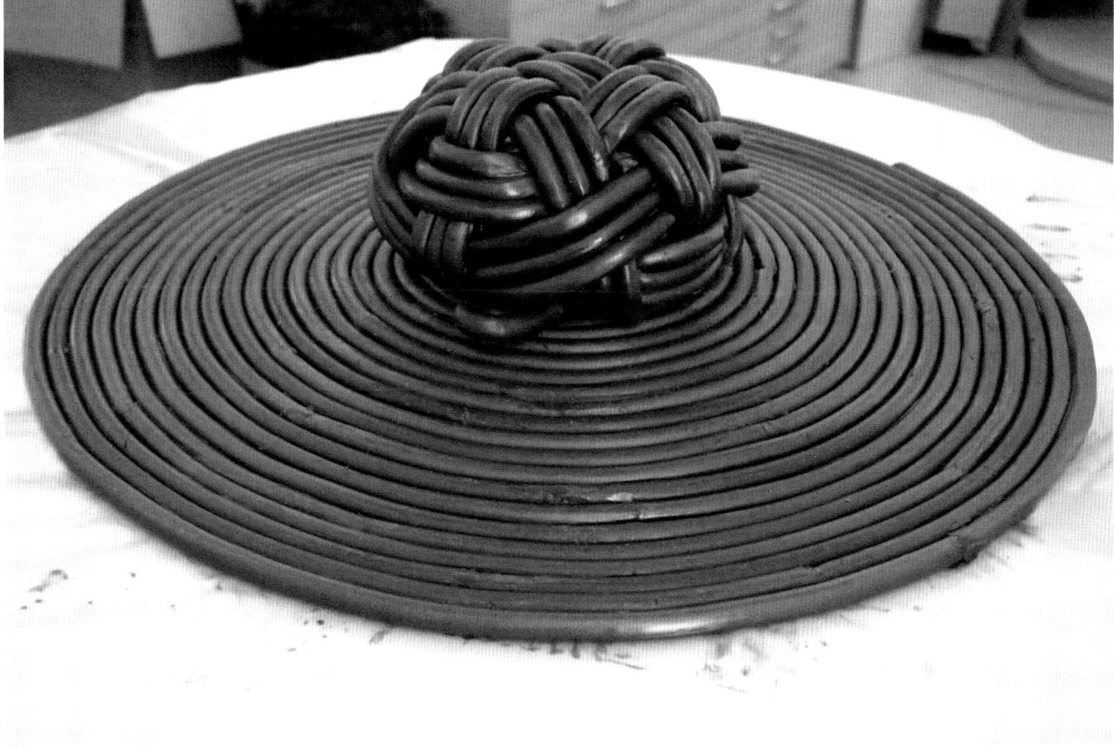

Arthur Watson's wax-resist rope components ready to be cast in bronze for the *Iolaire* memorial

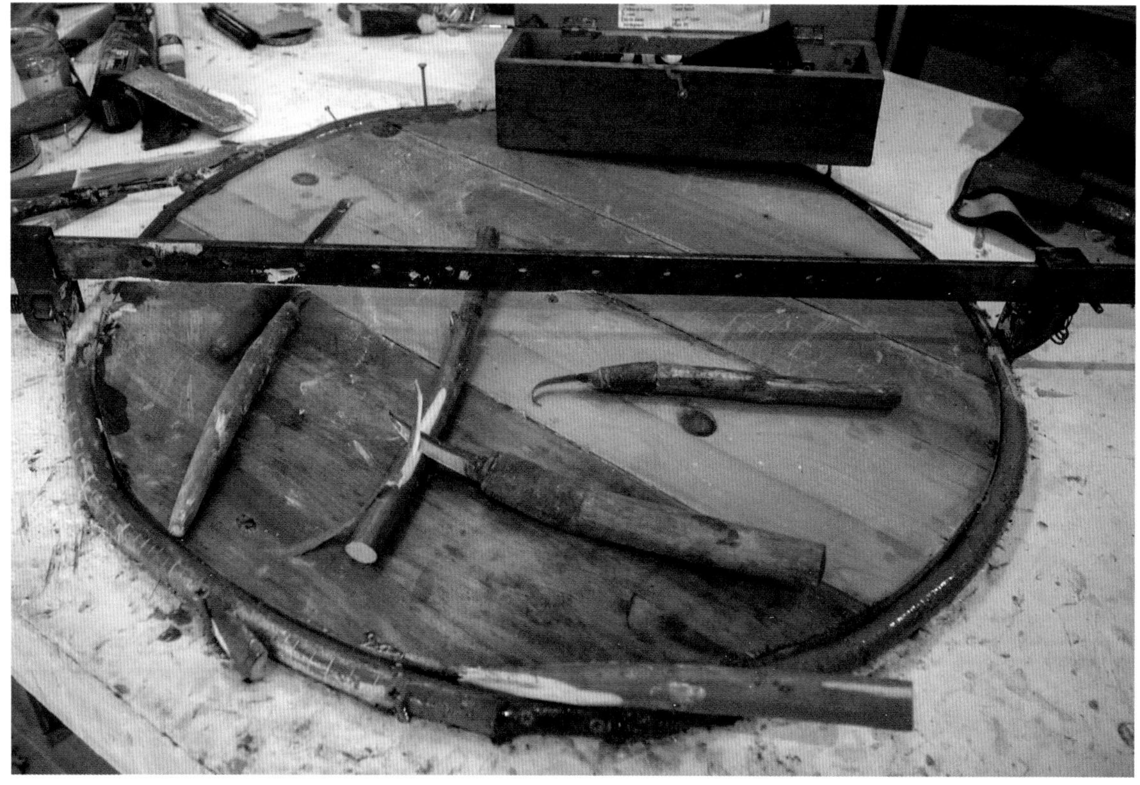

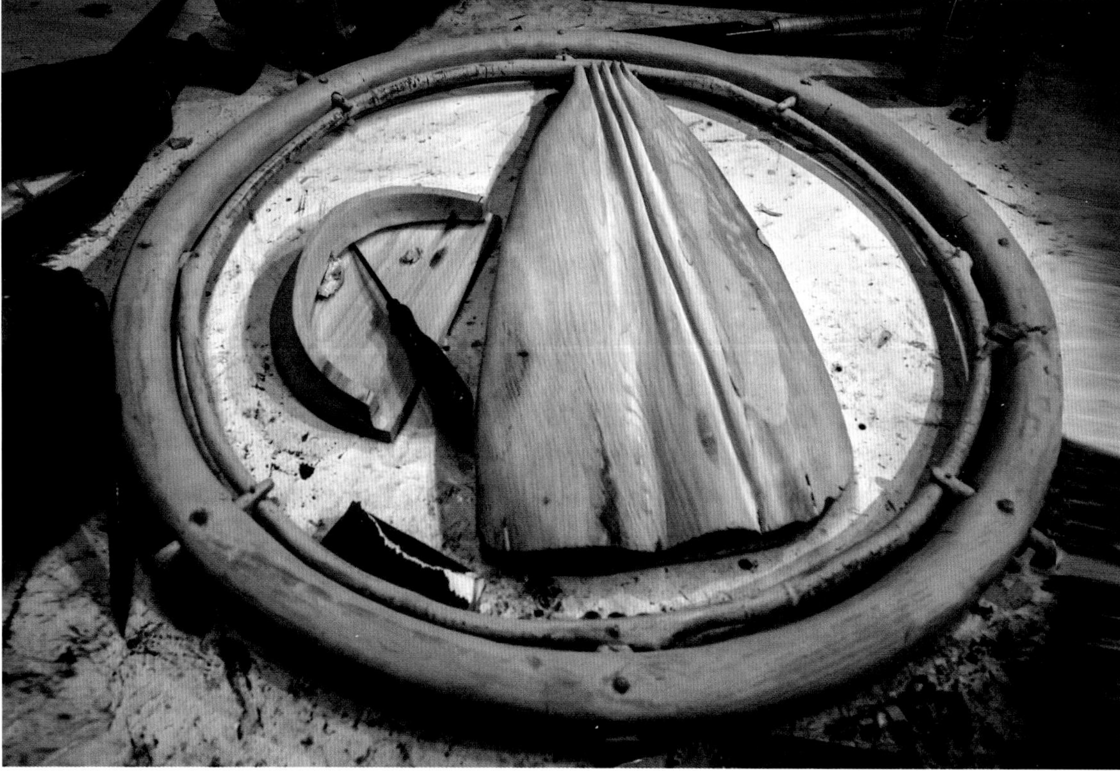

TOP Will Maclean's willow carving, with Canadian carving tools, for the *Iolaire* memorial wreath
BOTTOM Will Maclean's carved rating's cap and kitbag, in preparation for the bronze casting of the *Iolaire* wreath

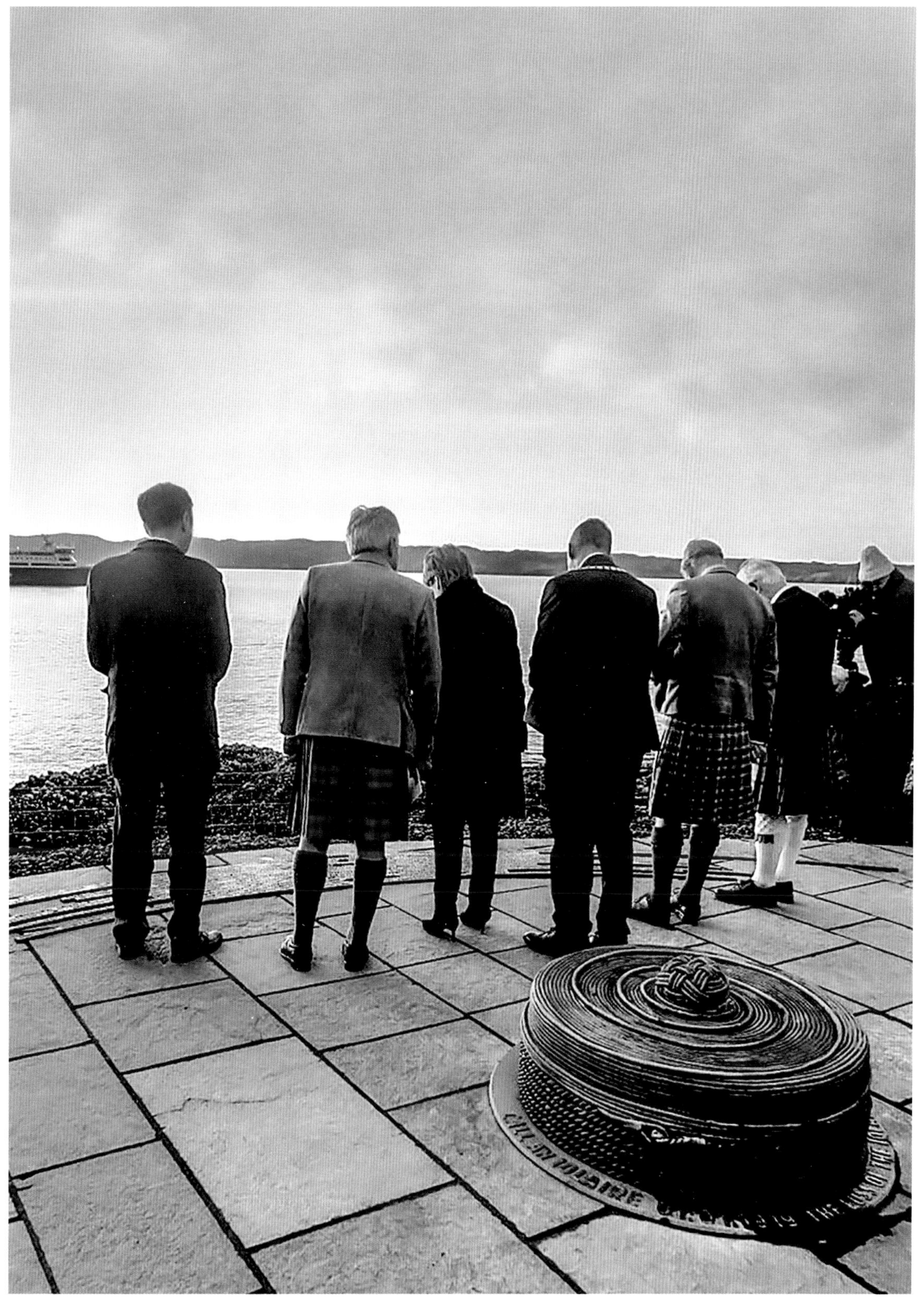

Opening ceremony of the *Iolaire* memorial, on 1st January 2019,
with HRH The Prince of Wales; First Minister of Scotland, Nicola Sturgeon; and Rear Admiral John Weale
among invited guests from the community (see Notes to Illustrations)

Notes to Illustrations

p.17

Eight numbered stones are set in the monument's interior wall to mark eight compass points. Six of the stones were taken from the homes of the six land raiders who were acquitted at the court in Edinburgh on 14 January 1888. In addition there is a stone from Ruadh-Chleit, the site of the reading of the Riot Act, and a stone from Airidh Dhòmhnaill Chaim, the site of the land-raiders' camp. See also Normand, p.37.

pp.56 – 7

Will Maclean's 1994 pen and ink drawings on Arches paper, each 50 x 70cm. Page 56: top: Balallan cairn; bottom: Aignish cairn. Page 57: Gress cairn. The drawings reveal Maclean's multi-dimensional response to the requirements of the commissions, demonstrating the sensitivity of his visual thinking and providing an informative record to accompany the finished structures. Collection of Museum nan Eilean, Stornoway, Isle of Lewis.

p.58

Two of Marian Leven's pen and wash drawings for *An Sùileachan*. The lower image describes the iron basket, placed on an old local millstone in one of the two enclosures, with its opening to views of the sea. Visitors can make peat fires here, turning the basket into a beacon of warmth and light, and welcoming wooden benches are set within the protective stone walls. See also photo p.60.

p. 62

Marian Leven's watercolour sketch for the *Iolaire* memorial gives an immediate sense of its form and setting. The plan below shows a 'bird's-eye view', demonstrating how it takes the form of an eye, with Watson's bronze heaving line sculpture as the iris.

p.98 top right

The opening of the Aignish cairn, on 16th August 1996, saw a gathering of more than 600, including a group of 200 local people in period costume carrying red flags, marching from Bayble School to the cairn, led by pipers. A play by Norman M. MacDonald, *The Aignish Riot*, was performed. John Mackay, the son of one of the 13 jailed raiders, opened the cairn officially.

p.99 top

For the opening of the Pàirc cairn, pipers led the descendants of the raiders and a crowd of over 500 through the town of Balallan, to music especially composed for the occasion by Ian Crighton. There followed a re-enactment of the events of November 1887. During the speeches the marchers enjoyed a taste of venison cooked over an open fire and the day concluded with a sell-out Gaelic concert in Balallan village hall.

p.99 bottom

Angus 'Ease' Macleod MBE (1916 – 2002) was a local polymath with experience in the weaving and tweed industry and a lifelong commitment to the preservation of local history. He was an avid collector of books and local artefacts (now housed in Stornoway's Museum nan Eilean) and served as the Honorary President of the Scottish Crofters Union. He took the lead in the Cuimhneachain nan Gaisgeach project to commemorate the crofters' struggle for land-law reform, which resulted in the commissioning of the three memorial cairns at Pàirc, Aignish and Gress.

Will Maclean recalls that the main criteria were that the structures should not intrude on the landscape; should withstand the weather; be low maintenance; the design should reflect the specific event; and there should be sufficient signage to explain the history and function of the memorial. Maclean was a natural choice to design the memorial structures. He worked closely with a local team, in particular historian and builder, James Crawford, and the project engineer, John Norgrove, who dealt with planning, roads, legal and safety issues.

p.105

A hundred years after the disaster of the *Iolaire,* on 1st January 2019, the solemn unveiling of the memorial took place in the presence of HRH Prince Charles, Scotland's First Minister, Nicola Sturgeon, and Rear Admiral John Weale. Invited guests included the artists and the families of the survivors and of those lost. On a ship anchored where the *Iolaire* sank, school children from the western isles witnessed a service on board and then threw 201 symbolic red carnations into the sea.

Artist Biographies

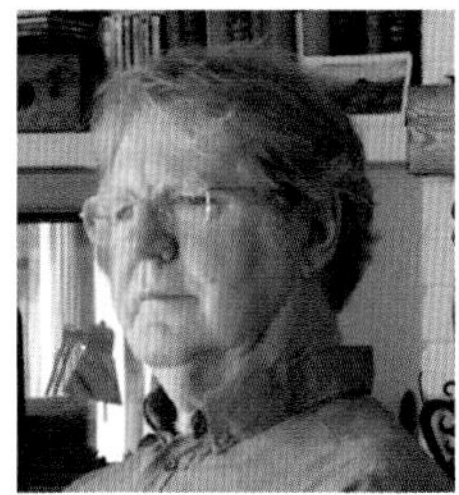

Will Maclean is Emeritus Professor of Fine Art at the University of Dundee and lives and works in Tayport with his wife and fellow artist, Marian Leven. He is a Member of the Royal Scottish Academy; Member of the Royal Glasgow Institute of the Fine Arts; Honorary Doctor of Letters, University of St Andrews 2000; MBE 2005; Honorary Fellow of the University of the Highlands 2008; Honorary Doctor of Letters, University of Aberdeen 2009; Fellow of the Royal Society of Edinburgh 2010.

His work is held in collections including: in Britain: Arts Council of Great Britain; the British Museum; the Fitzwilliam Museum, Cambridge; Gallery of Modern Art, Glasgow; Government Art Collection; Scottish National Gallery of Modern Art, Edinburgh; the Scottish Parliament; in North America: Art Gallery of Newfoundland; McMaster Museum of Art, Ontario; North Dakota Museum of Art; Yale Centre for British Art.

Widely published, books and catalogues featuring his work include *Sculpture and Box Constructions*, Woods/Runkel, London, 1987; *Symbols of Survival*, Prof. D. Macmillan, Mainstream, Edinburgh, 1992, updated 2002; *Atlantic Messengers*, T. Normand, Art First, London, 1998; *Selected Affinities*, University of Dundee, 2001; *Cardinal Points*, L. Reuter, Museum of North Dakota, 2001; *Driftworks*, Dundee Contemporary Arts, 2001; *Collected Works*, Fleming-Wyfold Art Foundation, London, 2011. In 2005 Maclean gave a valuable recorded interview for the British Library and Tate's shared *Archive of the Artists' Lives* series – a part of *National Life Stories*. He has been represented by Art First, London, since 1994.

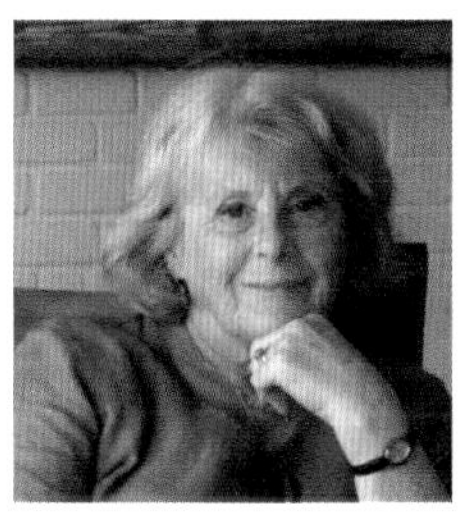

Marian Leven is a painter, printmaker and designer whose practice centres around the experience of living by the sea and the changeability of coastal locations. Awards include the Noble Grossart/*Scotland on Sunday* Painting Prize. She has collaborated on three key projects with Will Maclean, her husband and fellow artist: the *Waterlines* sculpture, University of Aberdeen, 2011; *An Sùileachan* land monument, Isle of Lewis, 2010–13 (winning the Saltire Society Award); and the *Iolaire* memorial, Isle of Lewis, 2018.

In 1999 Leven was a lecturer in Constructed Textiles at Duncan of Jordanstone, University of Dundee; painting Lecturer at Glenrothes College, Fife in 2001; and between 2002 and 2008, visiting Lecturer in Fine Art at Taigh Chearsabhagh, UHI, Lochmaddy. Her work is held in collections including the Fleming-Wyfold Collection, the RSA collection and the University collections of Dundee, St Andrews and Aberdeen.

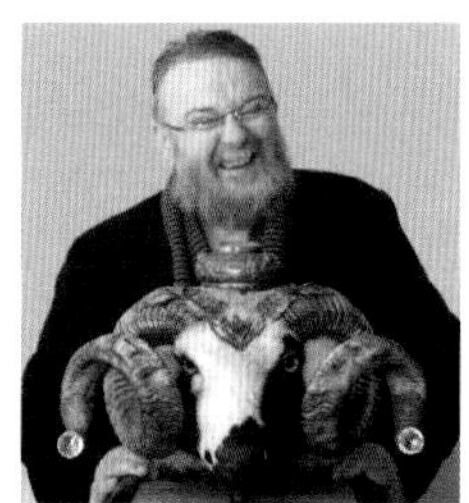

Arthur Watson trained as a printmaker and works across sculptural installation, text and curation. He established Peacock Printmakers (now Peacock Visual Arts), an artists' print workshop, publisher and gallery, in 1975. He has served on panels and committees of the Scottish Arts Council and the boards of several arts organisations, including the Scottish Sculpture Workshop, Arts in Partnership Scotland, the Richard Demarco Gallery, the Pier Arts Centre and currently the Demarco Archive Trust. He has exhibited across Europe, America and Japan, including at the 1990 *Venice Biennale* with Kate Whiteford and David Mach in *Three Scottish Sculptors*.

In 1995 he was appointed MFA Course Director at Duncan of Jordanstone College of Art, where he still teaches part-time. With close colleague, Euan McArthur, he created the Demarco Digital Archive and three subsequent publications, most recently *Demarco 2020: From Strategy: Get Arts to the Future*. A Royal Scottish Academician, he was elected the RSA's Secretary, then President (2012–18), acting as lead curator for *Ages of Wonder: Scotland's Art from 1540 to Now*, in partnership with National Galleries Scotland. Several collaborative projects with Will Maclean include public works on Cairn Gorm Mountain, at the Gaelic College on Skye and the *Iolaire* memorial on the Isle of Lewis.

Author Biographies

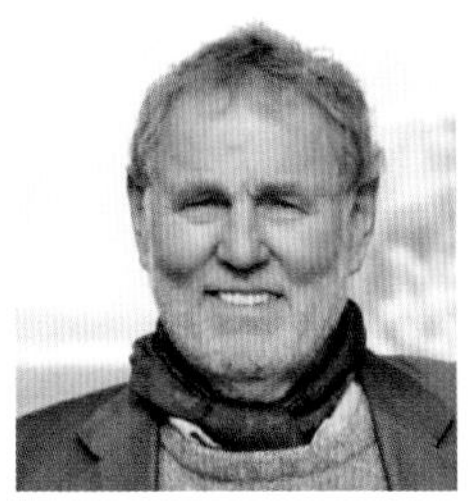

Duncan Macmillan is Emeritus Professor in the History of Scottish Art at the University of Edinburgh and art critic of *The Scotsman*. Among his published books are monographs on Will Maclean and several other Scottish artists, as well as *Scottish Art 1460–2000* (Mainstream, Edinburgh, 2000), *Scottish Art in the 20th Century* (Mainstream, Edinburgh, 1994) and *Scotland's Shrine: The Scottish National War Memorial* (Lund Humphries, London, 2014). He has published numerous articles and exhibition catalogues and won several prizes for his writing. He is a Fellow of both the Royal Society of Edinburgh and the Royal Society of Arts and an Honorary Royal Scottish Academician.

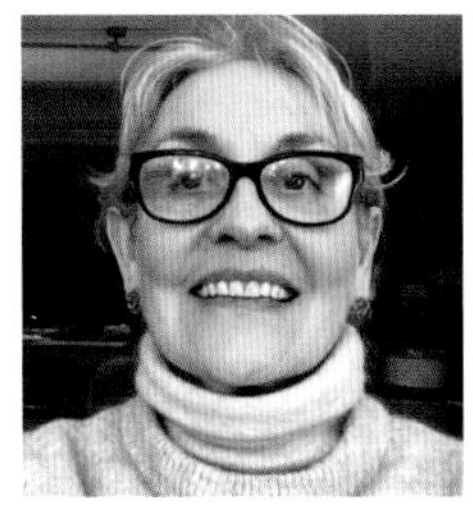

Dr Joni Buchanan is a native of Mangersta in the Uig area of Lewis. She graduated in economic history from the University of Strathclyde and gained a PhD from the Universities of Aberdeen and the Highlands and Islands. Her doctoral thesis, *From Gàidhealtachd Community to Shared Space*, followed the transition within her own home community over the postwar era and identified measures necessary for retaining population and maintaining the Gaelic language. Dr Buchanan is author of *The Lewis Land Struggle: Na Gaisgich* (Acair, Stornoway, 1996) and her research into the lives of island women will be published as a book, *Mnathan nan Eilean*, by Acair in the near future.

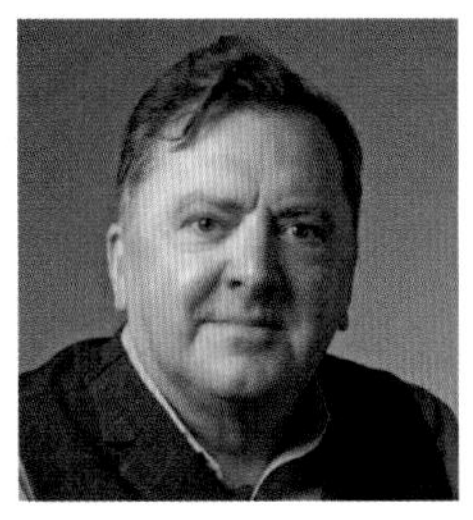

Dr Tom Normand is an art historian specialising in British, and especially Scottish, art. He is the author of several monographs, on Calum Colvin, Ken Currie and Wyndham Lewis, as well as books including *Scottish Photography: A History* (Luarth Press, Edinburgh, 2007) and *The Modern Scot: Modernism and Nationalism in Scottish Art 1928–1955* (Routledge, London, 2000). He edited the book *Ages of Wonder: Scotland's Art 1540 to Now* (National Galleries of Scotland, Edinburgh, 2017) and has authored numerous academic articles, critical essays and artists' catalogues.

He is Honorary Research Fellow in the School of Art History (University of St Andrews) and an Honorary member of the Royal Scottish Academy of Art.

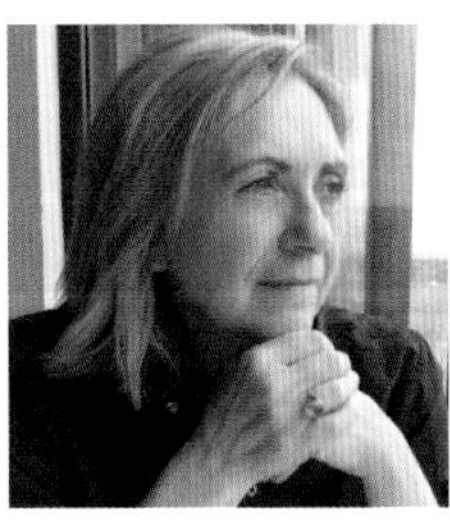

Dr Lindsay Blair, University of the Highlands and Islands, is a Reader in Visual Culture and Theory. Since 1980 her groundbreaking work on 'word and image' problematises codes of representation. Her monograph on Joseph Cornell is acknowledged as an outstanding contribution to Cornell studies (it has been reprinted and translated into several languages) and her BBC Omnibus documentary on Cornell was screened in 1991. Current research on visual culture in the Gàidhealtachd extends to an interest in 'place', 'mutations from below' and transnational representations. She is the Principal Investigator for a European network, Hands across the Sea, and part of the Arctic Sustainable Arts and Design network.

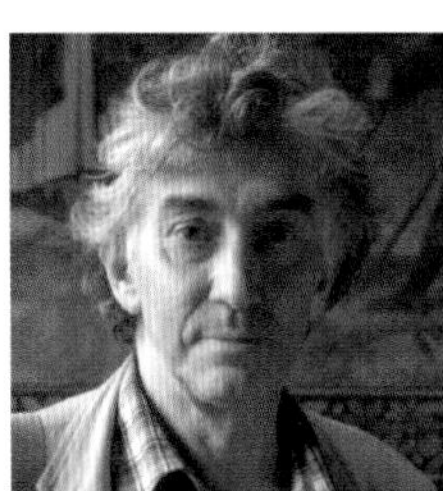

Robin Gillanders (commissioned photographer for this publication) is former Reader in Photography at Edinburgh Napier University and was awarded a Fellowship in 2016. He has several works in the collections of the City Art Centre, Edinburgh; National Portrait Gallery, London; Scottish National Portrait Gallery, Edinburgh; V&A, London. Publications include *Little Sparta: Portrait of a Garden* (1998), *The Photographic Portrait* (2004), *The Philosopher's Garden* (2004), *Highland Journey: In the Spirit of Edwin Muir* (2009), *A Lover's Complaint* (2016) and *Compelled by Memory: The Lewis Land Monuments 1994–2018* (2022).

He has exhibited widely and internationally, including at the Prada Foundation, Venice; Royal Scottish Academy, Edinburgh; and Scotland House, Brussels. He had a major retrospective at Stills Gallery, Edinburgh, in 2017–18. Gillanders is co-editor of the journal *Studies in Photography*, published by the Scottish Society for the History of Photography, and is one of the organisers of the Jill Todd Photographic Award.

Acknowledgements

The publication of this book has been made possible through the welcome support of the Gaelic Books Council, and with generous contributions by individuals whose hearts have been stirred by the stories behind the Lewis Land Monuments – and of course by the art of Will Maclean himself. For six decades Maclean has devoted his creative output to the subject of the Scottish Highlands, to its history, its people, and to the sea with its universal themes of fishing, whaling, exploration, navigation, emigration; to island life itself, with its culture, its poetry, and its instincts of survival.

I would like to give special thanks to Brian and Lesley Knox and to Ian and Tina Taylor, whose funding and good faith launched the project, enabling Robin Gillanders to undertake his evocative photographic documentation of the monuments, and enticing illuminating essays from the four wonderful authors: Lindsay Blair, Joni Buchanan, Duncan Macmillan, and Tom Normand.

The University of Dundee and the Royal Scottish Academy made contributions to artists' costs, for which they have all our thanks.

Quietly along the way, readers and friends have helped in their unique fashion and I thank especially Penelope Cummins, Malcolm Maclean, James Moon, Benjamin Rhodes, and Vicky Unwin. Thanks go to Clare Hewitt for her charming map marking the positions of the monuments.

The book itself is in your hands thanks to the Sansom & Co. publishing team, in particular, Paul Deaton, Clara Hudson, and the patient, dependable copy editors: Ann Kay and, for the Gaelic essays, Gillebride MacMillan.

The person who accompanied me throughout the preparation of this publication is Strule Steele, the book's designer, whose input and experience has been exceptional – enormous thanks to him.

The inspiration behind the book is Will Maclean, and I thank him warmly for all his help, and for the archival images and anecdotes. Also thanks for his, Marian Leven's and Arthur Watson's beautiful editions of prints of the monuments, created for the individual subscribers whose financial contributions have ensured the final phase of the book's publication.

To each subscriber, my heartfelt thanks. It is a pleasure to include your names on this page.

Clare Cooper
London March 2022

Subscribers

Bhaltos Community Trust

Donella Macdonald *from the family of the late Dr Colin MacDonald of Reef (remembering friendship and fun, yarns and fine drams)*

John Barker

Geoffrey and Rossanne Bertram

Ross and Vicky Cattell

Jonathan and Christine De Ferrars Green

Frank Cranmer and Helen Donoghue

Jamie Gibson

Charles and Hen Irving

Peter Lyburn, Stonehaven

James and Polly Moon

Malcolm Offord

Jeff and Cynthia Penney

Francis and Sarah Salway

David Sneddon

Martin Watson and Elspeth McAdam

Published to accompany the exhibition
Will Maclean: Points of Departure
At the City Art Centre, Edinburgh, 4th June – 2nd October 2022
www.edinburghmuseums.org.uk

First published in 2022 by Sansom and Company
a publishing imprint of Redcliffe Press Ltd.
81g Pembroke Road, Bristol BS8 3EA
www.sansomandcompany.co.uk
info@sansomandcompany.co.uk

ISBN 978-1-911408-91-8

Editor: Clare Cooper
Copy Editor: Ann Kay
Copy Editor Gaelic: Gillebride MacMillan
Design: Strule Steele
Printed and bound: Zenith Print Group

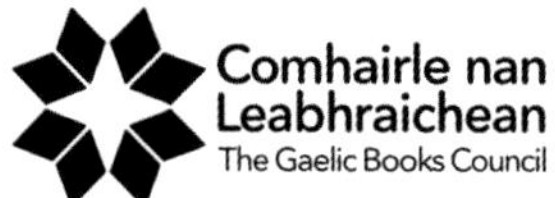

Art First, The Forge, 15 St Mary's Walk, London SE11 4UA

www.artfirst.co.uk

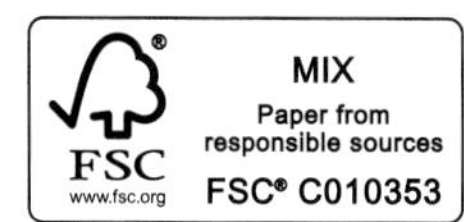

Chuidich Comhairle nan Leabhairhean am foillsichear le cosgaisean an leabhair seo